My Unusual Life

One woman's intriguing journey to the '68 Olympics, an extraordinary time at *Architectural Digest*, overcoming a brutish marriage, and the discovery of her soulmate.

Laurie Lewis Havel

ISBN: 978-1-916770-56-0

Dedication

To John, ever encouraging and still my inspiration, and to our much-loved daughter.

To our family and friends who made our life, and continue to make my life, so complete.

And with great gratitude to my editor, Maureen Lasher,who harnessed my written meanderings, and patiently prodded me to dig deeper.

Table of Contents

About the Author

Laurie Lewis Havel spent almost two decades on staff editing and writing for such publications as Architectural Digest, Society West, Goodlife Magazine, LA West Magazine, Los Angeles Home and Garden Magazine, Daily News, and Small Business Times. She freelanced for such publications as Palm Beach Life Magazine, Palm Beach Daily News, First Class Magazine, Western's World (bimonthly travel column), Los Angeles Magazine's Official Olympic Guide to Los Angeles, and California Gardens.

In addition, she worked for almost a decade in corporate communications healthcare for such companies as Blue Cross of California/UNICARE (nationwide), Maxicare Health Plans, and Unihealth Corporate marketing.

A credentialed education specialist, she taught special education to middle schoolers for ten years.

Her volleyball highlights include: '66, '67 USVBA 2nd place team; '67 Outstanding high school player in California; '67 USA World Games Team; '67 USVBA All American 2nd team; '67 US Pan American Team; '68 USVBA National Championship team; '68 US Olympic Team; '71 All Star Southern Calif. Intercollegiate Athletic Conference; '71-'72 UCLA First National Collegiate Volleyball Championship Team; ' 97 Named one of the top 25 greatest volleyball players at UCLA.

Photo by David Lustig

Introduction

Grateful is one of the words that comes to mind when I look back at my life - a pastiche, a combination of many unlikely parts. I took each part and built on it, moving on to the next. Learning all that I could along the way, it amazed me how skills, experience, and knowledge in one part could carry over to another.

Challenges, yes, but I persisted, armed with supportive family and friends and the patience of more than a few mentors. There were bright spaces and dark places, but thankfully, I could always ground myself.

At four years old, while already adventurous and risk-taking, I was full of love for people and pets as I scooped my goldfish out of the water and lovingly placed it on the pillow next to my head as I went to bed. I screamed and cried in horror in the morning when the goldfish would not swim in its bowl. I learned. I carried that heart and hope forward.-No doubt, I was a handful for my parents and perhaps for others later in life.

Each season of my time allowed me to meet a passel of intriguing people, to have unbelievable adventures, and to find myself on the continuum of ideas. Along the way, my experiences reflect the fractious sixties and the culturally evolving seventies, raw university life, and all manner of ideas then that shaped me. I reveled in a host of work connections made even with tweens. I lived through Y2K and am coping with the initials shorthand of the digital age. My life reflects the culture of sports, the power of art, and the impact of people, friendship, and, ultimately, love.

Ingenuous, positive, and sometimes naïve, I faced life head-on.

If any of this stirs thought, invokes humor, or points up life's lessons, I have achieved my goal.

Chapter 1: Road to the 1968 Olympics

Sea, Sun, Sand, and Sport

Spike Pop!

The ninety-mile-an -hour -plus volleyball exploded off the beach sand. Hit with an open hand and a whip-like arm with tremendous torque, the volleyball had its own trajectory up from the sand or off the forearms of a player intercepting it, popping it into the air for another play.

Fast-moving, with split-second reaction, timing, and movement, volleyball captivated me. Volleyball had become my passion. I was obsessed. I ate, drank, thought, and spoke volleyball.

At age sixteen, I was on the beach during the summer playing from 9 A.M to 5 P.M. I'd return home, gulp down some food, lace up my Pumas, Adidas, or Nikes, and head to Santa Monica City College to play for another three hours in the indoor gym. Incidentally, hardly anyone had heard of, much less, wore any of those shoe brands then.

I happened upon the beach volleyball scene at the beginning of its adolescence and mine. I met, watched, and/or played with or against the early stars. Who were these people? I didn't get to know them all, but over time, some became part of my extended family of friends.

A fair-skinned blonde with my hair pulled back, I was tan as can be at the end of summer. I think all my freckles filled in, and voila, I was tan. Years later, my skin knows and shows that I spent that time in the sun, but wouldn't have traded a minute.

Playing on the beach differed from gym play. The sand didn't give you the lift you could get from a springy gym floor. Sand and sun were legitimate timeouts on the beach. The first week of playing on the beach was killer.

The first day or two, players developed blisters on the bottoms of their feet and between their toes from the hot sand. The next few days were difficult with tender feet–then the blisters healed and turned to calluses. The hot sand was no longer a concern. Acquiring "sand feet" was the coveted mark of a beach volleyball player. Was the preparation worth it? It was to me then.

"Wonder what she is saying and about whom?" I used to muse watching players just two towels away.

For the really competitive players, State and then Sorrento Beach and later Muscle Beach was a place where you could sit on one end of the beach and watch players on the other side gossiping about you on the other.

There was a heightened sense of competition and perhaps tinges of jealousy underlying the gossip. Still there were, friendships, affairs, and bonds formed there that didn't fade. When one well-known tall lanky, slim female player, became terminally ill years many years later, another player made sure that she was taken care of until her death in the early 2000s.

Survival skills were essential in beach volleyball. It was reported then that the women hit the ball at a speed of ninety miles per hour and men even faster.~~Get~~ hit in the face with just one spiked volleyball, and it was amazing how quickly, no matter the circumstances, you could pop your hands up in front of your face for protection. You also learned to defend yourself from sand and sweat.

Beach volleyball had its own subculture of cars, fashion, and accouterments. On any given day in the mid-1960s, a quick drive-by, a scan of the parking lot, and instantly you knew who was playing. There was Johnette's Volvo, Selznick's Cadillac, etc.

There were the fashionable bikinis that had replaced the more modest suits of the fifties. These colorful suits of the sixties showed off the women's finely tuned bodies. The men wore loose fitting trunks, unless you were in from Hawaii where jams, wildly colored and flowered, trunks were the order of the day. Both were flattering since most male players were tall and lean.

Liaisons were another intriguing part of the subculture - who was married to or with someone else. Pairings were always colorful and interesting.

Johnette, a pert hard body, always bikini-clad, was married to Dave Heiser. Later she married the tall and quick-tongued lanky player/ coach Gene Selznick. Years later, she wed another. I was a fixture on the beach for several sixties' summers. In my teens, I studied the game and its greats on the beach. One summer, play shifted south of State Beach to the beach behind the Sorrento Grill in Santa Monica. The Grill, north of the Jonathan Beach Club and south of Barron Hilton's house and a line of others, had walls that were a photo gallery of beach volleyball players and tournament winners.

Did I know all these people? Some I knew in passing. Some, like Fran, my godmother, I knew. I just kept playing, and slowly, I proved my mettle and began to know the players, some better than others. Still, I was quite young compared to most who were in their mid-twenties or older.

Breaking into the scene was like slowly dipping your toes in the water and then immersing yourself in cold water.

It was during this time that I met Harlan Cohen. We chatted informally on the beach between games. I was fifteen, five foot eleven inches tall, almost a foot taller than he. We talked about health and medical issues between games, and I blushed with the shyness of a young teen girl. Conversations were varied, sometimes animated, and always interesting to me.

"I like to sleep on my stomach," offered Harlan, the dark-haired player who walked with deliberately cocked knees and a curious forward tilt.

"I prefer sleeping on my back," I blurted and blushed, realizing the implications of my comment. From there, the conversation wound all around, and hopefully, my tan hid my true color. Little did I know what impact Harlan would have on me later.

Each year was new on the beach. Summer beach play shifted to Muscle Beach just south of the Santa Monica Pier. The diehards went south again. The long, lanky volleyball players stood in stark contrast to the muscled weightlifters and bodybuilders for whom the beach was known and named. We volleyball players seemed to develop an addiction to Hot Dog on a Stick® and their lemonade, then a small concession next to the pier, and now a chain. In the later 1960s, tournament crowds grew and Gatorade® and other items became synonymous with the sport.

In addition to the daily play, there were weekend summer beach tournaments which were held from State Beach to the South Bay, but nothing like the scale now women's doubles, mixed (one man/one woman), and men's doubles. You couldn't help but get to know a host of people playing up and down the coast. And it was on a much smaller basis than it is now. Linda P. stands out in my memory blond, medium height, bikini clad, and terribly nice - and others were regulars in the South Bay and developed liaisons with some from the north.

This was a time when the players were the main audience at beach tournaments, so we rooted for each other. There were no professional leagues or teams yet, but there were rumblings, then late in the 1960s, of a professional league. In 1969 and 1970, audiences started increasing. As the game and techniques advanced, so did the number of people who become interested. Records started to be kept.

I played in a number of tournaments from State Beach to Redondo Beach and a host of beaches in between, such as Marine Street Beach. One year I won the State Beach Mixed Doubles tournament with Bob V. Vogie, as he was known, screamed and yelled the entire tournament - not necessarily at me, just in general – not a great courtside manner. In other tournaments, I partnered with Kathy G. and others. Kathy and I won the second Manhattan Beach Open, which some refer to as "The Wimbledon of Beach Volleyball."

When the landmark Sorrento Grill was razed for a condominium complex, the photos on the Grill wall and records vanished or disappeared into private vaults. There are few official records, although some started to be kept in the late 1960s, and author Art Couvillon later did much to reconstruct many. Records of beach tournaments were spare in those days. My records were comprised of a box of trophies in the garage which I absentmindedly tossed one day.

Sea, sun, sand, and sport -typified volleyball at State Beach at the intersection of Pacific Coast Highway and Chautauqua in Santa Monica. It was a unique experience.

Indoors Side Out

I was wowed several years earlier at fourteen as my high school volleyball coach, Sally Lewis, coaxed two volleyball players, Mary Perry, and Mary Jo Peppler, just back from the 1964 Tokyo Olympiad, where indoor volleyball made its Olympics debut, to come to our school and demonstrate what women's volleyball was all about.

I was riveted. In addition to fanning my wanderlust, this seemed so exciting, much more so than my tennis lessons, despite the fact that my tennis coach wanted to put me on the circuit. One of my high school classmates, Peggy M., had already played doubles in Wimbledon. Another schoolmate, Sarah B., a swimmer, had missed the Olympics by two- tenths of a second.

Why not try volleyball? It would be new, fun, and challenging. At the time, I suffered from that teenage mindset that I could rule the world and probably would. Well, I did try.

Besides, I was an avowed tomboy. At four years old, I borrowed the neighbor's twenty-four-inch boys' bike and took off barefooted down the street toward my house. I glanced back and heard a sudden crunch. I had run into a red brick planter, and, with surgery, my toe was saved, and I was saved from a permanent limp, but. ~~But~~ I spent a boring and immobile summer in a cast with my foot up, watching the horses run the paddock among orange trees across the street in mid-San Fernando Valley.

I played daily at lunch at Marymount High School, an all-girls school just across the street from UCLA, and down Sunset Boulevard from the infamous Dead Man's Curve in Westwood. I practiced after school and played indoors on weekends.

I had befriended my high school coach and P.E. teacher, Sally, who was a fount of volleyball knowledge. We shared a parallel sense of humor. I was 5'11" while she was 4' 2". She was full of enthusiasm and had a natural gift for mentoring and encouraging. Some disapproved of our friendship because I was so young compared to Sally. That didn't stop me, and our friendship has been lifelong. (Since we share the same last name, some still think Sally and I are related, which is not true unless you count the fact that I am godmother to her son Joe.)

"Try out for the Shamrocks," said my mentor, Sally, "You can do it!"

The Shamrocks were the number one women's team then and had the best political connections.

In the fall of 1964, I mustered up my courage and showed up at the Shamrock practice.

I was a nervous, hopeful young teen.

"Hello," said Jane Ward, captain and powerhouse player, and former beach great.

I gulped and responded in kind.

Blonde and medium height, she was fiercely loyal to her team. She led weekly practices with a firm hand and a dedicated demeanor.

I tried out and made my first indoor club team, the Shamrocks, originally the Ahern Shamrocks. This was a group of skilled and already accomplished volleyball players. I hardly knew them, but that would change. Some were physical education teachers in middle or high school. I had the double whammy since they could have been my teachers, and I had to relate to them as teammates. That hurdle soon disappeared. At fourteen, I was thrust into a world of adults - most were in their late teens, twenties, or older.

A series of monthly tournaments led up to the culminating nationals in May. I was agog watching all the players at the monthly Saturday tournaments. I recall standing at the door of Redondo Beach High School gym listening to the Mamas and the Papas sing "Monday, Monday," and watching intently as 150 or 200 players warmed up in preparation for the round-robin tournament. Deep inside me, I was thrilled watching all the volleyballs in motion.

The goal of playing in the next Olympics was always in the back of my mind. I was in awe of the former Olympic players who attended the first Olympics to include volleyball in Tokyo, in 1964.

Sheer passion and love of the game motivated the players then. I was no exception. My life revolved around volleyball. One summer night, after playing on the beach for eight hours, I happened to be at Santa Monica City College gym without shoes and was desperate to play. I decided to play doubles barefooted. Not recommended! I arrived home with big blood blisters on the bottoms of my feet.

It took days for them to heal, and it took no time to decide that I would never do that again!

This was a different time. Sports or strenuous activity for females was suspect at the time. Parochial elementary schools (first through eighth grades) that participated in interschool games only allowed two female basketball players per team to rove full court. Others were limited to half court, caught in the uncertainty that this much exercise might be unhealthy for young girls.

In high school, we had Mary-like gym uniforms with skirts! I reveled in the volleyball workouts and training despite warnings from quite a few that I would develop unsightly muscles. Perhaps related to this was the affidavit of commitment in 1964, that we club players were asked to sign attesting to the fact that we would continue in the volleyball program. We all signed.

Most players who had with a passion for the game also worked hard to incorporate the newest techniques and to develop strategies of offense and defense and how to make that package work overall. It was exciting to watch as these skill sets developed. Players started switching positions on the court.

Players with "good hands" (who could volley or set the ball smoothly or well) would be sent into the front row. Serving was overhead but without jumping. Still, skilled servers could deliver the ball to any desired spot or player in the opponents' court. Those who bumped (passed underhand or on the forearms) well were encouraged to cover more of the court when receiving serves.

Height obviously became a factor when trying to produce umbrella-like blocks to stuff the ball back into the opponents' court. All of these factors and more exploded on the scene like a volatile chemistry experiment. Trying to put together the balanced equation, to make all of these factors work at the same time and to add more, made the game of volleyball exciting and terribly fluid.

The Politics of Choice

There were others in those early days, names that loomed large in the politics of the sport and had tremendous impact on the players. The United States Volleyball Association (USVBA) Executive Committee members were very much empowered and an important political part of the game.

There was also "The Committee." This group of people, dedicated to the game of volleyball, were the ones who ran the sport and appointed subcommittees, typically groups of their members, to choose the national team members. I was cowed by the Committee at first. The Committee determined our fate. They decided who made the team.

In addition to the official politics, there were other factors and subsets of politics. In women's volleyball, the Shamrocks were more reserved and conservative, and the Renegades were more liberal and free- spirited. Both had much to recommend them. And both had the political passion, vitriol, and will to succeed.

Coaches, too, moved from the beach into the indoor arena easily. Gene Selznick coached the Renegades, an apt appointment, and Harlan Cohen coached the South Bay Triumphs and other teams. Both of these women's coaches also played indoors.

The always verbally colorful and frequently entertaining Gene Selznick was seen as a rebel by some, since he vehemently disagreed with the official Committee platform. Some saw him as a leader, and a few even thought of him as an anarchist as he railed against the politics of the sport. Mary Jo Pepplar, one of the greatest players, railed against the volleyball establishment too.

Lesbian liaisons figured as well. Some were. Some weren't. Most didn't pay much attention. I didn't pay too much attention. I was too wrapped up in the sport.

My mother did ask once, "How did X and X become roommates on this trip?"

Innocently and honestly, I answered, "They traded."

It was a different time then. High schoolers and college women played DGWS, Division of Girls' and Women's Sports, and AAU, American Athletic Union. There were no college scholarships, no professional teams. There was no money to be made then. When people started to discover the excitement of volleyball, as time progressed, things changed.

Starting out, I was only fourteen and didn't drive, I faced another hurdle. How to get to practices that were held in Long Beach one night, Pasadena the next, and the South Bay the next? That scope of fifty to seventy-five miles was daunting. Sally Lewis scooped me up in her pale green V.W. Beetle and made sure that I made all the practices. She mentored and shepherded me through what was then a volleyball maze. We did have great fun, though, talking and analyzing the game for hours. I was, and continue to be, most grateful.

Several years later, one night after a pre-Olympic practice in 1968, Sally and I were sitting on the den sofa at my house and talking volleyball strategies and politics. The T.V. was on. As our conversation became more animated, there was a sudden loud bang on the T.V.

Both of us became silent. Bobby Kennedy had just been shot at the Ambassador Hotel in Los Angeles, not far from where we were at my house in Westwood. This was just a scant two months after the assassination of Martin Luther King.

"Did you see that?" she asked.

I was speechless. Riveted to the T.V., we had just witnessed another historic milestone. Sadness and silence crept over us. We lived in turbulent and troubled times to be sure.

Was I a Typical Teen?

Marymount provided a springboard for me to indulge in silly schoolgirl antics and devote myself to academia and other endeavors. Since Marymount had and has a worldwide network of schools, from elementary to college, I'm still not sure of the origins of the traditions we practiced, but they were fun and memorable.

From the moment we started as freshmen, we were scooped up by seniors who "capped" us with the distinctive mascot sailor caps during a welcoming ceremony and then showed us around. There was a surprise kidnap breakfast where seniors kidnapped the freshmen, put us through our paces, and then met the whole group for breakfast. Those "paces" were humorous. I will never forget marching single file with classmates through a Los Angeles International Airport terminal in my pajamas at dawn-thirty in the morning, singing: "We are the goony girls, the goony girls, one, two, three, four," as we marched down the terminal concourse. Hardly anyone in the airport terminal raised an eyebrow after a glance at us marching in our pajamas.

Like any other fourteen-year-old, I joked, played around with, and intermingled with my classmates, except that I was laser-focused on volleyball. We were a small group of sixty girls, but there were no bullies that I experienced; no nasty girls. We were lucky, and we rallied for each other. We laughed, giggled, and freely sat Indian-style, cross-legged in our uniforms. There were only two males on campus, Mr. Ellis., the history teacher, and Thermos, the gardener!

I was a half year younger than most in my class who were already driving, so when sixteen approached, I couldn't wait to get my driver's license the moment I was eligible - as most sixteen-year-olds were in those days. I had the added motivation of getting to volleyball practices and tournaments that were held from Pasadena to Newport Beach. I wanted to be free of relying on others. I was at the DMV the morning of my sixteenth birthday when the DMV opened to take my test. I had bucked my father's new stick Mustang all around a parking lot for months learning to drive and shift, but when it came time for the test, I opted for my grandfather's automatic Impala, a boat by any description.

A rather dour DMV examiner walked out and got in the car with me. He instructed me to take off and get into the left turn lane. I was tense and tentative. I finally arrived on a side street, at which point he asked me to parallel park the car. I did nervously. He opened the rider's side door, looked at the curb, and dryly said,

"I said to park the car, not abandon it."

I quickly went into high gear and realized that I would have to loosen this guy up, or I was going to flunk.

"What a stressful, and sometimes dangerous job you have," I said. "I read an article in the paper last week about it."

That was all it took. He launched into a verbal tirade of all manner of hair-raising escapades he had had as an examiner, and I drove on and passed. And I was finally able to drive myself to all my destinations.

I'm not sure how, but the Marymount nurtured independent thinking, dedication, and passion. We were taught to question all that came before our path. Yes, all. The nuns nurtured and counseled, providing a strong grounding of common sense and other sensibilities. Although one nun, Sister Brendan, seemed to have it in for me. She pursued me on multiple levels, in algebra class and outside. If I stepped out of line for an instant, it was Sister Brendan who found me.

Academically sixty of us were divided into three groups randomly or perhaps by admission test scores or by I.Q.s, which were listed alongside scores. Yes, times were different then. I got to know and appreciate the humor of the twenty or so very bright girls that I was grouped with.

At lunch, the guys from Loyola High School would sometimes cruise up through the driveway rimming the playground. Classmates would talk with them until the nuns shooed them away. I, of course, was deeply involved in a volleyball game. No time for flirting. We designed our graduation gowns yearly, but with one caveat - it must be empire style. Despite birth control instructions from the lay teacher, Mrs. D., each year, we all knew who, if anyone, was pregnant at graduation.

All the girls in my class took off in various directions to college and adulthood, free-spirited, full of confidence and determination. Lest you think we were a homogenous group, we were not. The majority were Catholic, but there were other religious denominations represented as well. All were received with open arms and hearts.

Years later, I found out that some girls were undergoing some difficult situations at the time. For example, one girl was dealing with a parent who was undergoing a mental breakdown, and other similar earth-shattering situations.

The Westwood campus was a boarding school. My heart ached for those whom I later discovered were "parked" there by their parents not those who went home to their families regularly, but those who didn't.

Marymount provided a respite, a supportive family on multiple levels for those girls, and a wonderful expansive haven for me.

Most women I know complain about bad hair days. Not me. I complain about bad eyebrow days. Yes, I started out life as a platinum blonde and continue as such, with various other hues taking precedence. The downside? No eyebrows or eyelashes without makeup. If I don't draw my eyebrows correctly, I'm lopsided, crooked or condescending all day. I've always been a little different, full of contradictions, and up for a challenge. Volleyball was that challenge for me then.

Design Various international matches, many with Japan, held here in California's Southland, kept player interest high.

In April 1966, a U.S. Women's Volleyball team was chosen to go to Mexico City and play against their national team. I was one of the chosen twelve.

This was my way of leaving home, or at least that's how my mother remembers it. So, at age sixteen, I hugged my mother goodbye at LAX airport and took off. We took a plane to Tijuana and then changed planes to fly to Mexico City. The shanties lining the Tijuana runways were a sight that I will never forget. Nor will I forget seeing the Tijuana Mexican federales or police taking a fistful of money from a handsomely dressed male traveler who was waved through customs. The policeman detained the next deplaning passenger, a little elderly lady returning from the-U.S. He dumped her suitcase on the floor and said that she had not claimed anything - nor had she palmed him a fistful of money. The look of terror on her face was another part of the tableau that sticks in my mind.

We stayed at the Hotel del Prado in Mexico City, then a landmark that had obviously been there for a while. It was lovely, and made even more so by the stunning lobby mural by famed Mexican artist, Diego Rivera. (I had a deep interest in art and was dubbed the "artistic athlete" in my high school yearbook.)

Tall, lean, and lanky, Jean Gaertner, a volleyball phenome who participated in two Olympics in two different sports, was my roommate and ever so watchful of me. I was the youngster on the trip, most others were in their late teens or early twenties. None of my teacher teammates pulled adult rank on me. If I said that I was going to go somewhere, one of the others, like Jean, said, "Hold on, and I'll go with you."

The Sunday before we left to come home, on a day off, we all trekked out to the National Autonomous University of Mexico and were shown some beautiful Aztec artifacts and art. Volleyball trips always afforded expansive experiences. One of the professors at the university took us on a tour, and we came home with small, unimportant Aztec trinkets and artifacts.

We played the Mexican national team, and it was thrilling for me but not thrilling enough to remember the scores or the outcomes other than I remember coming home feeling victorious.

International matches at home in the U.S. were always a cause celebré and an enthralling contest, such as the one on December 13, 1965, at Cerritos College and another on December 14, 1965, at UCLA's Pauley Pavilion. We played against the Japanese national team. The U.S. team was comprised of a mix of familiar players.

A few scant months later, we played against the Japanese World Games team that had taken gold in the 1964 Olympic Games. We had taken silver. We played once at Los Angeles State College and then at Santa Ana College.

We again played against the legendary Japanese team again at the Veterans Memorial Auditorium in Culver City, California, on December 8, 1967. Did we win? I doubt it. They were flawless. The thrill of international competition was enough compensation for me.

Harlan Cohen had the nod from the Committee and was consistently named the women's team coach for national teams. He had understudied Hirofumi Daimatsu, the Japanese coach who had achieved tremendous success in the prior 1964 Olympics. In addition to inventing the "Japanese Roll," in which players slide sideways or forward on their sides to retrieve a ball and then instantly roll to their feet, Coach Daimatsu had ruthlessly drilled a factory team in Japan. The players' skills were almost perfect. They could play pepper (in which one player spikes the ball to another who digs it and then passes it back to the first to do the same thing all over again) for what seemed a half hour with nary a stray ball. The Japanese team, who trained 364 days a year, after working in the factory for a half day, were tall, several were six feet or taller, contrary to stereotypes of the time.

After the game, we asked the girls, through an interpreter, how they stayed together for the four or five years. They explained that they had signed a pact to stay together.

"Would you do it again?" we asked.

Without hesitating, there was a chorus of, "No."

Each player had her fingertips or parts of their fingers taped. I was curious, but I would find out why firsthand later.

On December 8, 1967, we played against the Japanese team again at the Veteran's Memorial Auditorium in Culver City, California.

Nationals always afforded the chance to meet and greet other players from around the country and to study how proficient they were or how differently they played. California was by far the powerhouse. I was so serious that I headed back to the hotel to rest so I would be at the top of my game. Some of the older, more wild players-I was among the youngest-would party in the halls into the wee hours of the night. After the tournament, or once eliminated from the round-robin play, it was serious party time.

Getting there, getting the money to go, and where to stay were always questions. The first year I played with the Shamrocks, Jack Kent Cooke, then the owner of the Los Angeles Lakers, was one of our sponsors, and hence we played one or more exhibitions in the Sports Arena in downtown Los Angeles. Surely, I thought this was a good omen.

The key players on the Shamrocks and Renegades were well acquainted from playing on either of the teams, from trips and exhibition matches. I was getting to know them.

Jane Ward, the captain, was also the coach who had a quick tongue or quip just the same. She was fiercely loyal to her club team and, yes, committed to the game. She was a solid player. Sometimes it seemed as though she had an invisible "guard all" shield on when she felt uncomfortable or under attack.

Mary Perry, an almost six-foot-tall lithe blonde who, when she felt stressed, used to go out and jog for nine miles, was a quick-witted comedienne of the first order. She liked to laugh and make others laugh. She would frequently speak in strange cartoon-like voices, and was quick to dub any one of us with a nickname based on whatever was happening.

Marilyn McReavy from Texas, a six-foot tall, freckled redhead, used to speak with a bit of a drawl. Strong- minded but nice, Marilyn tended to hang with Mary Jo.

Linda Murphy, another freckled redhead, and sometimes called "Red" was 6'3", not terribly talkative, but when she did say something, we listened. Linda held many honors, including the Outstanding Player of the S.P.A.-A.A.U. Tournament Helms Award.

There was "Feather" Sharon Peterson, a pert blonde from the South Bay area, who always sported a smile and a friendly greeting and had an indomitable spirit on the court. Hence her nickname, which grew from her ability to streak across the court on a moment's notice. She was a setter and was 5' 6 ½' tall.

My roommate Miki McFadden, nicknamed Miki McFoo by Mary, at 5' 9', was a blonde from Hawaii and had a contagious laugh. Miki and I were the babies.

"Otis," Nancy Owen, was a blonde who also was 5'8 ½'. She hailed from the South Bay or Palos Verdes area. Her nickname came from a pair of bib overalls that she wore one day.

Fanny Hopeau was a pure Hawaiian from the Islands who was full of fire, power, and spirit. Dark wavy hair and a booming laugh were her trademarks. Fanny, who had a heart of gold, was 5' 8'.

Bobbi Perry, 5' 8', also from Hawaii, was dark-haired, spoke melodically, and always seemed to have a smile on her face. She tended to be serious, but with a ready laugh.

Ninja Jorgensen, at 6' 1', was blonde and had a reassuring quality to her voice and a lilt to her laugh.

Patti Bright, a Chicago transplant, was only 5' 3 ½', a bit shorter than Feather, and was remarkably even-tempered. Altogether we were an affable group. It didn't take much for one or more of us to launch a barrage of good-natured humor barbs.

This was the core of women that I lived with, trained with, and worked with sporadically off and on for months at a time over four years. It was a good group and, thankfully, compatible.

World Games Journal Vignettes

After a series of international matches here, several international trips, such as one to Mexico in 1966, nationals, and much training, it was late 1966. Harlan Cohen was the women's USA coach for the international matches, and he had been named coach for the World Games. The World Games Team was chosen in the fall of that year, and I was one of them. The Games would take place in Tokyo, Japan, in January 1967, and the athletes would be billeted in the 1964 Olympic Village. We would also be stopping in Hawaii for a week before and after the games. I was on cloud nine when I found out I made the team. Not only did I make it, but I was also going to feed my travel lust. Airports were magic for me then. Stepping inside meant the world was at my feet!

A month before leaving, I was playing a "jest" game of volleyball at Marymount with some of my high school classmates. I jumped, came down, and twisted my knee. After multiple trips to the orthopedist, I was sore from a slightly ripped, but not severed, cartilage in my right knee.

"Will you be okay to play in January?" the Committee asked.

"Absolutely," I said, determined that I would be going to Japan.

The normal treatment was surgery which left a Frankenstein-like scar up and down the leg. This just didn't fit into my plans. I worked tirelessly before and after the trip to build up the muscles around my knee to compensate. It hurt and ached. I took a cloth bag filled with whatever weights I could find, usually telephone books, and slung it over my knee. I raised and lowered my right leg exercising the muscles around the knee while reading, watching T.V., or sitting. Still, standing on concrete or hard surfaces or putting all my weight on the knee caused a maelstrom of pain.

A senior at Marymount in Los Angeles, I would miss a month of school. My grades were good, so that wasn't a problem; however, packing for the trip was. We had warm woolies to pack for Tokyo, sometimes freezing in January, and jams and bathing suits for the Hawaiian tropics. I developed blisters on my hands from carrying and dragging my suitcase all around airports on this trip. But I did learn how to pack the maximum possible in a suitcase, thanks to my mother - everything was flat, and I fit a month's worth of cold-weather and hot-weather clothes. Big suitcase!

The United States Volleyball Association, paid for the trip and provided us with fuzzy warm coats for the chilly Japan January.

Warm, tropical, and rainy in January, Hawaii was magic to me as a seventeen-year-old, there for the first time. As the seasonal warm rain passed, I learned to step under a palm frond.

We played practice matches in Honolulu, hung out at the Outrigger Canoe Club, and, of course, practiced. I tried surfing for the first time near Diamond Head but didn't dare stand up for fear of falling on the jagged coral just below the water's surface.

The native Hawaiians on the team, Miki, Fanny, and Bobby, and our hosts indoctrinated us with Hawaiian lore and superstitions. We tried poi and other native dishes, and I had my first lesson in how to use chopsticks. Miki's mother gave me my first foot massage - which I thought rather eccentric until I experienced it. Nirvana!

Before I left, I was given a travel journal by students and teachers at my high school, which I kept during the World Games, documenting the trip.

Journal Vignettes January to February 1967: Los Angeles to Oahu Island, Waikiki...

Nine-hour flight to Tokyo at 10 PM. The sun came up at 3 AM as the stewardess was offering breakfast. I stretched out in the plane aisle to try to get some sleep...Walked to the military base, so nice out, had dinner, and played slot machines. Fun! Then to the gym...practice, practice, practice...and to Noncommissioned Officer's Club for show Kabuki dancers... watched the Japanese subtitled "Man from Uncle" on T.V...Our translator Katsuko wrote out Nancy's and my names in all three Japanese alphabets: Katagana, Hiragana, and Kanji...Before; before the game, photographers took pictures of Jane and me, oldest and youngest...At dinner, we spoke a common language French. The president of the International Volleyball Association very nicely told me that my French grammar was terrible. I agreed, but he agreed that he understood me!

Alice doesn't feel good, and Metrow is sick. Linda's knee hurts, and Fanny has a cold... pictures with Katsuko and Mamasan...To Olympic Village, to the enlarged ice box for practice - it must have been 30 degrees in the gym very hard to warm up .... Practice, practice, practice, practice...Took a Japanese bath with Nancy, Sharon, and Fanny. Shower first, then soak. So relaxed I could hardly move! Practice, practice, practice, practice, practice...

Cal also ordered some pink champagne for us...U.S. servicemen from Vietnam were all over...in the cocktail lounge talking to Bob, Roger, the Commander, and the other Navy guys....Kobe...steak.... Practice, practice, practice, practice....According to new roommate Ninja, "We're three logs." Bobbi, Nancy, and I really don't have too much trouble sleeping...

Off to the Budokan (the 1964 Olympic venue for volleyball) for a warm-up and opening ceremonies. We played the Korean team. We took two straight and then took the fourth game...

WE DID IT—WE WON! We beat Peru today...Second Place, silver medals...The president of the Japan Volleyball Association, Masaichi Nishikawa, invited each of us to a friendship party on January 28 after the closing ceremonies at the Nippon Budokan...Osaka, and a one-hour bus ride to Nichibo Company. Change and warm up with the Nichibo team. After match-back to a Japanese-style hotel with traditional Japanese-style toilets (otherwise known as a hole in the ground) and baths...Went to the Golden Pavilion. It snowed - beautiful - a sight that I will never forget... Took the Bullet Train to Tokyo past Mount Fuji... Hard to believe that we're on our way home. What an experience chockful of memorable people, places, and experiences!

Pan American Primer

"We're driving, and we'll meet you there," said Mary Jo.

The second year, I had joined the Renegades, led and coached then by Mary Jo Peppler and Mary Perry, the two '64 Olympians who inspired me. The atmosphere was different from that of the Shamrocks, intense but infused with humor and some silliness. The nationals were in Detroit, Michigan, where it was cold and rainy. The dark brick buildings were so different from what I knew in California.

A renegade politically and philosophically herself, Mary Jo was poetry in motion. A beauty with high cheekbones, she was six feet tall, and explosively powerful, yet every movement of her almost perfectly sculpted body was graceful. Bright, curious, and ever-pushing to improve the game, she would study and implement new playing approaches–spiking and passing techniques. She bristled at the politics and railed at the hierarchy of the sport.

Mary Jo also had a silly schoolgirl side too.

"Do that again, and you'll get the spin-around," she'd threaten, if the mood was right. None of us were petite, but that didn't stop her. If the teasing continued, she would pop the person up over her head and start twirling like a gymnastics act. Most impressive. We all laughed until our sides ached as the spinnee landed on a bed or sofa.

"I'll take the t-shirts and wash them," she'd said.

At nationals, Mary Jo collected all of our white jerseys and headed off to the laundromat so we would have clean uniforms the next day. She returned and pulled out the T-shirts.

"Good work, Mary Jo!" was the refrain amidst a sea of laughter.

So much for the uniform color! We teased her unmercifully about washing the previously white, now pink shirts with red shorts.

I connected with Mary Jo on multiple levels. Her poetic side was as expansive as her play was inspiring. She and I would stay up until the wee hours of the morning writing poetry and talking philosophy in the off -season.

It was the summer of 1967. I had just graduated from high school. The Association's "Windy" was playing nonstop on the radio, and Sidney Poitier's To Sir, With Love was playing in the theaters.

The V Pan American Games were to be held in Winnipeg, Manitoba, Canada, from July 23 to August 6, 1967. Eighteen prospective players were chosen for the Pan American Games at the Detroit Nationals. We worked out doggedly between nationals in May and the onset of summer.

On July 1, 1967, we flew to Minneapolis, Minnesota, where we trained intensively for two weeks at the University of Minnesota. There we lived in the dorms and worked out in a grueling daily schedule. It was early July, and the weather was sultry and humid. The mosquitoes were out in force.

We practiced twice daily for three hours except for Sundays when we only practiced for four hours. We were judged by The Committee during three nights of drills and play at Hamlin University Gym.

One afternoon between practices, we were reading and amusing themselves. The sirens went off, and all the Californians and Hawaiians looked at each other, puzzled.

"Please go directly to the basement," the authoritative voice boomed over the loudspeaker system, "tornado warning!"

With alarm in our eyes, the other Californians and I trundled down to the basement. After what seemed an eternity, the all-clear whistle blew, and we resumed our normal activities, but not without comparing the pros and cons of tornadoes and earthquakes. Most of the Californians chose earthquakes over tornadoes.

On the third night, the final twelve were selected by the Committee.

"I made it!" I thought to myself with a thrill. "I made the team!"

We were outfitted with traveling and playing uniforms and luggage.

With eleven others, I was off to the V Pan American Games in Winnipeg, Manitoba, Canada. The games showcased top competitor countries in the Western Hemisphere. Brunette former player, Alice Englert, was the manager, and Harlan Cohen was again the coach.

We arrived in Winnipeg and were driven to a picturesque castle-like building in the countryside outside of Winnipeg. The turreted castle, a scene out of a European postcard, was a school for the deaf and very quiet.

Opening ceremonies were held on Sunday amidst pouring rain. Britain's Prince Philip, representing Queen Elizabeth, greeted the countries as they marched into the stadium in the festive parade. Don Schollander, the four- time gold medal winner in the 1964 Olympics, was the flag bearer. Track star Ralph Boston carried the flag during the closing parade two weeks later, but then with the sun shining brilliantly.

I was agog watching the other athletes and sports. This was the first time that we met and interfaced with other teams and sports. Prior to this, it was volleyball only. I had never before seen cyclists cruising by in practice with perfectly chiseled and clean-shaven muscular legs. The United States sent a full contingent of 429 athletes in an array of sports: track and field, swimming, diving, fencing, gymnastics, judo, rowing, shooting, weightlifting, wrestling, yachting, men's basketball, baseball, water polo, soccer, and men's and women's volleyball.

Somewhere during the Pan Am Games, I met basketball captain Mike Silliman for the first time. He was good-looking with a dry sense of humor and a ready smile.

He was 6'5', the perfect height as far as I was concerned. A graduate of West Point, he was a lieutenant in the army. Later, in the fall, he called me and asked me out to see one of his favorites,

Bob Hope, who was performing at UCLA Pauley Pavilion. Oh, I was smitten! What a crush I developed. I frequently added seeing him to my list of why I wanted to go to the Olympics - to see him again.

We worked out regularly until the games began. We would face Canada, the host country, Brazil, Mexico, Peru, and Cuba.

One day several of us made our way to the basketball stadium to take in some games. Brazil was playing. Brazil had a center who was well over seven feet tall.

The team finished playing, and the center and several teammates sat several rows ahead of us. The center stood up and kept standing up, and then he made his way up to where we were sitting. One of his female teammates called out, asking him to get something at the concession. He leaned over, stretched out his arm and hand across all the rows. She put money in his hand, and it looked like toy money since his arms were so long and his hands were so big. Quite a sight!

We had an early morning game one day, and Alice feared that we wouldn't get out of bed. We awoke in disbelief, crawled out of bed, wiped our eyes, and peered out to see if we were dreaming. There was a suited bagpipe player marching up and down the hall. Alice had hired him to ensure that we would be up and on time for the match. It worked.

Alice also had a cure for mosquito bites. "Yahoo! She's here." you could hear the mosquitoes say as they licked their lips in anticipation of my stepping outside. I wasn't alone. Half the team walked around scratching red welts as though we had fleas. Alice pulled out Preparation-H . To my amazement, it actually worked to relieve bug-bite itches.

We were introduced to one of the U.S. team trainers, Jim, who wrapped our ankles when needed, and massaged our tight and sore legs. Tall, red-haired with freckles, Jim had a gentle speaking voice that was instantly reassuring. He took good care of us, and we appreciated it. This was the first time that I had experienced the care of a good sports trainer. They're worth their weight in gold. At the end of the games, Mary Perry and I presented Jim with a signed volleyball one day at lunch just to say thanks.

The U.S. vied against volleyball teams from Peru, Cuba, Brazil, Mexico, and Canada. With five wins and no losses in the fifteen-game round-robin tournament, we won the gold medal! Pan American Games gold medals are not real gold, but they still held

great meaning for us.

I was amazed by the simple fact that the Brazilian women's volleyball team had a standing thirty-six-inch jump. Without a running approach, each could jump as high as a yard stick which was quite intimidating until we realized that they weren't that strong a volleyball team! The sport had come a long way from its origins in 1865, when William G. Morgan invented the game in Holyoke, Massachusetts, and called it mintonette.

There were colorful Pan Am flags flying everywhere. It was, of course, the athletes' job to get them. One night six of us went out in a car, and we stopped at several flagpoles. Nancy "Otis" shimmied up one pole and got one. Mary Perry shimmied up another and so forth. I came home with a beautiful Pan American flag, blue background with the stylized red insignia of the games, and, of course, the maple leaf.

One night the men's and women's teams met and went out for a drink. I joined the volleyball players who ranged in height from mid-five feet to mid-six feet with age spans of seventeen to late thirties. I was seventeen and went along for the ride.

"I'll have a whiskey sour," I said.

The waitress didn't flinch. Baby-faced twenty-something Danny Patterson ordered, "I'll have a beer." The waitress asked for I.D. immediately. We all laughed.

One day after the competition, a Canadian spectator, blond and buff, eighteen-year-old Robert whom I befriended, asked, "Would you like to go waterskiing?"

"Never been, don't know how, but I'm game."

"That would be fun," I said.

He picked me up, and we drove out to Lake Winnipeg. He introduced me to the lake area and its beauty. He coached me, and in a little amount of time, I was up and waterskiing all around the lake on two skis. One ski still challenges me, and I don't water ski without thinking of and thanking Robert for teaching me.

Feeling victorious, gold medal in hand (well, it looked like gold), I headed back to Minneapolis to visit my Swedish and Irish relatives and then returned home to Los Angeles.

Summer was ending, and the competitive indoor volleyball season was about to begin. I had missed the summer beach season, and I was readying to rejoin the Shamrocks. We worked out intensively all fall/winter season, playing in and winning most of the tournaments until Nationals in Portland, Oregon in May 1968. I was included in the group invited to try out for the Olympics. It would be a long and arduous season, running, weightlifting, training, and playing.

I was dedicated to my Olympic dream. I met a nice chap, Nick, through my high school friend, Terri. I had gone to grad night with him at the Coconut Grove, and he had asked me out several times. He took me to dinner at a charming Scottish-themed restaurant in Glendale quite a distance from Westwood, where I lived. He took me to dinner in Newport Beach, then an hour's drive away, to a charming yacht transformed into a restaurant.

We chatted and had a good time, but at ten o'clock, I asked, "Mind if we head home? I have an early practice at 7 A.M. tomorrow morning."

Poor guy.

Chapter 2: UCLA A New Chapter

It was a familiar sight, even as a tween in elementary school (first through eighth grade) at Saint Paul the Apostle in Westwood, UCLA. After Saturday volleyball, basketball, or softball practices and skirmishes at our school, the boys and girls would group and walk to Westwood for lunch and a movie. After my embarrassment at Sophia Loren emerging from the sea with a wet top, leaving nothing to the imagination, in *Boy on a Dolphin*, I experienced my first kiss at the Bruin Theater one Saturday afternoon.

Another Saturday afternoon, en route to the Village, we stopped at Pierce Brothers Westwood Village Memorial Park with gravesites and a mausoleum. Pranking overcame us. We wrote "Help Let Me Out" backward in chalk on Marilyn Monroe's crypt and then continued to the movies just a normal Saturday.

Other times we would trek a couple of blocks north of the Village to the UCLA Ackerman Student Union. This was a new world with a bowling alley, snack bars, a large assembly hall, and a huge student store. These were impressive symbols of independence to me as an eighth grader. Later, I learned that UCLA had its own post office. This was indeed a microcosm of the world and society. Families with young children, the elderly, international students, and a diverse student body populated the area. Westwood Village, where my teenage father, in the late thirties, stood in front of the Bank of America building and sold daily papers, was a hub of upscale department stores - Bullock's, Desmond's, and FedCo and a host of up- and down-scale smaller shops and restaurants such as the Swedish/Danish Chatam. I had explored them all, alone and with friends.

Bullock's was a familiar haunt for me for all sorts of things, from clothes to hairdryers. I remember a day when, as a small tyke, I went shopping with my mother and grandmother; I must have wandered off.

When Mother found me, she said, "You were lost!"

I quickly retorted, "I wasn't lost; you were!" asserting my strong mind at an early age.

An impressive clock tower heralded the drug store on the corner down from Bullock's, and just down the street was Henkes jewelry store frequented by all in my family. Hamburger Hamlet, down the street, was a regular haunt in high school. Westwood Village and UCLA were familiar parts of my hometown.

I was going to attend UCLA in the fall of 1967, and I was excited, nervous, and filled with anticipation. I remember watching the 1962 film *Whatever Happened to Baby Jane?* The Sunday night before starting, knowing full well that I was so excited I might not sleep that night. A slightly scary movie fit the bill.

The college experience overtook me. I was learning about the campus and its social and political parameters. It was thrilling. UCLA was a multidisciplinary tinderbox reflective of the sixties that I took for granted at the time. This was normal for college in my mind.

Activism and Innovation

The groundwork had been laid before I arrived and continued with speakers of every description: conservative William F. Buckley, Dr. Martin Luther King, Black Panther Eldridge Cleaver, Timothy Leary of "Turn on, tune in, drop out" fame, President Lyndon Johnson stopped by to speak along with other world leaders. And a host of dignitaries. Arthur Ashe reigned in tennis. Coach John Wooden had started his winning ascent. The Kingston Trio, South African Miriam Makeba, Thelonius Monk, and others entertained in various campus locations or the Ackerman Union Ballroom.

Nobel Prize-winning chemist Willard Libby was celebrated for the radiocarbon dating process.

And in Boelter Hall, Professor Leonard Kleinrock and his student logged onto ARPANET (Advanced Research Projects Agency Network) and communicated with Stanford University, the origins of the first internet. This all took place toward the close of the sixties. And UCLA celebrated its fiftieth anniversary.

I managed to start college during the start of a politically explosive time. Before I arrived, the social justice and equality platform moved from Hyde Park between the men's and women's gym below Janss Steps, a little south of Bruin Walk and Kerckhoff Hall. As you walked up the hill to class, tables and sometimes speakers of every description graced the campus amidst loud demonstrations and acclaim.

Apart from stellar speakers of all sorts, who represented an array of political and social views, UCLA students joined in the Free Speech Movement, which began in and was supposedly fiercer at Berkeley, although hard to believe in retrospect. Walking up Bruin Walk, students were greeted with political, ethnic, religious, and social ideas of every persuasion. It was exciting to hear the names and see some of the speakers. However, I was not a particularly political animal at the time, other than fiercely advocating for social justice, equality, women's rights, and abortion rights.

Yes, it was my college generation that fought for Roe V. Wade. (While I was not a placard-carrying demonstrator, I remember walking out in the morning at age twelve and scanning the front page of the Los Angeles Times to read about a woman who had used a coat hanger to end her pregnancy and, unfortunately, her life. Even then, I felt this to be unfair. I was fully behind the women's choice movement even though I didn't think I could personally have an abortion.)

I was initially overwhelmed, coming from a class of sixty girls and now facing 33,000 students. Freshmen classes were frequently lecture classes of 500 students. Professors graded the curve based on the class scores. If you had problems with the lecture, the professor recommended that you read the book, which he typically wrote, and which parroted the lectures - not much help. It seemed as though some professors were anxious to weed out any borderline students.

I took my first final in psychology, a multiple-choice test in which all four choices were correct, one more correct than the others. I didn't even open a book for the final. I figured everyone in my class was as bright as the girls I had gone to high school with - most in my academic group of twenty received scholarships and awards. One girl received a scholarship to every college she applied to and went to Harvard! Even though I had held my own in high school and graduated cum laude, I was initially intimidated at UCLA. Little did I know as a commuting student - I lived at home with my parents only a mile away – that tests were on file in the dorms, and there were many other details of matriculation that I quickly caught onto later.

The problem for me was going to the Olympics. Even though I was in my first year at the university, I was obsessed with training for and participating in the Olympics.

In some ways, the oldest of three, with a younger brother and sister, I was my father's first "son." At five years old, I used to don red shorts and swim out past the breakers with my father at a locale in the Pacific that we nicknamed "Knucklehead Beach." It was great fun, and I so adored him. Then he told me I had to put on a top before we went to the beach. I was indignant. Why? I thought. He didn't wear a top. I acquiesced.

When I was older and in the running for the Olympic team, he was my biggest rooter.

Sports ran in my family. My six-foot-three father played basketball and ran track at UCLA, and his six-foot-six brother put the shot. It was a tradition that I wanted to continue; besides, I was a natural tomboy.

The Olympics hung like a bright star in the sky that I wanted. No one in my high school or family had gone to the Olympics. One high school classmate had gone to Wimbledon, and another had missed making the U.S. Olympic swimming team by two-tenths of a second.

I was on probation at UCLA after getting a D in psychology after not studying for the final. Balancing reading Shakespeare eight hours a day and training multiple days a week was a gamble I didn't want to risk. Both were too important to me. So, after several quarters at UCLA, I went to my mother and explained that I couldn't study to keep my grades up and train without jeopardizing one or the other. I was never one to do things halfway.

My mother told a friend many years later, "Laurie always knew what she wanted."

I wanted the Olympics. Campus life was fun, and I had made some friends, but I had barely dipped my toe into life on campus. In my mind, I had to pursue the Olympics before college. I was torn, but I knew that this was my chance. College, for the moment, took a willing back seat.

My parents agreed to let me drop out of school for a year to train and work toward going to the Olympics. Their friends chided them, telling my parents I would never return.

Even at seventeen, I never doubted that I would return.

Now I could devote myself full-time to training for volleyball. And I did.

*E*n route: Long Beach, Lake Tahoe, and Denver

"Mom, I think I have a fever," I said.

"It's probably a reaction to your travel shots," Mom explained.

About a week before reporting to the Olympic training camp, I had the recommended inoculations for traveling to Mexico. The day after, I spiked a small fever. The next day my fever rose higher, and by the third day, my mother packed me in the car and drove to our pediatrician.

I exited the car and said, "Mom, I think I'm going to faint."

"You will not faint here. I'll have none of that," she snapped in an uncharacteristically strict voice.

It worked; I stayed conscious till I lay down on the examining table in the doctor's office. I don't run fevers well. He examined me and announced that I had a mighty case of strep throat. He knew that I had to be in tip-top shape in a week. A horse shot of antibiotics later, and I was home recuperating. I was back in full force in a week, but it took a while to get my volleyball timing back.

Before entering the training camp, the selected players worked out intensively for three months. In addition to volleyball, we ran a minimum of two miles a day on our own. I hated running. I started stiffly but managed to run the four laps around the track. Once finished, and I usually ran only a minimum of two miles, I felt good. I envied others like Mary Perry, who seemed to run effortlessly and would run multiple miles to loosen up when needed.

Sometimes during practice, Harlan would have us run up and down the stadium steps for what seemed like an eternity, all the while I was fighting pain and deep burning leg muscles. Stadium stair running is bona fide torture. Then after practice at Long Beach State University, we would weight train. I have less than fond memories of the Universal Weight machines there.

Harlan's philosophy at the time was to simultaneously work on strength and endurance. He had us increase reps or sets and weight. Was this the proper way, the most proven way? Did he know about such things? I don't know now and certainly didn't know then. We were careful, though, and no one was injured.

This was when the term "jock" negatively affected women. It did change but not for a while. The team had the weight room reserved for certain times at California State University at Long Beach.

One night we walked in, the weight room attendant said, "Room is reserved, Guys," Clear out."

We walked in and reset all their weights up several hundred pounds from where the guys had them. There were audible gasps from the guys who had stayed to watch. We could hear the term jock, bandied about. Leg pressing 500 pounds or more was standard for all of us.

The Olympic trials were held in Long Beach from August 24 to September 2, 1968. Players to try out had been named at nationals in Portland. Eighteen of the usuals were chosen along with a list of alternates: Patti Bright, Ann Heck, Fanny Hopeau, Ninja Jorgensen, Laurie Lewis (me), Miki McFadden, Marilyn McReavy, Nancy Owen, Barbara Perry, Mary Perry, Sharon Peterson, and Jane Ward made up the core.

These were the women I had played volleyball, lived and traveled with for four years, and knew from nationals, club teams, or exhibits.

During those four years, we were scheduled to put on an exhibit one night at March Air Reserve Base in Riverside, California. Ninja drove. The exhibit came off without a hitch, but upon leaving to return to Los Angeles, the fuel pump in her car blew. We spent the night awaiting the fuel pump delivery while buying candy and chips from the vending machine. I arrived home at seven A.M., just in time to hand the morning paper to my father, who listened intently as I explained I had spent the night in a gas station in Riverside.

I met Patti Bright, married to Mike Bright, on the Olympic men's team, at State Beach. A beautiful couple, they had an adorable two-year-old who adroitly put her hands on her hips and would frequently exclaim, "*Diculous!*" I still quote her today.

Miki, Bobby (Barbara), and Fanny, I knew from nationals, previous teams, and our stop in Hawaii en route to the Tokyo World Games, when all three introduced us to Hawaiian lore and tradition. Miki had attended USC while I was at UCLA, and we had played against each other in the cross-town rivalry.

Sharon hailed from the South Bay area and then later moved to Hawaii. I was on several teams with Sharon and Nancy Owen. I played with Marilyn on the Renegades, and, of course, I played with Jane Ward on the Shamrocks.

Mary Perry, the Mel Blanc of the team with her ever-changing voices and impressions, had a terrific sense of humor, and we connected famously. She and I would go horseback riding and get together in our free time (between teams and practicing) to enjoy ourselves.

This was a unique, amiable group, supportive of one another, and each with an iron-clad competitive spirit!

There were others integrally involved in the game who had not been selected this time but were part of former international teams. Among the scorekeepers at the trials were Adelaide Packwood, who had served as manager for some U.S. teams, Sally Lewis, my friend and high school coach, and Ann McLoughlin, who later married Wink Davenport, a member of the men's 1968 Olympic Volleyball team. If the name is familiar, their daughter Lindsay Davenport became a power in women's tennis.

I'll start at the beginning. We were in Long Beach for two weeks for the Olympic Trials, starting August 23; after weight training and running two-to-four miles daily or wind sprints, we worked out every day for six hours a day - from nine to noon and then from seven to ten at night. It was summer, and it was hot.

A typical workout was like a disciplined rally of volleyball parts. We started a workout by stretching to prevent pulled muscles. We jogged at the gym and then started drills. In a pepper game, one spikes the ball at the second player, who digs or passes it back and repeats. Harlan then spiked ball after ball at us quickly in staccato fashion as we dived across the floor to dig the ball or keep it in play. Miss the ball, and there were always more to come.

Setting and spiking ball after ball with only moments in between followed. Serving practice capped the pre-scrimmage set. We had to do a hundred sit-ups in the morning before leaving the gym to run two miles or do wind sprints. Repeat at night with some slightly different drills interspersed.

We hoped this regimen would help us fend off the daunting Japanese and others we would compete against.

Fatigue and soreness got to some, but much energy remained during the afternoon downtimes. We would create our indulgences, whether enjoying Adelaide's Packwood's homemade cookies, talking, or playing pranks. I have some good pictures of Marilyn bombing others with shaving cream and other pastimes. We learned how to rub each other down by virtue of where we hurt. Hot to cold, and then constant working out many times left us stiff and sore.

Humor was our cornerstone. During training camp, a regular practice had just ended in Long Beach, and someone had contacted the coach/manager to see if we could sample protective bras. The coach opened a box, and there were Madonna-like pointed plastic cups hooked together with elastic. These were meant to be worn over our regular bras. We slipped them on and proceeded with Japanese rolls and Russian dives on the floor. These rather firm pointy cups are inverted. Owh! We quickly slipped our hands under our tee shirts and into the cups and poked them out again. There was a chorus of click/pop in the gym - the same noise that clickers or frogs made when we were in grammar school and the nuns clicked to get us to genuflect on cue. Jane Ward quickly picked one up and poured her water into it.

"Here's to protective bras," she said. We followed suit and toasted each other and the not-so-protective bras.

That was sheer experimentation and unsuccessful at that. We were being studied since, physiologically, women in sports were a relatively new phenomenon. A revelation at this time was that some women stopped menstruating during training and competition but returned to normal about a month after returning home. The same was not true of all the women on the volleyball team. Some had mighty uncomfortable days during training.

Aches and pains were nothing new. All of us had suffered at one time or another from sprained ankles, knees, jammed fingers or knuckles, or worse. These were typical volleyball injuries. Torn knee cartilages were not uncommon either. I had worked intensively on my knee, which was fine now.

While we all had very strong hands, we worked out so often and touched the volleyball so much that most of the natural skin oil from our hands and fingers disappeared. The leather balls sucked up the natural skin oils. Many of us had dry, cracked, bleeding fingers, which we slathered in cream or lard nightly and then taped our fingertips before practice or games to preserve the little oil we had left.

To acclimate to the altitude of Mexico City, which is 7,342 feet above sea level, the team was scheduled to go to Lake Tahoe on September 4, where the final twelve would be selected. We left Long Beach and headed for the small town of Camp Richardson in Lake Tahoe, elevation 6,225, with one post office, hotel, and gas station. If you drove too fast, you missed the town. It was rustic and charming.

I can't say the same about the food. The menu had a sameness about it that became monotonous. There was a nice enough chap who always wore a ski cap and prepared the food - like a character from a movie. Among other things, we were served Jell-O with dinner every night. I have nothing against Jell-O. I like it but not night after night after night. And to complicate matters, this Jell-O® was made like Jigglers before Jigglers were invented! One night after dinner, we snapped.

"Food fight," someone yelled. We immediately launched into a Jell-O basketball game against the wall and the Jell-O bounced back!

We worked out in Tahoe at the pace we had in Long Beach. Harlan gave us three days to acclimate. On the first day, he had us run two miles. It turned into a four-hour jog walk -a challenge when you have just arrived at a 6,000-foot elevation. The second day was three miles. The third day was four miles. And by the fourth day, I was ready to say forget it! I want to go home. All of us had such spurts, though. We were all ready to quit at one time or another.

Harlan and I butted heads and traded barbs frequently. But then he butted heads with just about everyone on the team.

"Laurie, you need to lose some weight," he told me.

"Harlan, what more can I do? I eat sparingly and am working out. I can't stop eating altogether." I responded. No matter. Exercise and eating sparingly produced no weight loss results. It didn't come off.

We worked out, ran several miles, and did wind sprints one day. It was hot, and I lost several pounds of water weight from sweating, which, of course, went right back on after rehydrating myself.

"Great," he said when he weighed us after practice.

"Harlan, it's water weight which will return as soon as I drink water," I said.

The next day he weighed me, and the few pounds had returned, so he sent me out to run the track several more times. I still remember the hot tears streaming down my cheeks as anger and resentment rose at the unfairness as I was directed to run extra laps around the track.

Despite a hail of caustic complaints aimed at the coach, we acclimated quickly. We were in good shape and had been working out for years, running two to four miles daily. Most recently, in training camp, we would work out playing volleyball for three hours in the morning, do 100 sit-ups, and either do wind sprints or run for two miles after practice. After a few hours off, we reconvened again in the gym for another three hours of volleyball practice. Prior weight training had helped too.

It was the end of summer, so we were still walking around in shorts and sandals when we weren't practicing. By the time we left Tahoe, it was snowing. This was only the second time I'd seen snowfall - here in Tahoe and the first time at the World Games at the awe-inspiring Golden Pavilion in Kyoto, Japan.

Up in Tahoe, we were joined by the track and gymnastics teams. We met many of them. Muriel Grossman was the team coach and seemed to have things well under control - the team too. The gymnastics team was incredibly disciplined and diminutive. I watched them eat one day and was struck by how meager their diet was - but they were also half our height. Cathy Rigby was part of that team. We watched as they entered the dining room and ate a pittance.

The U.S. Men's Volleyball team was there as well. We knew them all and managed to fraternize with them regularly. The team consisted of: John Alstrom, D. "Mike" Bright, Wink (Winthrop) Davenport, H. "Smitty" Duke, Tom Haine, Jack Henn, Robert May, Danny Patterson, Larry Rundle, Jon Stanley, Rudy Suwara, and Pete Valasco. Jim Coleman was the coach, and John Lowell was the manager.

The makeup of the men's and women's teams was almost a mirror image. California was home to the majority of players, with one from Texas and three from Hawaii on both teams. Those states were the three powerhouse teams at the time, and all the players knew one another from previous teams, nationals, or the beach circuit.

This physically demanding sport, requiring grueling training, performance, and strength, rarely allowed those over the age of thirty to excel. With an average age of twenty-six, the men's team ranged from twenty-one to thirty-one. The women's ages ranged from eighteen to thirty-six and had an average age of twenty-four.

The men's and women's teams had quite a party before we left Tahoe, and everyone joined in. The Camp Richardson Lodge, at the time, was a homey, oversized cabin with slightly worn furnishings and paneled walls on the main road. We all emptied into the great room on the last night, where we reveled for hours sharing stories of training woes and anticipating what was to come.

While we were housed in a lodge in Tahoe, the track team lived in trailers not far away. They came down to watch T.V. at our lodge. The trailers they stayed in were supposedly terrible. A team doctor visiting the team said that if they didn't clean them up, he'd move the guys out the next day. Apparently, someone cleaned them up because the guys continued staying there.

The track qualifying finals would be held on the nearby track, half of which was dense forest and the other half clear. I couldn't wait to see Jim Ryan run, the first to break the four-minute mile run. One day off, Mary Perry and several of us trekked down through the forest to the track and watched. It was quite odd to see the runners take off and sprint on the track into the forest, only to emerge shortly on the other side. Afterward, we set out to walk to the car and had to cross the track. There was a gaggle of press around Jim Ryan, who, like other runners, typically lost lunch, breakfast, or whatever after pushing himself to his speed sprinting limit.

"Let the guy have a moment of peace and then barrage him with questions and snapping cameras," I thought.

There were no T.V.s in the rooms, so I listened to disc jockey Wolfman Jack on the radio at night. Strangely he seemed to soothe the tinge of homesickness I had for Los Angeles.

We went to L.A. for a day to play the Japanese in an exhibition game and then were slated to go back up to Tahoe for a week and leave for Denver. I was glad to see my parents and family, and friends.

After the exhibition match ended, I asked, "Mom, can we give one of my teammates a ride home?"

"No," she said very atypically. I was puzzled. Without stopping, she explained that she had just had surgery, a lump removed from her breast.

I was stunned and concerned. I gasped and quickly offered, "Mom, I'll come home and stay with you."

"Absolutely not," she said. She assured me that the lump was benign, but she was still recuperating. She would hear nothing of my returning home, but I was sincere. My mother was my rock, and this news jarred me. Still, after her repeated assurances, I decided to continue.

After the Lake Tahoe training camp, we headed for Denver via Reno. We were in Reno for only several days, but after a workout one day, we managed to take in Bobby Gentry's show at Harrah's. We also visited Virginia City and hung in, on, and over the top of fake jail bars mugging for each other's cameras. The camaraderie was thick and genuine.

On September 25, the team would travel from Tahoe to Reno to Denver on October 3 for official outfitting with clothing, luggage, and processing of official papers. In the Reno airport, track athlete John Carlos dressed in full traditional African dress (but

I don't know from which group or country) won a slot machine jackpot for me. This was great fun. Little did I know what was in store. The Olympics was the culmination of years of hard work for many, and you could feel the tension and desire in the air.

Denver is when all the big fun started and the first time that we felt alive in a long time. We stayed at the Denver Hilton, which was quite nice. To be away from the cold weather in Tahoe, away from the same old gym, the same practicing routine, and to mix with other people was a revitalizing change. All the athletes that were going to Mexico went through Denver. That's the first time since the Pan American Games that I saw 6' 5" Mike Silliman, who was the captain of the 1968 Olympic basketball team and a West Point graduate.

The lobby elevator door opened, and there across the lobby was Mike Silliman. I looked at him, and he at me. We smiled and waved, and my mouth fell open like a deer in headlights as I stood in the elevator. Yes, I had a crush on the then twenty-four-year-old. And what better way to enhance an already magical time?

They routed the athletes through Denver in shifts since there were quite a few of us 389. The basketball team, the fencers, and others were all there. The swimmers left for Mexico the day that we got there.

The four-day stay in Denver was a whirlwind. We were told to report to a conference room, and there was Jesse Owens.

"You are representing the United States..." he said in a kind and supportive voice. Most of the athletes listened politely. He continued for a short time, and another speaker took over. His words were prophetic and impacted us, not to mention his experience in the 1936 Olympics, as he won the "fastest human" right in front of Hitler. We were each given A Competitor's Handbook, put out by the U.S. Olympic Committee.

We were outfitted with clothes, a travel and parade uniform, emblemed jackets, and red Samsonite luggage. The luggage was the same as it was for the Pan American Games in Winnipeg, but these had Olympic logos on them instead of Pan American Games stickers. And we were alerted that we would receive per diem from the U.S. Olympic Committee, $3 a day. I came home with more money than I had left, but it wasn't huge.

We were given hemoglobin shots to combat hepatitis and a host of other sundries. We sent home extra clothes that we didn't need. We had more talks and instructions regarding hygiene, such as washing your hands before every meal and ensuring that you didn't touch your mouth if you had touched a banister or anything without washing your hands. They were fearful of us contracting Montezuma's Revenge.

In Denver, Mike stopped me in the lobby and asked me out. I was walking on cloud nine. I was agog. The first night, he took me to this little New Orleans-type street, Old Towne, I think it was. We sat and talked and had great fun. Nice person. The second night we went to a nice restaurant with some former schoolmate friends from Denver. My spirits soared.

We still kept a workout schedule of two or three hours a day in Denver. One day in Denver, the volleyball team left the hotel after lunch for a short two- or three-hour practice. We passed the restaurant where two large wrestlers were eating. When we returned several hours later, we passed by again, and they were still eating!

Sunday morning, we were up bright and early en route to mass. About four or five of us were Catholic, and Mike walked us over and then came back with us. I was wowed and then some. Then we all hopped on different buses - men were segregated from the girls. We went to the airport. We waited about half an hour and boarded the planes for Mexico. On board, the flight attendants gave us little Western Airlines pins, a curler caddy, and different little mementos similar to those they had given us the previous summer en route to the Pan American Games.

These athletes were larger than life. When we were being outfitted, track athlete George Woods had just put his coat on and said anyone wants a coat hanger?

I said, "Sure," and took it.

This was a well-made, sturdy coat hanger, and I packed it in my suitcase. When I returned home, I quickly pulled it out and discovered that nothing I had, sort of a tent, would fit on this coat hanger. This shot putter had shoulders that were broader than any skirt I had. Undoubtedly, the hanger had to be specially made for his specially-made jacket.

Similarly, on the plane from Denver to Mexico City, I was amazed that one athlete was sitting alone amidst the three across seats. Well, it became apparent quickly that there was a reason. J. Randy Matson, who put the shot, was given one seat for his body and one for each arm and he filled them!

Chapter 3: The 1968 Olympics

For those who don't follow sports, this was a time of firsts and records despite the mountain-high Mexico City as the setting. This was the Olympics of Willie Davenport, Jim Hines, Bob Beamon, John Carlos, Tommie Smith, Richard Fosbury, Wyomia Tyus, George Foreman, Cathy Rigby, Mark Spitz, Don Schollander, Debbie Meyer, and Arthur Ashe, to name a few. It was the time of the Vietnam War, and Lyndon Johnson was president. "The Mod Squad," "Gunsmoke," "Andy Griffith," "Gomer Pyle," "Ed Sullivan," "Smothers Brothers," "Star Trek," and "Green Acres" were popular T.V. shows at the time.

This was a time of social unrest both in Mexico with the Tlatelolco Massacre (student riots in Mexico City), and in the U.S. It is not surprising that these Olympics would be controversial. Many doubted that records could be achieved because the altitude of Mexico City provided thirty percent less oxygen than at sea level. This was the Olympics of Bob Beamon's phenomenal long jump, a record that would last for twenty-two years, the fisted protest of John Carlos and Tommie Smith, and the time when America fell in love with Cathy Rigby.

The final selection had been made: Jane Ward, Mary Perry, Marilyn McReavy, Patti Bright, Sharon Peterson, Miki McFadden, Nancy Owen, Fanny Hopeau, Bobbi Perry, Ninja Jorgensen, Ann Heck – and me!

Miki was born in January, and I was born, in December, the following year. She was almost two years older than I was, making me, at 18, the youngest athlete on the volleyball team. While each of us came with a list of accolades, I was officially listed in the Olympic Press Book as "'67 Outstanding high school player in California;'67 USA Team to World's Championships; '68 UCLA Women's Volleyball team; '66, '67 USVBA 2nd Place Team; '68 USVBA National Champions."

Dr. Marie Rose Liba, named a leader in volleyball in 1964, was the manager of the team. Marie had multiple degrees and hailed from the University of Wisconsin. She was a member of the "The Committee," those USVBA dignitaries who selected the players. At that time, she wore culottes almost as a daily uniform, which we quipped about regularly. The only challenge was she typically sat with her legs apart, so we always made sure one of us sat in front of her, especially when on camera.

As anticipated, Harlan Cohn was again named coach. Even the newspapers referred to him as "Napoleon." The dark-haired former beach and indoor player Harlan put us through our paces, some players more than others. The team always rallied to provide support to whoever was low or had sagging spirits.

Back in the U.S., during the last few years, we had all been giving volleyball exhibitions and teaching seminars to high school and college teams and coaches to show the tremendous strides that volleyball had made and to teach the sport. The innovations of the Japanese and others were fresh and new. Mary Jo was frequently the first one to understudy these techniques and implement them. Mary Jo and Mary Perry brought back the Japanese roll from the Tokyo Olympics. The Japanese ball handling was amazing at the time. Little did we know that the Russians had taken the game a step further with a daunting umbrella block.

All teams blocked spikes, jumping and spreading hands apart to stop the ball. But the Russians jumped very high at the net and formed an almost two-foot-wide umbrella over the net, stuffing the ball back into the court of their opponents. As simple as this sounds, it was a devastating wall that stymied the other teams. Later, teams caught on to the ploy and hit the ball off the block's hands to outside the court, taking the point. But it took a while for teams to counter the Russian team's play.

The field we faced consisted of Poland, Czechoslovakia, Japan, Russia, South Korea, and Peru. The competition was set up in a round-robin tournament. Each team played each of the teams once. The winning team of those that had lost only once would then play the winning team that hadn't lost.

On October 6, we flew to Mexico City, a three- or four-hour flight. We deplaned and had to show the I.D. cards that had been given to us in Denver. We were ushered into a new airport addition, a special area in the airport set up for Olympic athletes. It was painted in bright colors with the Olympic rings and insignia. The distinctive design logo of the games, created by Lance Wyman for the 1968 games, is still vivid in my mind. We boarded buses and were taken to the Olympic Village.

The Olympic Village

The Mexico Olympic Village was totally different from the Tokyo Olympic Village when we were there for the World Games. This village was alive with people, decorations, and pulsing with Olympic excitement. This village was for athletes only since all press, reporters, etc., were housed in a different nearby village. While picturesque, there were a few drawbacks. Chief among them was the fact that there wasn't one washing machine. With 5,516 athletes working out and showering multiple times daily, you can imagine what the village looked like. Everyone was flying their own flags - laundry - from every possible perch.

Each team had an apartment in one of the multi-story buildings. They were nice buildings, but there was no heat. It was fall and getting colder. We were at an altitude of 7,000 feet. I had sent all my winter clothes home when we were in Denver. I wore sweats whenever I could to stay warm.

The U.S. Women's Volleyball team, twelve of us had an apartment with four rooms. It was a little cramped, but we managed. The beds were nice, and we were given our bedspreads as souvenirs. The bedspreads were actually plain gray but featured the Olympic insignias and the Olympic rings.

The 1968 Mexico Olympics were postponed until October due to what some refer to as the Tlatelolco Massacre, the student riots in Mexico City, but we felt safe. The Olympic Village security was good by the standards of that era - at least everyone thought so until the massacre of 1972. There were guards posted at the front gates and female, brown-suited guards in the lobby of each apartment building for female athletes. (Australian swimmer Dawn Fraser's book about the 1964 Olympics, chronicling the hanky-panky, alarmed Olympic Committee members and, no doubt, set the stage for the guards and security.) I was only asked for my I.D. once, but then we usually all had uniform USA sweats on. We'd smuggle friends in, friends of friends, friends of the team, by taking out a jacket to them, and then we'd walk in and show our I.D. Usually, if you had sweats on, they didn't ask you for your I.D.

There were scores of people waiting outside the village daily to try to get in to see the athletes or where they were living or meet them or get their autographs. Some waited for a bus tour of the village. The big thing for some of these little kids who did get into the village was trading. They'd say, "Change" or "Cambio?" They wanted to trade for pins, Olympic pins because they couldn't buy pins at the stores. I traded two huge Mexico posters for a pin.

It was unnerving to stand on the corner in the village, which was pretty big, and have a bus go by. The guided tour bus was jam-packed, with not even standing room left in the bus for the people who had been waiting outside at the gate. We would be talking on the sidewalk, and everybody on the bus would stare as they drove by. They were speaking Spanish, and you couldn't help but wonder what they were saying.

"And here on the corner are two Olympic athletes talking..." Not everyone had competed yet; most were just working on their sports. Achievements would soon be known.

When we arrived in Mexico, our practice sessions were cut. We were working out only two hours a day. Our practice gym was outside of the village.

People were just arriving and getting ready for the games. The first day or two we were there, they let people in the village more freely. You couldn't walk from your dorm to the dining hall without getting asked for an autograph. It was unnerving, quite a sensation. I'd never before had someone walk up to me and ask me for my autograph. The first time it happened to me, I quickly turned around to see who was behind me.

There were three women's buildings in the village. These were surrounded by six or eight-foot fences. Also, there was a gate that was guarded by intimidating female guards who were dressed up in off-putting eighteenth-century-like getups. Most were nice but didn't speak any English. If you couldn't communicate in Spanish, well, it really didn't matter most of the time, but if you wanted to get a phone call, a long distance or collect call through (pre-cell phones), you had to go to the main administration building. I know that my mother tried to phone me unsuccessfully. It was really a hassle. The coaches had a tough time. Even the doctor had to be accompanied by a guard to gain access to the building to see any sick female athletes.

The first week was exciting. Everything was new, and we were all wide-eyed and walking around checking things out, finding different corners of the village. They had a practice track and practice areas for shot putting, discus throwing and boxing, wrestling, and fencing in the village. Other sports had to go out off-site to practice. We were no exception.

In the Olympic Village, there were free Coke stands, and meals were readily available. Three large countries shared a dining hall. There were about six dining halls. They opened up in the morning from six to nine and then lunch from twelve to three, and then dinner from six to nine. If you couldn't make it to one of these sessions because of your practice schedule or whatever, then you would go to the International Club, which opened when your dining hall closed. So, the International Club was open from nine to twelve and three to six, and nine to twelve again at night. You really couldn't miss out on food.

The International Club in the village was the meeting spot for all the athletes at night. There you could exchange pins from different countries. Unfortunately for us, the American rowers and swimmers who arrived a week before we did, had traded their pins and gathered up all the rest of the athletes' pins. But we still managed to collect some when we got there.

We would walk out of the apartment building in the Olympic Village and walk past the Tartan-paved track over to the International Club. Along the way, we couldn't help but be amused by the competitive walkers. Lean and lithe, these male walkers would walk all over the village as they trained. The rules, as I understood them, were that your feet could not leave the ground completely, so one foot was always on the ground in a heel toe, heel toe. This combination of heel-toe produces an incredible rear wiggle. Most entertaining.

At the International Club, athletes could find newspapers in their native languages. It was a place where the athletes could assemble, meet, and talk either verbally or with wild gesturing if a common language couldn't be found. We usually checked in to see what the headlines were in the papers and what was happening.

In the main center, the main administration hall, they had free papers, so every day we'd go through there, and we'd pick up one of everything. Spanish or English or anything and go through it and cut out the pictures - almost like comic strips pictures of us or people that we knew and send the pictures home. There were grand color pictures of the opening ceremonies and nice color pictures of different events. Back then, there weren't a lot of color photos in newspapers.

Thankfully, at least one American newspaper down there was in English. One day we were in the trainers' room, which was on the ground floor of the men's apartment house. We picked up a paper there too. One morning, I guess it was the day of the basketball finals, their big star, 6' 8" Spencer Hayward, had diarrhea. He made the headlines, "U.S. Cage Star Ill but Will Play Anyway." You open it up, and across the inside page, it says, "Spencer Hayward has diarrhea but will play anyway."

"How would you like to make the papers with headlines like that? Ugh," I thought.

One night I was at the International Club with a handful of basketball players and my pal Ken Spain. Ken was 6'8" tall, blond, and a heck of a nice guy. Without even thinking, he straddled every doorway he entered. I asked why, and he quickly showed me that if he straddled the door sash, he just cleared it. Otherwise, he would coldcock himself on the top of the door jamb. We managed to form a nice friendship and hang out just talking even though I was dating Mike and Ken was seeing a swimmer. The basketball guys were tall, another dimension tall.

We were all observing the athletes from different countries. Communication was largely hand gestures unless a common language could be found. Several attractive female Swedish athletes wearing sleeveless dresses entered. They reached over to pick up something from the table, revealing tufts of underarm hair. There was an audible "argh" from the guys.

The village also had little shops, a jewelry shop, a book shop, a travel shop, a barber shop, a drugstore, a camera shop, and a clothes shop. These offered the bare essentials and Mexican products. We all waited to go into Mexico City. We were about half an hour away, but we would go in to get the regular things that we needed, shampoo or lotion, among other sundries.

When we were in training camp during afternoon downtimes, between practices, if we weren't sleeping, we would massage each other to loosen the muscles in the upper and lower back, which became stiff from spiking, passing, and bumping the ball and from sweating and then cooling down. It wasn't difficult to learn where the sore muscles were since we shared them. Here at the Olympics, there were official trainers such as Joe, a short, rather round, jovial fellow, who would tape up ankles, knees, etc., and rub us down after matches. Ah, those were the days!

The venues for different events were anywhere from fifteen minutes to an hour away by bus. You could hop on buses that ran through the main building that took you to any desired event. The number six buses took you to the basketball stadium. Number five buses took you to the volleyball stadium. And some would go to two or three venues or just make the rounds. There were special entrances for the athletes at the different stadiums.

One memorable night after a practice game with Russia, but before opening ceremonies, several of us were heading out for a night on the town. I was still head over heels in crush with Mike. There were no matches the next day, so we were clear. We all rendezvoused at the American Ambassador's residence for a reception for American athletes on Thursday, October 10, 1968. We had all received special engraved invitations. We donned our dress U.S. travel uniforms. After proper introductions and polite conversation, four of us – Mike and I went out with another volleyball player Wink Davenport and Chris Van Salsa, a swim team chaperone. bid the partiers adios and headed for La Fuente, a nightclub in Mexico City. We laughed and joked and then took off for drinks at one of Mexico City's nicest new hotels just finished for the Olympics. As early morning approached, we decided to go to Shakey's Pizza for some American fare. Yes, American logos and icons had made their way to Mexico even then, but Shakey's was almost the only sign of Americana that we saw. We hailed a cab and arrived shortly in a rather unpopulated suburb. Our taxicab driver didn't speak too much English, but we did learn that his wife had just had a baby. We congratulated him. Soon we headed back again to the Olympic Village.

It's surprising how much you can communicate when you don't speak a language.

Opening Ceremonies "I can't wait," I thought and wondered and fantasized what the opening ceremonies would be like.

We had been in the Olympic Village for a week before the opening ceremonies. The last two nights, Friday and Saturday, movies were offered for the athletes. We all piled into the International Club for some amusement. Friday, we watched *Mary Poppins*, not exactly adult entertainment, but certainly fit the bill for our rather taxed minds and bodies at that point. There was much chortling and laughing in the audience.

Saturday evening, they aired the documentary *The Tokyo Olympiad*. There was rapt attention; adrenaline was pulsing, and the athletes were psyched and pumped. They all walked out about a foot off the ground, ready to go and ready for the opening ceremonies the next day. I half expected some to walk out the front door and flex their biceps like a Hans and Frans skit on "Saturday Night Live." It was exhilarating.

The opening ceremonies were scheduled for Saturday. I was sure that the sky would open up and a loud voice would speak, although I wasn't sure what it would say. I was so excited that I could hardly contain myself.

We all dressed in our opening ceremonies uniforms and piled into the bus. We were all like taut rubber bands - emotionally and physically primed. We had been working for this for years – at least four and some longer. At this point, our anxiety - the good kind, if that's possible – was fever-pitched, ready for competition. After playing, running, training, and aching, we were about to begin.

We stood and waited almost five hours that day. We waited for an hour or two before they started. The throngs of people waving in the stands brought goosebumps.

We lined up outside the stadium in the country order designated and then in the U.S. contingent according to height. I was taller and toward the back. The Parade of Nations began. The athletes entered the stadium through a tunnel with hundreds of spectators peering down at them—so many people.

We had guards all around, but the people were so excited it made you feel good to be there. We marched in, the crowd gave a good roar, and my heart sang. There was noise and cheering. We had been instructed to be very dignified and not wave. But when we got in there, we all started waving and smiling. It was overwhelming. We marched around the field during this rousing ovation and then slipped into our slot on the infield.

We waited there and stood on the field for a couple of hours more. Meanwhile, a female athlete two down from me passed out. A doctor who was on the track team and three or four guys carried her off.

Despite what they said in the newspapers back here, we were greeted warmly. Of course, Mexico was greeted warmly also since they were the host country. Whenever Mexico did anything, the crowd went crazy, absolutely crazy.

We watched the Olympic flag come around. We didn't have a very good viewpoint from where we were standing on the field unless we happened to be very tall and could see over everyone in front of us. But it was exciting to watch and listen. There was an archipelago of athletes amidst a sea of people from around the world.

The President of the International Olympic Committee, Avery Brundage, began to speak. He bellowed into the microphone, "Let the Games begin!"

They released the balloons, and immediately, some snagged and hung on the lights. They released the doves. About three delegations over, a group of men had a tarp over them. I was next to several athletes from other sports, one of whom pulled out a large see-through plastic tarp.

"Quick, step under the tarp," one of the athletes said to me.

Curious, I did and was very glad. The next thing I knew, hundreds of doves flew into the air and directly over us. There were some colorful comments as these agitated avians left their cages and their marks on the athletes below. It was chaotic. All most athletes could do was duck.

Then we saw the runner come in with the Olympic torch. Seeing the torch made emotions swell. The athletes stood erect, proud to be there, to watch it all happening. Then we went out; we paraded around the stadium again. It was good to move again. We paraded around and went out through the same tunnel, waving at the people and guards.

It took us hours to get back to the village because all the athletes were waiting for buses, and the buses were in short supply. So much for logistics.

The next day we had our first match against Japan. Some athletes and teams competed for the first day or two and then were done for the rest of the games. Some athletes didn't compete until the middle or the end of the games. We worked the whole time. We had practices on the days that we didn't play, but we managed to sneak in plenty of fun.

After the games started, schedule permitting, we went to the track stadium, where we got in free with I.D.s. Richard Fosbury won the gold medal in the high jump at the Olympics that year with his revolutionary Fosbury Flop. It was remarkable then because he was the first to use that technique amidst a sea of nay-sayers. Fosbury took off running to the high jump bar, ascended with the help of a pole, twisted, and went over the high jump bar backward. Today this is the standard method used for the high jump.

The first track competition I attended changed me. One of the U.S. track athletes won. The U.S. national anthem played, and my heart swelled. I was there representing my country. Strong feelings welled up inside me, love of my country and countrymen, a stronger desire to do well. These emotions stayed with me, and today, hearing the U.S. national anthem can still move me to tears.

The Tommie Smith/John Carlos fisted protest is seared in my memory, having met both of them. In what is now an iconic photograph of the 1968 Olympics, Tommie Smith and John Carlos, two black athletes stood on the dais with black-gloved fists in the air, heads bowed. Smith had just broken the world and Olympic record in the 200-meter. Carlos took third. On October 16, 1968, the two shared the dais with Aussie sprinter Peter Norman, who took second and wore a badge of support for the two American athletes protesting the treatment of blacks in the United States.

There was quite a different perspective down there. The athletes were still intently focused on their individual sports and competition. Smith and Carlos's quiet protest of blacks' treatment in the U.S. may have caused a media storm in Mexico and the U.S. newspapers, but as soon as it surfaced in Mexico, the incident was quickly swept under the rug by the U.S. Olympic Committee. Tommie Smith and John

Carlos disappeared from the Olympic Village. The athletes took note of the event and then went on with their lives. They had a job to do.

Years later, in celebration of the 1984 Olympics in Los Angeles, Disneyland planned a parade of former Olympians. I rode in a car with Tommie Smith, and we both wore Mickey Mouse-shaped pseudo-gold medals. He was polite, and pleasant, and the same cross-sport courtesy that existed at the Olympics in 1968 was evident then. Did he remember me? Probably not. He was coaching track at Santa Monica City College at the time. I was sorry that, according to what I had read, both he and John Carlos had a very difficult time after their fisted protest. Neither could find jobs, and other former Olympians scraped money together for them. Carlos's wife was bereft and committed suicide. Both paid a hefty price for calling attention to racial inequalities in the U.S.

After the games started, it was fascinating to watch competitions in other sports. It was fun just to be there with the other athletes who were tense, just like we were, over their own sport and had the same or parallel political problems. I would have liked to have seen all the sports, but time didn't allow.

When we finally arrived in Mexico, there wasn't that kind of nervous atmosphere that you would think people would have. However, we were in a team sport. Hanging out with other athletes who had parallel problems was relaxing and certainly enlightening.

I visited the sauna one afternoon and talked at length to one of the doyennes of fencing, Maxine Mitchell, about the politics of sports, the general frustrations and information. Surprisingly, sports are like people - they are ever so much alike. She had been a member of the 1952, 1956, and 1960 Olympic teams as well as the 1955, 1959, 1963, and 1967 Pan American teams, and she had an expansive perspective.

"Volleyball politics can be most frustrating," I said.

Without skipping a beat, she agreed, "We have it too in fencing." We talked for an hour.

Television coverage in Mexico City was via Wide World of Sports on ABC. There was limited coverage of events, and it was spotty either because of time allotments or sponsorship, I'm not sure which.

During one match being broadcast, although I didn't realize it, I was a spiker in the front right row. The ball came from the back left over my shoulder and to my right hand near the net, referred to as off-hand. I spiked it, but it went into the net. Apparently, a lot of people saw that because when I returned home, several people mentioned it. I couldn't remember the match or the off-hand set, but that happened to have been showcased.

Our volleyball competition reached a crescendo in Mexico. Why? Harlan panicked, and rather than relying on proven defenses and playing cliques, he started changing everything. We worked on different techniques. We played some practice games, and when we didn't do too well, he changed everything. He changed defenses and offenses. He started a six on the court with our first match against Japan, who had not even played together - even in practice.

Then he walked out one day and said, "Here's the defense I want you to play, Girls."

We had never practiced or played that defense. It was chaotic.

Our competition in Mexico was rough going. His panic attacks and constant changes had our best hitter so afraid to go out on the court and do something -one mistake, and he'd pull her out. Everyone was so buffaloed and so talked down that we lost to teams that we never should have lost to. We had never lost to South Korea, Peru, or Mexico. We even lost to Mexico without a fight which was unthinkable and a new precedent. It was sobering.

Not winning matches at the Olympics only made me appreciate the victories. The years of time, tenacity, and hard work that go into competing all underscore the possible mishaps or efforts that can go askew.

When people asked me how we did, I always say, "We had fun."

Still, the irony of winning a spot on the team but not medaling at the Olympics, not winning wasn't lost on me. The hurdles I handled and the skills I learned through the trials and training stayed with me and helped me through all manner of life situations. This was a summary of my ultimate competition in life - the contest with myself, testing myself, striving to do my best.

More Humor

"How will they do this new test a test for chromosomes?" I mused.

This was the first Olympics where there would be female chromosome testing. For years there had been scuttlebutt that some of the Russian athletes had been taking hormones. Interestingly, two of the suspected female athletes from Russia didn't show up that year - Tamara and Irina Press - claiming that their mother was ill. One put the shot, and the other was in track. Rumor had it that one was a female taking male hormones, and one was a male taking female hormones. True or gossip? I don't know.

Manager Marie Liba came in one morning and told all of us that we had to report to the medical office no later than 5 P.M. the next day for a chromosome test or we would be disqualified individually for competition. Well, this was a new experience, a new chromosome test that had just been invented – and I was quite curious. I headed over in the morning and was taken in by a pleasant Mexican doctor.

"What do you do? How do you do it? What are you looking for?" I asked, so curious about this new procedure.

"Don't worry," he said, "You will pass."

A quick tongue depressor swab of the inside of my cheek, and I was on my way out the door. Later I received the "sex" test, as we called it. Signed by Prince Alex. R. Merch, the certificate says in three languages that I passed, but it doesn't say what sex I am.

Cars were parked outside the Olympic Village, except those for official business or emergencies. One night we were returning from a match, and we were all exhausted. Several people decided that we would tell the gate guard that I was sick or injured so that we wouldn't have to walk the distance. We arrived at the gate, and the driver explained. The guard looked at me to assess my illness, and I burst out into laughter. (I'm a rotten liar.) The guard laughed, too, and waved us in. My teammates agreed that this would be my last stint as an ailing actress.

The games had started. We had practiced in the morning, and the basketball guys had a game that night. I wanted to see it, so I caught the bus and met Estelle, a high jumper from the United States who had a boyfriend on the basketball team. After about an hour, we arrived and sneaked downstairs. We sneaked in with the newspapermen who sneaked in with the reporters, the ABC sports guys. Show your pass and just walk in right behind them. We got five people in one night doing that. We were on the ground floor and had the pick of seats. It was fun. Except for track and your own sport, you had to have tickets, but we always managed to sneak in.

We watched the game. Afterward, Mike came up and said, "Hello. I would love to get together with you, but I'm going out to dinner with the Kentucky Colonels, a basketball team from Kentucky."

Apparently, they wanted him and Bill Hosket to play with them the next year or whenever Mike was to get out of the army. They were going out to dinner with the team officials.

I ended up going back on the bus with Ken Spain from Houston. He was seeing a female Canadian swimmer.

"Laurie, I forgot that I had a game tonight. I'd asked a Canadian swimmer on a date. I asked her out for five o'clock," he explained. Could you deliver this note to her apartment?"

Communications were unheard of with the guards at our dorm or apartment house. I did deliver the note, but apparently, she never got it.

We came back to the village on the bus that night, and it was raining. The bus driver came in a special entrance to try to pick us up and keep us out of the rain. It took us twenty minutes just to get out of the parking lot, and we got back at about 7:30. It was pouring, so we stopped at Ken's dorm. The United States guys stayed in this apartment house near the main gate. Ken had his hat and his raincoat, and with the two of us underneath it, we went back to the dining hall. On the way, we stopped at the girls' dorm to look for the Canadian swimmer, but she wasn't there.

When they built and dug the village, they found pyramids. They left the pyramids amidst the village. They were striking. Stairs which led up to the dining hall were unpaved and surrounded by gravel. It was loose-filled gravel that flooded when it rained.

Ken said, "Well, hop on."

So, I hopped on his back piggyback, and he carried me. He started up the stairs.

Fear welled up as I looked down, and the ground was getting farther away.

"I'm good, thanks," I said. He put me down. Whew.

"He's really strong to be able to carry me," I thought.

Ken, the Canadian swimmer, and I met quite unplanned in the refectory, the name for the mess hall or cafeteria in Mexico City. Food had been flown in from the U.S. in the hopes of avoiding any possible intestinal irritation.

The three of us had dinner together. Then we started back to the apartments. We were coming down the stairs, and there was about a twenty-foot puddle below these stairs, the same stairs that Ken carried me up piggyback. A passel of people was trying to straddle fences and plod through this foot or so of water. They were getting sopping wet. Many paused on the last step and pondered the puddles trying to figure out how to avoid them. Some braved them and came out shaking their feet and legs like cats who accidentally stepped into the water. Ken said, "Okay. Put your arm around my neck."

There were two of us.

I said, "Ken, you carry Nancy, and I'll walk."

Certainly, this was not a balanced fulcrum with a five -foot-two-inch swimmer and me, a five-foot-eleven volleyball player. He would hear nothing of it. She put her arm around his neck, and I put my arm around his neck, and he carried both of us all the way, about twenty/thirty feet, through this puddle, and applause rang out, a standing ovation from the people standing on the stairs. I looked down, and the water had only come up to the tops of the soles on his "larger-than-life" sized shoes. The sheer size of some of the athletes was impressive. Most of the onlookers had to wade in ankle- or shin-deep water to get to dry ground.

In addition to chromosome tests, there was drug testing. One would think that was a simple matter, but not always so. We had a four o'clock match one day. By that hour, we were all warmed up, loose, and ready to go. The match ended, and two Mexican guards approached my teammate, Ninja.

"You are wanted for a drug test. Come with us," one of the guards said.

"Fine," she said and marched off to the restroom to comply.

Simple physiology tells you that when you are sweating profusely, full of adrenaline, and in the heat of competition or just after, visiting the restroom is not an issue. Well, it became one. At eleven P.M., seven hours later, the guards took Ninja back to the team apartment so that she might feel more comfortable, more at ease and give the two guards a urine sample. Finally, success.

Other People

"I've read about all of these people in the sports pages," I thought, "and they're almost all here." I met an amazing assortment of people down in Mexico City. Some before they became famous.

Bob Beamon, the long jumper, was a fantastic guy, though quiet. The pictures of him in the paper crying when he made the jump touched me deeply.

I met Arthur Walker, the triple jumper, an All-American nice guy, the 200-meter runner Larry Questad, my pal cager Ken Spain, most of the basketball players, some of the swimmers, who were friends of my roommate Miki's, and others.

I met many women too. One girl, Inge, was from West Germany. She was about twenty-three and had defected from behind the Iron Curtain in East Germany the year before. She was an only child. She spoke a little bit of English, thankfully. She said it was so drab and dull over there in East Germany that she would never go back - even though her parents were still there, and they were older. She wouldn't go back. It was too terrible for her. And if she did, it would be all over for her anyway. She had defected.

Ian, a videographer, had come down to record the games. He had been with us in Long Beach and Tahoe too. He brought two of the volleyball alternates down just to see the games. He managed to take us around and arrange some fun nights out in Tahoe. He took us to an amusement park in Mexico, where we all rode the roller-coaster, then we went back to the village.

There was an Olympic Center in downtown Mexico City, decorated with huge balloons with Mexico XIX on them and the logo of the Mexico '68 games. Balloons and logos were in the Olympic Village dining halls and around the village too. By the end of the first week of the Olympics, they were all gone. Everybody had scavenged them from the dining halls, which, I think, was expected. I didn't get there in time to get one, so I bought one in a store in town.

People at the games from the United States and from all different countries were extremely friendly. We met and befriended a family, husband, wife, and three children from the San Fernando Valley who had come to Mexico to watch the games. He was a teacher on sabbatical. They'd been there for, I don't know how long, and they knew their way around the city. It was good to see people from home that spoke English and had the same reference points. They were nice enough to pick us up and take us on a tour. They also took us to the city, where we shopped.

We dressed normally, but we had the United States team's white jackets on. Well-wishers were everywhere. The night we went to Shakey's Pizza, we had a Mexican couple come up to us and say, in English (many did speak English), "We wish you the best of luck. What sport are you in?"

"Volleyball," we answered collectively.

"What are your chances?" they asked. People expressed their support everywhere we went. It was a remarkable feeling to be in a foreign country and have such an outpouring of good feelings and friendliness. If you passed an American athlete in the street, athletes would say hi to each other automatically whether you knew each other or not. It was just a natural kind of camaraderie. They were from the United States, and so were you. Quite remarkable.

One of the personal thrills that I had was being called to the front gate of the Olympic Village to greet my eighth-grade gym teacher/coach, "Tink" Turner. She was accompanied by her husband and daughter. I was able to take all three on a tour of the Olympic Village.

Surprisingly enough, a lot of people came down toward the end of the games. I don't know whether it was the student riots in Mexico that caused them to cancel a lot of room reservations, but people who came down unexpectedly didn't have a problem finding a place to stay even though it was advertised that everything was sold out years beforehand.

Towards the end or after the first week, some of the competitions were over. Athletes started leaving. One night we watched the whole Czechoslovakian track team leave in a group because their track competition was over. Olympic officials announced that only six athletes per country would be admitted into the closing ceremonies. I think all of the athletes that were still there managed to get in.

After the athletes started leaving, there was a different atmosphere. There were many people left, but it was different from the heightened excitement at first when everybody had just arrived.

Then towards the last week, things became tense for the U.S. basketball team. The media and most said that this team wasn't as good as they could have been if Lew Alcindor (later Kareem Abdul-Jabbar) and other star players had been there. This just fanned the team's desire to win. Hank's Boys (Hank was Hank Iba, U.S. Olympic basketball coach) did well without any help from the players who decided to sit it out. They had no problem beating Russia – they never got to play Russia. Russia lost to Yugoslavia, which was a really big upset.

The precautions we took and being in good shape must have worked in our favor. One team member got sick down there. A few had diarrhea but managed to play anyway. I didn't get sick until I got home. Nice timing. The majority of people weren't that sick, at least sick enough to stop them from participating in any of the activities. I imagine it was a big mental hurdle for some of the athletes in individual competitions. In addition to the altitude, it could impede top physical performance. Still, impressive records were set.

I left that Sunday morning before the closing ceremonies. I had had a running cold for the last week, and it seemed like an eternity since I'd been home, not to mention that I was dejected to find out that Mike Silliman had taken a diver out on a date toward the end of the games. I just kept traveling around and writing letters to home, but I didn't really have a home. It was a funny sensation. I'd been living with twelve girls for two months. We all did pretty well. We were really a compatible group for the two months that we had to live together. We're all still friends.

I came home with five bags of bibelots souvenirs, glasses, bedspreads, all sorts of key chains, a "sex test" (my chromosome test), and things that meant something to me, that reminded me that I had been there and been a part of the Olympics. I had to buy an extra bag just to get home.

And then I got to the airport, and the man at the airport said, "Your bag is too big. You'll have to ship the rest of the stuff."

I panicked because I had twelve drinking glasses with the Olympic logo, my camera, and a slew of other items. I had visions of it all being broken.

"I'll put it in a safe place on the plane," said the steward.

Sure enough, he did. When we arrived in Los Angeles, and I retrieved the bag, not one glass was broken. Everything was intact; everything was fine.

When the competition was over, we traded uniforms with teams from different countries. I traded my parade uniform for a West German parade uniform. They thought ours was better, but I thought we got the best deal. Their dresses were stylish, and they had a hat to match. A lot of people traded purses and other items. The other U.S. travel uniform I kept and wore home. Coming through customs on the way home was challenging with five bags of stuff.

(Years later, I donated almost all of this to the Smithsonian Museum, which had set up an Archives Center 1968 Olympic Games Collection.)

It turned out to be fortunate that I was wearing my Olympic uniform when I went through customs.

The customs official said, "Were you in Mexico for the Olympics?"

I said, "Yes."

He said, "You're free to go."

It was good to be home.

I played on one more international team on October 3, 1969, in which the U.S. Women's team vied against Japan's Yashica team. The U.S. team had some new faces internationally, all of whom I knew. Former 1968 Men's Olympian, Wink Davenport, was the coach, and Adelaide Packwood was the manager.

The Nationals in 1969 were slated for Knoxville, Tennessee, and the next year they were to be held in Hawaii. I didn't make it to either of those. Instead, in the fall of 1968, I decided that it was time to return to school. I had watched some of my teammates take approximately ten years to finish their bachelor's degrees while playing internationally and traveling. I wanted to move on with my life.

Ah, yes, time to return to college.

Chapter 4: UCLA Redux

I was raised in a home in which it was typical to be dispatched to get a dictionary if a word came up at dinner that we didn't all know. My father started studying architecture, but WWII intervened. He joined the navy, was sent to Saint Mary's pre-flight at Occidental College, and then went to UCLA where he played basketball. He went into education, coached basketball, and taught high school math. We had well-constructed playhouses in our backyard that could have withstood the strongest of earthquakes.

My mother was one of three, the oldest with two brothers. When she graduated high school, she talked to my grandfather about going to college. He was amenable but emphasis was on her brothers, who went to Santa Clara University. My mom attended Mount Saint Mary's College (now University) for a year and then told a nun that she was going to go to UCLA. The nun gave her a D disqualifying her from UCLA, so she dropped out of St. Mary's and went to work since she and my dad were engaged. She never let the lack of a college degree impede her progress and she worked extra hard to be informed. Her determination was legend in the family. While she was the shrimp at five- foot- two inches tall, she still kept my tall, long-armed father running on the tennis court, and told each of the three of us, almost six-foot tall children, that she could still stand on a chair to scold us. She was gentle and kind but could be fierce.

These lessons weren't lost on me, and it always rankled me that her education seemed to take second place to that of her two brothers. The importance of education was a strong theme in our family my brother became a geophysicist and geological engineer, and my sister graduated UCLA magna cum laude, raised six children and became a registered nurse working in hospice care.

When I was new to UCLA and had been reading literature for eight hours a day, I went to my mother in a low moment and baited her saying, "I don't think I'm cut out for college."

Surely, she would disagree and then I would have a handy excuse to quit.

"Laurie, if you intend to be with people like Mike (Captain of the 1968 Olympic basketball team and a Captain from WestPoint,) you need to be able to engage them intellectually. It's your decision," she said.

"She outsmarted me again," I thought.

Her words stuck with me. To this day, I am driven and work to make sure that I can engage folks I meet intellectually.

It was time to return to UCLA, but the school was on a quarter system and my scheduling was slightly off. To fill the gap time, I enrolled in West Los Angeles College, a junior college in Culver City. Curious to see how different it would be from UCLA; I was pleasantly surprised. I wanted to take chemistry for dumbbells, a requisite at UCLA for non-science majors and, of course, the UCLA professor wrote the book. I will never forget one night in chemistry class when the teacher at the community college had little nests of hay that had a chemical on them. Just a couple drops of water dropped on them made them burst into a small explosive fire. Most impressive! But he wouldn't tell us the name of the chemical in case there were any budding pyromaniacs in the class.

Classes to Last a Lifetime

I also took an English class and studied like crazy for the final. I can still remember the final exam which turned out to be a good-natured joke. The first question was Sophocles who? I didn't know Sophocles' last name. No one else did either. There was a loud chorus of groans across the room. All the questions followed suit.

The teacher smiled and said, "Have a great Christmas holiday!"

The teachers/professors at community college seemed to be more interested in teaching. At UCLA, "publish or perish" was the mantra. UCLA students needed strong self-motivation at the university.

When the semester ended, I returned to UCLA. This was only a little over a year after leaving, so it was almost like I had never left. I sometimes recognized people in my classes for my major, English literature, but everyone took these classes in their own order, so it didn't seem that much had changed. My return was almost seamless. Perhaps I was more attuned and aware when I returned. Returning was like riding a bicycle.

A special moment: One day while walking through Westwood Village, I saw a man almost hit his head on the stoplight. At seven feet two inches tall he caught my eye, and I took a double take.

"Oh, I thought, there is Lew Alcindor –soon to become Kareem Abdul-Jabbar."

Ducking Demonstrators and Weaponized Telephone Poles

Chancellor Franklin Murphy was stepping down. His successor, Chancellor Charles Young, then the youngest chancellor to lead a major university, took the reins for three decades. It was he who hired and rehired Angela Davis after the Regents fired her for her communist ties. During his tenure, Chancellor Young helped shape the fabric of the university and propel it in a progressive direction.

Had anything changed since I left? Well, the pitch of anti-war and activism was higher. I had acquired a Vespa to transport me to and from home. Parking a car was a nightmare at UCLA - *Butterflies Are Free,* the movie, even poked fun at parking on our campus.

I had taken a part-time job in the intramural sports office in the men's gym doing office work. I worked with three other guys, who were full-time, and ran the intramural sports program for the university. Jovial, fun-loving, and low-key jocks best described the crew in the office. It was a perfect fit for me. But times were tense. Students had just been shot at Kent State and animosity toward the war in Vietnam was mounting.

One day there was a great deal of foment outside the men's gym. Students rallied and massed outside the men's gym trying to get to the ROTC office just down the hall from us. The mob somehow got hold of a telephone pole and managed to beat down the almost two-story heavy gym doors. Quickly, the director announced that we were evacuating, and we ran quickly out a back door to safety. No one was seriously injured, but it was scary facing down an angry mob.

That was not always the case though. In 1969, two student leaders, who were part of the Black Panthers, were killed in Campbell Hall over a dispute about leadership. It was a turbulent time, fueled by passion.

Many of my classes were in Royce Hall, up Janss Steps and to the east. I remember being stopped by students one day, who were advocating a boycott of classes for whatever was the current activist crusade.

I was bent on going to class. These students weren't going to stop me from getting my education and I did not favor their crusade. This was supposedly a "Hippie" time of love and tolerance.

I quickly cited, "We are the generation of laissez-faire, letting people do their thing!" to the students who finally let me pass. I was back at the university, and I would like to think I was more aware.

President Lyndon Baines Johnson came to campus to speak one day, and my mother joined me before lunch to welcome him as he arrived.

I did chuckle decades later when my mother asked me if UCLA was wildly liberal. My thoughts shot back to that time, to the incredible exposure to right and left ideologies, to the gamut of then radical ideas, celebrated ethnicities, religions, and political thought. That experience made me examine where I stood in the continuum of thought and ideas.

For decades after, I thought college generations had lost the passion that we brought. They seemed tame, unmotivated.

My father had pledged a fraternity when he attended UCLA. He encouraged me to look at sororities. I did and met some very nice women. Still the conversation at one such meeting was dominated by what dress a sorority sister would wear to an event. I had just returned home after witnessing the politics and the fallout of racial politics in Mexico City. I had experienced different cultures, our military abroad, and other worldly adventures. My initial interest in sororities quickly dissolved.

At this point, I was starting to tune into politics and current activism more. Still, I attended political science and constitutional law classes in Bunche Hall. It wasn't until much later that I learned Ralph J. Bunche was the first African American to receive the Nobel Peace Prize and was a former valedictorian of his class at UCLA.

Hanging around the gym was always interesting. One day as I walked out, I saw a car which had snagged a parking place just outside the gym. I glanced inside and noticed that there was no front seat on the driver's side. In short order, I saw basketball player Bill Walton walk to the car, get in and drive off siting in the back seat. This so reminded me of the "oversized" Olympic athletes I had encountered.

I originally thought of going into child psychology but knowing the statistics courses necessary and remaining realistic about my less-than-optimum math skills, I decided against it. Despite doing complex business budgets much later, I opted for English Literature. No one told me to pursue a field of study that made money. Still my study of English Literature allowed me to support myself and has been a strong foundation for many adventures in my life.

My college experience included classes that shaped and changed me, but not in the ways that one might expect. One such class was "Jazz with Tanner." Yes, I still remember the name of the professor. It was known as a "Mick" class, a Mickey Mouse class that was an easy grade. I enrolled and was mesmerized. After learning the structure, history and evolution of this music genre, I developed a life-long love and appreciation for jazz, soft, hard and everything in between.

It wasn't until decades later that I discovered that the professor, Paul Tanner, a UCLA alum, was the last surviving member of the Glenn Miller Orchestra. After earning a Ph.D., he taught the popular jazz class at UCLA for twenty-three years. A trombonist, he conceived of the class and co-wrote the text.

Another life-changing class was a journalism class that I took from author and essayist Robert R. Kirsch, the longtime book critic for the *Los Angeles Times*. He was remarkably approachable, kind and exceptionally human. One of his assignments, much to the groans and reticence of his class, was to keep a dream journal. I didn't remember my dreams, so this was a daunting, scary task.

Mr. Kirsch stood in front of the class, smiled at the audible gasps in the class, and said, "It's easy. Just chew each bite of your food for a minimum of twenty-five times and you will remember your dreams."

Ah, it worked for me and every other student in the class. I learned about the power of suggestion firsthand.

He also gave weekly news quizzes that required us to read Time or *Newsweek*, The Los Angeles Times, and watch television news shows in order to do well. Those quizzes made me a life-long news junkie. I love learning about what is going on.

One day I went into talk with Mr. Kirsch during office hours.

"I just wanted to apologize for missing your class the other day. I had a bad case of Shakespeare's green sickness," I said, referring to having coffee with a chap I had a crush on instead of going to class.

He was warm, welcoming and we talked for a time about what, in retrospect, were probably mundane personal college topics for him, but were salient to me. I knew of his reputation as a writer and reviewer and marveled that he could take interest in me. Mr. Kirsch probed my thoughts and the current zeitgeist to get to know me and I him. And, yes, I still have the textbook from that class that served as a springboard for me, then and now.

Another class which helped form me and taught me life's lessons was an English class with a young handsome professor, whose name escapes me. We were studying Lewis Carroll's Alice's Adventures in Wonderland among other novels.

Very simply he walked in, advised us to take out our books, and said, "Once you get into the world of the novel, you understand it. It all makes sense."

Sage advice that worked for me in any number of areas. Once I understood the world being presented, the rest was easy - tests, people who thought differently than I, politics, well just about everything.

I vowed after analyzing and dissecting literary classics for four years that I would reread many of these novels for the sheer joy.

Many other classes were fun, insightful and broadening. The quarter system was perfect for me. If the class was good, I could really get into it. If the class wasn't, it went away quickly.

I did return after my sports escapade and was off probation the first quarter. My grades were good, good enough to get into graduate school for a Ph.D. when I graduated.

I went out for the volleyball team and knew many of the girls. It was like old home week. A few were cowed by the fact that I had been on the Olympic team. I worked hard to ensure that intimidation went away quickly, and we could be a well-rounded team. Coach Andy Banachowski, acclaimed for having one of the winningest records of all time to this day, had just graduated UCLA. Laura, my college and post-college roommate, and a host of other talented women were on the team. We had great fun. There were no scholarships, no perks other than traveling to nationals.

We won the first national championship for UCLA in 1971-1972. We had an impressive record there.

Decades later when the UCLA team got together for a reunion, Andy said, "It was very different then."

It was.

Chapter 5: Paige One at Architectural Digest

Enough academia, I wanted the real thing. My classes at UCLA had finished. I wouldn't officially graduate until June, but I had decided to postpone pursuing a Ph.D. or a master's degree and to go out into the work world.

Laura, my always animated college roommate, decided to go to the graduation ceremony. There would be hundreds of students in caps and gowns, many with bathing suits on underneath since it was hot. The real diplomas, machine-signed by Governor Ronald Reagan, would be mailed later. I stayed home that day and cleaned our Westside apartment.

I started combing the newspaper for ads. (This was the preferred means of job hunting with no internet then.) Not long afterwards my mother talked with my Uncle Bill, an executive at Zellerbach Paper Company.

"Laurie saw an opening at a magazine called *Architectural Digest,* an advertisement for a receptionist's job," she relayed.

"It's a great opportunity," he said, well aware of the magazine since his company provided paper at that time. "Tell her to go on the interview."

On the appointed day, I hopped into Yves, my red VW Beetle, and sped off to the 5900 Wilshire Boulevard building across from the Los Angeles County Museum of Art in the Miracle Mile district, just east of Beverly Hills. At the time the building was owned by real estate mogul Walter Shorenstein, who had wooed many of the big advertising agencies as tenants such as Ogilvy and Mather, Doyle Dane Bernbach, and publications such as the West Coast offices of T.V. Guide.

After working as, a temp at Skin Diver magazine in college, with photos, stories, and adventures coming in from all over the world, I set my sights on television or publishing. ABC had offered a temp job, the insecurity of which put me off. This building was a West Coast hub, an electrifying destination for me.

Bon Mots and Personal Style

I arrived at the eighth floor and stepped into another world. As I later described to many visitors: the foyer had a bleached and pickled white parquet wood floor; the walls had black, silver, and white argyle foil wallpaper; the two facing white kid leather sofas were by Thayer Coggin. Glass coffee tables sat in front of each sofa, and the receptionist's desk was a rich wood plank atop two Plexiglas walls so that it would appear as though the desk was suspended or floating.

I sat studying the room design - quite a departure from the typical seventies green shag carpets and iridescent colored walls until I was called in by the business manager, Howard. An older gentleman, he was studied and somewhat scripted but affable, a little round in stature with a thinning hairline. I followed him inside the twelve-foot-high dark wood doors and entered the office inner sanctum double doors down the hall.

"So, tell me about yourself," he began. He was pleasant and we chatted for about fifteen minutes. I was just out of school with a bachelor's degree in English Literature, so I didn't have a lengthy job history to talk about: selling fine jewelry at Bullock's, teaching volleyball to high schoolers and coaches for Youth Services, and working as a secretary (filling in for the full-time secretary during lunch) in the intramural sports office at UCLA. The Olympics was listed on my résumé. Finally, he signaled that the interview was over, and he escorted me to the lobby.

Several days later, I received a call that I had landed the job. I was overjoyed. I loved magazines and art, so this just fit the bill. There was no question in my mind. I opted for AD and quickly set my sights on becoming an editor.

At about this time, I moved to a very tiny apartment with eight units in Westwood on Santa Monica Boulevard, an easy drive to work. There was a sign atop the street entrance for yoga lessons. The apartment was inexpensive since I was fearful of not being able to pay my bills. But the tenants were fascinating. One neighbor had a master's degree from UCLA in scientific instrumentation. He created the machines to measure whatever was the corporate order of the day. He walked into my apartment once night and my stereo stuttered. Dave immediately reached down and adjusted a wire, fixing it, and said, "You had a short." I was amazed. We are still in touch years later.

I started at *Architectural Digest* as receptionist in May 1972, the first of five incredible years at the magazine. I greeted all visitors and, of course, answered questions about the then avant-garde lobby design, as I sat at the long plank desk atop the Plexiglas sides in the lobby.

The linear L-shaped offices were divided into two parts with the reception area or foyer in the center. One side was devoted to subscriptions. Dagmar worked in fulfillment as did Anna and Florence. Each was so different and came from different backgrounds, but all were exceptional and skilled at interfacing with the public.

I was in and out of this area multiple times a day interceding on behalf of subscribers or relaying new subscriptions. As I asked questions for subscribers, one of these ladies would answer and explain the ins and outs of fulfillment or how foreign subscriptions work. I started to learn about the labyrinth of subscriptions and fulfillment in the magazine business.

The other side of the "L" was advertising, editorial, art, accounting, and the office manager, Howard.

Soon I met the two main editors Paige Rense and Dennis Murphy, who was a prodigy of Cannell &Chaffin, the famed design firm.

My assignment was to assist Dennis Murphy and Paige Rense in editorial. It became very obvious very quickly that Dennis and Paige were vying for the attention and the editorial power of the magazine run by the young handsome Cleon T. (Bud) Knapp. Bud was the astute, young scion running the family-owned magazine now.

Upon meeting Paige, I was awed. She oozed strength, intelligence, wit, resolve and a personal softness. Instantly I felt admiration. Paige dressed with great style. Her artistic flair was evident in the clothes she put together, simple, tasteful but with eye-inspiring artfulness. Diminutive about five feet two, the same height as my mother, she stood straight and spoke softly.

She was frightfully different from the harsh stereotypes of female executives. She spoke with great candor, not to mention insights. Her people skills were profound. She, I found later, was a master at verbal chess. Always speaking softly, she could and did support her staffers but could verbally eviscerate foes, corporate or otherwise, in short order. Once done, the recipient would walk away smiling and then replay the conversation only to find that he/she had been unraveled, dissed and verbally dissected. In fact, one secretary whose verbal expressiveness coupled with slow and unreliable work, had a meeting with her once and came out with a smile on her face. After replaying the conversation in her head, the secretary gasped and said, "Oh my, she just told me that there is no place for me here. She just fired me!"

Dennis was also in his mid-forties but dressed conservatively. He was soft-spoken and about six feet tall with a receding hairline. The jobs he gave me were simple straight-forward and rote.

Dorothy, secretary to William Warren D., advertising head, quickly showed me the ropes and tempered my hopes after I asked if she had seen the gorgeous guys who just walked into the office.

"Come here," she said, kindly. "Laurie, I wouldn't get your hopes up too high, if I were you. They're all interior designers."

"Drat!" I thought.

I loved going to work every morning. I loved the people, the work, and the setting. I was learning the ropes of the magazine business. It was a small office, so I was exposed to all phases. I was told that at the time, Architectural Digest was an anomaly in that it made its money or profit from subscriptions alone. Advertising was gravy.

Bud was in search of a new editorial leader since the tragedy that happened months before I arrived. Former A.D. editor, Bradley Little, had been shot and killed in the parking lot of a Westside restaurant.

There was really no contest in the caliber of design material that Paige and Dennis brought in. Paige's was cutting edge, exciting and fresh. Dennis had ties with the old doyens of design, Cannell & Chaffin, and others, but these were staid, formal, if not tired at this point. They were much more like the early days of the publication when it was more of an "architectural" journal than a design publication. I should know; I later cataloged all of it.

It didn't take much time until Paige eclipsed Dennis and received the nod from Bud. Dennis was leaving. I felt bad for him. He was nice and tried hard but he was no match for Paige.

The magazine was small. Bud and Paige shared a secretary and there were only about twenty staffers at the time.

Paige had hired another editor, a young lady name Andrea Levinger Smith, a graduate of one of the seven sister colleges, Radcliffe, I think. Mid-five feet tall, with long dark hair and a special sparkle to her eyes, she prepared a crib booklet for problem verbs etc. and started assembling a custom magazine stylebook for the magazine. She was quite bright and an equally talented proofreader and editor. For nine months, Andrea taught me proofreading according to the Baedeker of magazine style manuals, A Chicago Manual of Style. I was awash in cedillas, circumflexes, accents aigu and grave and a tome's worth of hows and how nots, when and when nots. Far beyond other style manuals, A Chicago Manual detailed magazine nuances in capitalization, historical eras and proper names, commas, and other conventions of the English language

Since we sent copy out to typesetters to be printed in manuscript form pre-computers, it was necessary to know how to correctly mark up these manuscripts. We had to know proofreader marks and how to treat copy. Andrea made a daunting amount of information clear through her interpretation, and she was great fun. I never stopped learning from her.

By this time, Paige had taken me under her wing and, even as receptionist, assigned me to research and write several articles. The first was "Antique Scientific Instruments." I was thrilled and combed everything I could for information. I interviewed my college roommate Laura's father who had one, if not the best, microscope collections in the country with original Leeuwenhoek's, among others. I would take off in the afternoon in my little red VW for an appointment with some dealers in Hollywood. I interviewed them, wrote up the article, and turned it in to Paige.

Paige reviewed it and said, "It is very well organized."

"But dull," I said, and she agreed.

"Forget everything you learned in school," she advised.

I did so immediately and well, then on April 11, 1973, a year after I started there, Paige sent out a memo to in-house staff and correspondents.

"Staff addition: You received a communiqué from Laurie Lewis. A UCLA graduate with an English major, she contacted us and took the job of receptionist with the opportunity for upward mobility. She has become a great asset and we are pleased to promote her to Editorial Assistant."

In addition to systematically reading every book in the AD library at home at night or on the weekends, I also understudied both Paige and Andrea. There was a wealth of information to be gotten from both of them. I handled most of Paige's outgoing correspondence which taught me a great deal.

Eventually, she would hand me letters and say, "Send them a bread-and-butter response."

That meant a one sentence response- yes, no, or whatever the case may be. I reveled in this and soon was able to mimic her style quite proficiently. She was a brilliant writer whose handling of words, cadence, subject matter and even coining new words such as affluentials was beyond compare. In everyday matters though, brevity was the order of the day.

Paige would conduct designer/client interviews for the magazine on a small tape recorder and I would transcribe the interviews. Some were quite entertaining. Pre-computer, typewriters, IBM Executive typewriters were a challenge but inevitably the interviews or interviewees were intriguing. After she returned from one interview in Montecito, south of Santa Barbara, I set to work transcribing the interview. The owner of the Montecito house had gone out to buy a 28-foot sailboat at a nearby boat dealer. He decided on the boat and asked the dealer, "How much is this boat?"

"It is XX thousand dollars plus $12 dollars," responded the dealer.

"What is the $12 for?" asked the owner.

"The $12 is for a license to sail it on a lake or the ocean," said the dealer.

"Here is the money for the boat less the $12," said the owner. "Just deliver it," instructed the owner.

The dealer did deliver it and the owner had the sailboat put in his front yard reflection pond, where he sailed it up and down.

Other incidents were bemusing and amusing. We joked for quite a while when Joan Crawford's New York apartment was slated to be photographed. The photographer had to wait a week while the plastic furniture covers were removed. Eccentricities were universal.

Not all incidents were happy. One time noted Los Angeles designer J.P. Mathieu (Pepe) was slated to appear in the magazine. His design was to appear on the cover. (This was pre-internet, so the papers carried the most current news.) I awoke to the front page of the Los Angeles Times that morning, as the magazine was about to go to press, featuring a front-page story on the murder of J. P. Mathieu. That headline ruled the morning. Quickly another feature was pulled to replace his design and the cover. We were all a little in shock for we knew him well. Pepe was a nice chap but obviously he was in the wrong place at the wrong time.

Photographs, usually transparencies, were pored over with intensity. The art director, Henri D., Andrea and I would examine them carefully on one of several light boxes. Paige would come in for final approval. It was standard operating procedure that backs of chairs be minimized and wall sockets were airbrushed out of photographs. The optimum time for photography seemed to be the middle of the night. White walls were captured in a steady light. If one transparency of a room didn't match another, well it was sent out and the walls were painted to match. Voila! Great pains were taken to ensure the finest quality and consistency.

Despite attention to minute detail, life was never dull at A.D. The firm across the hall had an ongoing stream of celebs traipsing in and out. The then darling of commercials, Rodney Allen Rippy, came to visit one day and half the building floor came out to gawk. Rippy became an instant celebrity when he starred in Jack in the Box commercials in the early seventies and later went on to produce the Six Million Dollar Man and other works.

Another day, while still working as a receptionist, two suited gentlemen entered the lobby.

"Good day," one said, showing his credentials. "We're here from the U.S. Senate Investigatory Committee. We'd like to examine your files on Nixon's Western White House in San Clemente."

La Casa Pacifica, Nixon's Western White House in San Clemente, California was part of the investigation into Nixon. The Committee had been tasked with looking into the Watergate break-in and any other questionable activity or cover-up. Our files would have provided a road map for tracking costs and expensive furnishings.

I asked them to wait momentarily while I shot down the hall to Bud's office. Without hesitating, he instructed me to decline them access to the files.

"Tell them no, Laurie." Bud said. "Tell them that the files and copies of the magazine are under the publisher's embargo."

I immediately returned and relayed the message to the two men who said, "Thank you," and departed.

Bud immediately dispatched me to the legal firm, Latham & Watkins, in downtown Los Angeles with the files. Intrigue. I loved it.

Later I fielded a call from a Washington Post reporter who asked if we had copies of the Western White House issue of the magazine in our warehouse. I put her on hold and checked with Bud who said,

"Tell her that we have fifty copies, but they are under publisher's embargo. However, we will sell them for $100 a copy."

I relayed the message verbatim. However, the reporter altered it slightly when she wrote the story saying that we were buying copies of the issue for $100. Yes, I was the lucky one who answered every letter via typewriter explaining the facts. My belief in the written word and the veracity of reporters was clearly redefined.

Paige seemed to enjoy mentoring and teaching Andrea and me. She would have us critique designs that came in. Once a week we'd report to her with our comments on designs: the good, the bad, the ugly, the details, the ones that worked and those that didn't and why. This appealed to my sense of art and design in a big way.

She brought us along gently until we were d'accord with her visions. "Traditional is more difficult to pull off well than contemporary designs," she would explain, Over the years, I have to say that I agree with her. Clean simplicity is not as challenging as layers of warmth and visual intrigue.

In those pre-internet days, libraries were a research haven. I spent much time across the street at the Los Angeles County Museum of Art library and talking with the curators. One day I took the LACMA curator to lunch on behalf of the magazine. A delightful friendly chap, the curator and I lunched and discussed art and upcoming exhibits etc. It was time to return to work, so I requested the check and the bill came. My first business lunch and I was chagrined to be told that my credit card had expired - most embarrassing. The curator picked up lunch to my extreme embarrassment. I reimbursed him later with a note of apology.

Paige, ever setting the course, decided that the magazine should have a Letters to the Editor section. We actually received few, if any then, and laws weren't as stringent. Paige called Andrea and me into her office and said, "We're going to start a Letters to the Editor section. Since we don't have any to start, I'd like the two of you to write some for this issue."

Andrea and I set to work and wrote letter after letter to the editor about all different topics and signed them by imaginary people. Creating names and places, lauding and critiquing was great fun. Shortly thereafter, we started receiving a stockpile of letters. Paige's plan worked.

Meanwhile, there were a slew of invitations that came in daily to gallery openings, parties, and other events. Bud and Paige took the "A" list invitations and Andrea and I made the rounds on the others.

One night Andrea and I attended a gallery opening in West Hollywood for etchings on glass by an artist whose name escapes me.

We were greeted by the gallery owner who was most gracious and said, "You undoubtedly know all about glass etchings."

Andrea responded, "No, actually I don't know anything about it."

"I didn't either until this show came in. Let me explain the process to you," the gallery owner said.

Voila! The stereotypic gallery hauteur exposed.

For those intimidated by art, their knowledge or lack of it, art is personal. There is no right or wrong answer. But attending gallery openings was also running the gauntlet of personalities. Most cared nothing about Andrea and me, but rather cared only about getting exposure in the magazine.

Another evening I was sent to a gallery in West Hollywood to view a showing of Erté lithographs, his alphabet. Each letter was carefully created from a human figure in a rich Art Deco style. Art, like wine, is very individual but I was entranced not only by the alphabet but by

Erté, a self-effacing man, about five feet tall, dressed in a purple, yes, purple, suit. He was charming and spoke with a lovely French accent.

One night I was dispatched to cover a party hosted by the Canadian Tourist Bureau at the Beverly Wilshire Hotel in Beverly Hills. I arrived and was greeted at the door by the host who immediately ushered me to the bar and then the hors d'oeuvre table.

"Have an oyster," he insisted. I had never had one and remembered asking Laura my college roommate about them.

Her response was "Think of a jellyfish slithering down your throat."

Not my idea of heaven, aphrodisiac or not.

I complied and took one, thinking, "How embarrassing to be sick in the middle of the Grand Ballroom of the Beverly Wilshire Hotel."

It went in, down and thankfully stayed. Success. Whew. I made my way around the room, working the party for any possible magazine contacts. When I again neared the door, the gentleman host approached me again and insisted that I have the largest oyster on the table.

"Thank you, no," I said. "I'm still working on my wine. Why don't you have it?"

"Oh, no," he answered. "I don't like them."

I harrumphed to myself silently, bid him good night and trundled home.

After attending gallery openings and parties multiple days a week, I developed a different outlook. I used to tell friends and family that shaking hands at these events was tantamount to getting a plastic cut from people who had an overriding interest in getting coverage in the magazine, but certainly not in me or others. "Nice being met," I used to say in my head.

Early on in my time at AD, Paige ran a piece on table settings. Some of the photos featured showed plates atop a bare wood table - anathema at that time after the prim and proper 50s, the rancorous 60s and now the 70s in which life was loosening. We received letters from countless readers asking what had happened to the etiquette of dressing the table. Paige reviewed the letters and told me to respond with "style," personal style knows no bounds.

Whole new worlds were opening up to me. No longer was I in school dreaming about going out into the work world. I was there learning, enjoying, dreaming, and doing.

After almost a year and a half at the magazine, I was promoted to assistant editor. I moved into the editorial section with a small office right next to Paige's.

Dutch Treat, Castles to Wee Country Cottages

In September, Paige called me into her office and said, "Laurie, you need to get a passpo rt. You are going on a three-day press junket touring Holland, compliments of the Dutch government and travel bureau. You will be there with journalists from other European countries."

I almost did summersaults out of the office. I thrilled at the thought of feeding my wanderlust.

I flew from LAX en route to Canada where, thankfully, I was upgraded to first class after hours of being sardined into a corner window seat by two seatmates who had managed to bring an entire department store on board the plane. We flew onto Scotland for refueling and ultimately Amsterdam.

I arrived twenty-four hours after I departed, and it was a different day and 9 A.M. in the morning. I was exhausted, exhilarated, and excited. I checked into the hotel and after a half-hearted attempt to sleep, arose and took off to see some sights nearby.

Europe. How exquisite, how different, how wonderful! What an impression. The detailed and decorated Dutch architecture, the wondrous canals, the corner pubs all captivated me. Tall narrow buildings one after another, side-by-side, lined the streets. I watched as a baby grand piano was being hoisted from the roof of one building to the second floor where it would be gently prodded into the second-floor picture window. Certainly, there was no room to take it up the narrow stairs or halls.

I met at the appointed five o'clock hour for a reception with the other journalists, a Brit, a Swede, and a host of others. We had a remarkably savory dinner which instantly reminded me of my mother's melt-in-your-mouth pot roast.

"What is this?" I inquired.

"Hare," was the response. It took a minute but then it dawned on me, rabbit! A first for me, but delicious.

We were greeted by a Dutch burgemeester, or civic leader, and traveled far and wide outside of Amsterdam to Kampen in the north and elsewhere.

We gathered the next two days for tours of city and country, historical ornate castles, and thatched-roof cottages in the country. The castles were elaborate with minute detailing and finishes, adorned with art, a stark contrast to most buildings I had experienced in the U.S. The country farmhouses, with four-foot-high doorways, allowed us a window into the peasants of a different century. The tiny doorways reminded me of a shrinking Alice making her way through Wonderland. It was quite a comical scene actually. My five foot-eleven-inch stature and that of the others, just under or over six feet, were challenged. In single file, the journalists lined up and crouched down to waist height or lower to gain entrance. Once inside though, thankfully, the ceilings were normal height, and we could stand up.

As we rode back to the city, there under the bridge pass ways were exquisite Dutch paintings by unknown artists. Seeing these beautiful paintings out in the open, hanging for everyone to see and admire stunned me. My faith in humanity was bolstered since there was not a hint of graffiti nor any damage. Years later I read that these treasures were covered to protect them from vandals.

The Van Gogh and Gauguin museums offered tours of breath-taking art. I purchased books at every turn so that I could later revisit the art.

While in Amsterdam, I was assigned to meet with a well-known photographer who might work out as a scout/photographer for the magazine. I called and set up a dinner with him. Not wanting to miss anything, I chose a five-star restaurant. Once I was in the taxi with the photographer, I directed the cab driver to take us to the restaurant via the red-light district."

He smiled and complied. I gawked. The two men laughed. Here was a street of storefronts variously decorated with recamiers, sofa-like beds, all backlit in blue. The working ladies reclined on the sofas gazing out on the small coterie of men looking longingly from the sidewalk. With a wink, the woman would summon one of the onlookers and voila, the man entered the building. The window was empty. It was quite theatrical. Novels I had read came alive before my eyes.

There was a brief respite one afternoon and the six-foot-tall, late twenty-ish, fair skinned Eric, the Swedish journalist said, "I need to get the locks on my luggage fixed. Do you want to walk with me and see if we can find a store to fix it?"

"Sure," I said. Most of the other journalists spoke multiple languages so I was feeling somewhat like a lazy American.

We sauntered down the street and finally found a locksmith. We entered and the short stout man behind the counter was abrupt and brisk with Eric, much to my surprise. Eric and the shop owner started bantering until they found a mutual language. Instantly the owner's demeanor changed. He was friendly and accommodating. I was puzzled. Eric had his luggage locks fixed and we bid the shop owner goodbye.

Once outside, I quickly quizzed Eric asking, "What was he saying?" "Simple," he said. "The Dutchman thought we were German, and he has no love for Germans. Once he found out that I'm Swedish and you're American, he was pleased. He lived through the German occupation of World War II."

The last evening was free and since all of the other journalists had left, I took off, in my long suede coat, up one of the windy, damp canal streets to Anne Frank's attic. I had been planning this visit since I arrived. Having read her book several times, the first time when I was her age, I wanted to see the attic where she wrote the book, where she hid for so long.

I walked up the street and saw the sign. I looked at the door, the building, and replayed Anne Frank's story, the cruelty in my head, I started to cry and was overcome with emotion. I continued walking on down the street, never entering.

At age twenty-two, I was stunned. World War II was a history-book lesson to me. The reality and the lesson sunk in.

I returned home wiser, I hope, and awash with a new cultural and historical awareness.

A Postcard from the Heartland

Sometime later, the governor of Missouri Christopher "Kit" Bond, later a U.S. senator, was hosting a dinner in Missouri and invited Paige.

"Laurie, I think you might like to go to this," Paige said. "I'm sure that he wants the governor's mansion to be in AD so check it out."

We had featured then Governor Jimmy Carter's home sometime earlier so this followed naturally.The heartland. I'm ready," I thought. I'd visited my relatives in Minnesota, and this would be similar, I surmised, but with added pomp and circumstance.

I flew into Kansas City and was greeted by a lovely lady who worked for the local newspaper. Mrs. Wharton and her husband were to drive me to the capital, Jefferson City, several hours away. She was a candidate for correspondent for the magazine and was most generous in filling me in on the local lore and information. I was wowed by the huge Hallmark Center as we drove through the city.

"All those cards paid off," I couldn't help but think.

My hostess regaled me with stories of the Kansas City "jet set" and what active travelers they were.

We drove for several hours and arrived in Jefferson City. I checked into a hotel and changed for the reception that evening. Thank heavens for a basic black dress and pearls.

It was sunny and a little cool. The couple scooped me up and we drove to the governor's mansion. The tall handsome Governor Bond was warm and friendly. This nattily dressed sixth-generation Missourian, the state's youngest governor and his wife greeted guests with ease and an air of hospitality.

"Welcome, please make yourself at home," he said in a melodic voice, ushering people into the main salon. Guests and friends mingled and chatted after drinks were served followed by the appetizer, tray-passed cups of cold strawberry soup.

The Governor's Mansion was quite grand and chock-full of Missouri memorabilia but certainly didn't fit Paige's bill of "haute design."

It was a challenge for me when dispatched on a trip like this. I perhaps erred on the side of grand rather than return with a mediocre design.

Later Paige received an invitation to the opening of John Portman's Peachtree Center Plaza hotel in Atlanta, Georgia. The prototype for the Bonaventure Hotel in Los Angeles and similar hotels in other cities, this hotel is seventy-five stories high with more than 1,500 rooms.

"Laurie, I thought you'd like to attend this," said Paige, with a smile, as she handed me the invitation. The thrill of traveling, of experiencing Southern hospitality that I had only read about mounted.

"Oh, yes, I'd love to," I said. I glanced at the invitation and realized that not only was I invited to attend the opening, but that Portman was hosting a ball Saturday night at the hotel.

"This," I thought, "is more like a Cinderella story and I get to meet a famous architect."

"You'll be met by X and her husband X. She may be a candidate as a possible contributing editor. She'll have houses for you to check out for the magazine while you're there.

I made sure that I had the obligatory basic long black dress and pearls for the ball, as well as the appropriate dress for other engagements.

Upon arrival, I hailed a taxi and started chatting with the cabby. I always learned about what was going on in town from cabbies. He mentioned a murder in a hotel downtown just across the street from where I was to be staying.

"Hmmm," I thought.

The hotel was huge and the lobby on three levels was mobbed by locals who came to view and eat at the restaurants and experience the bars. I finally found the front desk and checked in. A bellhop escorted me and my luggage to the lobby level which had room access and then to my room on the fiftieth floor.

"Gulp," I thought." Sure hope they don't have earthquakes here. I'm awfully high up."

The view was expansive and lo, the earth was red. All I could think of was the "red earth of Tara." Other parts of Gone with the Wind replayed in my mind.

I couldn't help but notice a hanging lamp over a table. It was swinging from side to side. I checked out the bathroom and watched with intrigue as the water in the toilet bowl gently rolled from side to side.

"Argh," I thought.

I was up and out the first morning, greeting my host and hostess who took me to a lovely suburb of Georgia. My jaw probably dropped open as we passed a whole block of homes that had been leveled by a tornado the day before. What destruction! Earthquakes? Tornadoes? Both can be nasty, but I think I'll take earthquakes.

The home was nice but certainly not "designy" enough. I returned to the hotel and climbed into bed for a quick nap before the evening's events.

About an hour into my nap, I heard a key in my door and my heart sank. I harkened back to the cabby's newsflash of a murder at the hotel across the street the week before. To make matters worse, there were only about fifty guests, mostly press, staying in the 1,500-room hotel. My adrenaline was high; my heart was racing. I pretended to be asleep while peeking. I watched as the hotel staffer entered my room, spotted me on the bed and then quickly exited and closed the door behind him. I breathed a sigh of relief!

The evening festivities in the Grand Ballroom were full of guests and press who mingled, chatted, and enjoyed a sumptuous dinner. At the last minute, John Portman had bowed out, a tad anti-climactic but the party was nonetheless entertaining.

The next morning, I toured downtown Atlanta by car with my host and hostess and then headed to the airport and happily flew back to my home in LA.

Once I was back in Los Angeles, I dived into another interesting assignment, at least interesting for me. I was dispatched one afternoon to an antique bookstore in West Hollywood. Paige wanted to purchase a set of encyclopedias for the magazine library. At the bookstore on Melrose Avenue, I met two older men who tended their books like doting parents.

Encyclopedias, I figured, couldn't be that complicated. Think again. Another lesson and I soaked it all in. The two men took me on a tour of all the previous years of encyclopedias they had in stock - an almost complete inventory of different published sets. They explained the pros and cons of the different publishers and finally we decided to study Encyclopedia Britannica. They took me on a virtual tour of each year. Some of the more recent years were underwhelming according to the two. Other years were good but did not have the best input from scholars and researchers. I was awash in facts and figures and more than mildly surprised that there was such a difference in editions. Finally, we decided on an edition several years earlier, thought by the two men to be the best edition in every possible way.

I returned to the magazine and reported on my findings. Paige ordered the check and voila, we acquired probably one of the best Encyclopedia Britannica sets published, parts of which I personally perused.

This paralleled my experience with dictionaries which I had learned from Andrea. Dictionaries also vary widely. Spelling and pronunciation preferences differ depending upon edition and publisher.

Writing was still a priority for me. Assignments were divvied up and I was assigned to cover then hot designers Kalef Alaton and Janet Polizzi. I did and attributed a "painterly" touch to the designers. Paige approved and praised it and I was delighted. Later the design and story were adapted and included in Paige's first book, California Interiors.

Books weren't the only area of study at the time. The corporate world was there in black and white, with all the attendant pitfalls.

We had a great Christmas party at a staffer's home in the Hollywood Hills during the early years. Henri D., the French art director who spoke with a slightly raspy accent, Bud, Paige, Bill D., Dorothy, all attended. Several people over imbibed.

The next day I was called into Paige's office, and she asked if I heard Henri make any comments about a particular situation. Quickly my mind shot to the implications of a corporate inquisition. I liked everyone. I didn't want any part of this or the office politics. And I hadn't heard anything, only rumors.

"No," I said, "I didn't hear him say anything about that."

Lesson learned. What goes on at office Christmas parties would stay safe with me.

I was still feeling my way and studying more than books. The corporate pendulum swung back and forth. Liaisons and corporate alliances formed before my eyes. The trick was to be on the right side of the relationships and the pendulum. One day early on while reviewing the political landscape and during a mini meeting, the subject of trysts came up.

Paige was quick to advise, "You never have to sleep with anyone to get ahead in the company."

Good to know but curious that she thought she had to say it.

I had graduated to an apartment in Beverly Hills which was quite sizeable. It was two stories with an attic, basement, a large master bedroom and second bedroom, a living room, and a small dining room with a classic black and white checker motif linoleum floor. It was located just a few blocks from the high school and within easy reach of Wilshire Boulevard and work. This was an ideal location.

The staff at AD was ever entertaining and as diverse as can be. From the accountant who went to Las Vegas for a weekend and came back married, to Bill D., who headed the advertising department, with Dorothy as his secretary. One of his salesmen was Richard McL. Personable in every way, personality, looks, intelligence, and athletic, Richard and I developed a fast friendship fostered by the fact that he only lived a few blocks from me in Beverly Hills, and we both liked tennis. The Roxbury tennis courts were a scant block away from each of us. We were in 90212 near the high school, a charming area with older buildings and large pricey apartments with service porches, basements, and attics.

Extra-curricular fraternizing was frowned upon at the magazine at this point so he would stop by my office door and say, "Court four at six." We were on for a rousing game of tennis sometimes followed by dinner and long discussions about the world. The world may have been what went on at work or what was happening in the news. Both of us liked to cook, so we traded off. He definitely had his own unique style.

We played tennis for years and checked in with each other when I spent a year in San Francisco where he had frequent business meetings. We remained lifelong friends until his death decades later.

Dr. Sam He Was One of my favorite people at the magazine was Sam Burchell. He had attended Oxford and Yale, taught at Yale and had written books for Time Life. I called him Dr. Sam since he had a Ph.D. and spoke four or five languages.

I learned quickly and absorbed as much as I could from him.

When he first started at the magazine, he arose in gentlemanly courtesy every time one of the four of us, all women, entered his office.

Finally, I said, "Sam, you can't stand every time each of us enters your office or you'll be exhausted by the end of the day, not to mention, you won't get any work done. You work almost exclusively with women."

He agreed and willingly gave up this chivalrous gesture.

Sam authored *Imperial Masquerade, The Paris of Napoleon III,* as S.C. Burchell. This was his third book. Erudite and polished, Sam was full of social niceties and uncanny largesse. He was terribly kind. He would come into my office and say, "Could you cast your orbs over this piece and let me know what you think?"

I turned around to see if he was talking to someone else. No, must be me. He knew how to level the playing field. Sam had great heart, humor and humanity. It was not uncommon to get encouragement or teasing from Sam, verbally or in the form of a note: LL in the rough and carnival atmosphere of the publishing world you cannot afford to be a Sensitive Jelly Bean. SB

Sam lived in Brentwood when he first joined AD. He was single then. He explained that he had married the only poor contessa in Italy and then after a divorce, married the daughter of Victor Fleming, the director of Gone with the Wind. He and his second wife had one son Alexander. Sam had adopted his second wife's daughter. Both lived with their mom although Sam took them regularly. He was a well-known Indian Chief camping chaperone and when I stopped in at his apartment as we were off to Santa Barbara, he offered me something to drink. Upon opening his refrigerator, there was a container filled with live worms – food for his daughter's piranha.

Sometime later, he had grown tired of his Brentwood digs and was hunting for a new apartment. I suggested that he talk to my landlord about an apartment for rent in Beverly Hills. He did and while I think he initially had some misgivings about living next door to me, they soon dissipated. He saw the apartment in my building, liked it, and took it. We saw each other at work and only socialized at home with an invitation.

There were only five units in the building and the landlord's granddaughter lived in one. All of us were friendly but kept private lives. One day, though, Sam's twelve-year-old son Alexander was waiting outside for Sam to return home. I invited him in so that he was not sitting out in the cold. Alexander walked into my apartment spied an antique typewriter, a trip gift from Paige, and proceeded to explain to me why this was called a "Qwerty" keyboard. Intellect ran in the family.

One morning during an editorial meeting, Paige declared that shag carpets were out of style.

Dr. Sam joked dryly, "You should have seen the shag carpets sitting on the sidewalks as I drove through Beverly Hills on my way to work."

We laughed and realized that there was great impact in what she stated. We knew the reality. We answered etiquette questions for visitors in the lobby and then jumped rope trying out new fitness fads behind the huge doors leading to the editorial department.

One weekend, there was an event in Santa Barbara. Paige headed up and I rendezvoused at Sam's. We headed up in Sam's car. There we were beautifully entertained by a Santa Barbara resident. Later Sam met up with an old pal and bon vivant, Barnaby Conrad. A terribly nice chap, tall and good looking with a slightly receding hairline, he welcomed me readily and I listened to their badinage about all manner of things. The dashing Barnaby was about the same age as Sam, early 60s. Articulate, prone to double entendres and friendly, he welcomed me with open arms as a friend of Sam's.

Soon the conversation topic turned to books.

"Ah, you are an aficionado," I said with a smile to Barnaby.

"The truest kind," he replied and readily handed me a copy of *La Fiesta Brava,* one of his books about bull fighting.

To me he was a Yalie friend of Dr. Sam's, but upon closer scrutiny, I was fascinated, particularly since I had gone to Mexico while in college to see a bull fight.

This San Francisco native was a man of many talents. He had served in the Foreign Service as U.S. Vice Consul at Malaga, Vigo, and Barcelona, and as Consul in Sevilla. He studied bull fighting in Spain, Mexico City, and Peru under famed toreadors. He served as Sinclair Lewis's secretary and chess companion and branched out to become a portraitist. He is perhaps better known as the author of La Fiesta Brava, The Innocent Villa and Matador, and as a writer for Collier's Magazine, Esquire, Reader's Digest, True and others.

Barnaby picked up a copy of his book, smiled and graciously signed "Best wishes to Laurie," on the title page and sketched an "Old matador for Laurie" on the opposite page. I was reminded of a modern-day Papa Hemingway and his escapades because Barnaby had many as an artist, bar piano player and, of course, bull fighter.

Not long after I joined the magazine, we received beautiful transparencies of a home in Italy. The only snag, it had shag carpets. No problem. We just sent it to the retoucher and had all the shag carpets painted out along with the usual wall sockets and any differences in wall color.

About six months later, a lovely lady appeared in our lobby and explained that the house in Italy was hers. Sam quickly appeared to translate. She would love to have some extra copies of the magazine. We quickly complied. She very nicely mentioned that the shutters on the exterior of the house were not purple as they appeared in the magazine.

Whoops. Not purple, "What color were they?" I asked.

"Yellow," she said.

"Oh dear!" I thought.

We never did figure out what happened.

As the magazine was expanding so too did the staff to accommodate added sections and circulation.

There is no doubt that Paige wielded influence in a number of ways. Some were more obvious than others. J. Kelley Younger was hired to step into the Managing Editor position. As Managing Editor, she would be scheduling, tracking, and prodding to ensure all was on time and ready. The magazine had expanded with a West Coast edition. It was Kelley's responsibility to ensure that three and four planned issues were on schedule and material was being processed properly. Her office was wallpapered in charts tracking each issue, each feature, and its status.

J. Kelley Younger was Boston-born but she had very little residual Boston accent. She was tall and slim with tousled free flowing, slightly tinted hair. She was bright and a new light at A.D.

Kelley, no doubt, admired Paige. Imitation is the sincerest form of flattery, they say, but Kelley took it one step further. Over time, all five- foot-seven-ish of her slowly transformed in Paige's likeness.

Kelley had her hair streaked and tinted to mimic Paige's coiffure. I worked with Kelley for several years and watched the transformation firsthand. Although Kelley was thin and maybe all of ninety pounds, she adopted Paige's mannerisms and eventually a hauteur which she exercised universally. This didn't sit well with Sam, me and a host of others. The iron hand was not delivered in Paige's soft-spoken way nor had Kelley earned the respect from the staff. She managed to rankle quite a few people.

Paige went to New York frequently to talk up designers and would ask me to take the New York Times to her house in Marina del Rey to her husband Arthur, a PR executive for one of the aerospace companies. (Poor chap was the chosen one to go on camera when one of the early space crafts burned up.) Arthur was a nice chap, who had two grown sons. I dutifully dropped off the paper one Sunday morning and he invited me in for coffee. Alarms went off in my head. To be nice I accepted, sipped, and departed. Later when Paige returned, I told her how delightful Arthur was and that he invited me for a cup of coffee." She smiled and thanked me, knowing that my radar was up and all over any potential problems. She assured me that Arthur enjoyed the company, and I breathed a huge sigh of relief.

Sadly, after quite a few years, Paige's marriage deteriorated, and she and Arthur divorced (only to remarry years later). Paige was unplugged at work to say the least. Her concentration turned into distraction. We just carried on in our orderly fashion. Dr. Sam made sure that there were no blank pages in the magazine and after a period of months Paige returned to us, ready to rev up the magazine.

One fallout of her divorce that we witnessed firsthand was the revelation that Paige had her husband's credit cards. Companies wouldn't give her a credit card in her own name. Shock set in my mind. How is this possible? Slowly she built credit in her name. The lesson stayed with me and to this day I still keep a credit card in my maiden name.

Another effect of her divorce and later in my tenure at the magazine, were her dual Rolodexes - no, not Rolexes, Rolodexes for cards, numbers, and addresses. Paige kept one for business and another for social contacts.

Up until this time staff lunches were typically held at a nearby Mexican restaurant, colorful, free flowing and expansive. Now the staff was growing, and staff lunches became departmental. Paige now took us to the chic French restaurants such as Le St. Germaine or later to posh restaurants on La Cienega or at La Maison in West Hollywood.

I began to learn the basics of foreign menus and the mouth-watering phraseology describing the food. Acquiring a copy of Larousse Gastronomique helped. There are various versions and attributions of "Know the rules and then you can break them." I still had a lot to learn but I was getting wise to restaurateurs who threw in a single word that didn't exactly follow. When asked, the wait person would explain that it was a brand name of a type of bacon grown on a small farm in Washington state. Ah ha! I thought, harkening back to my college professor who taught: Once you get into the world being presented, the rest is easy.

Everything Paige touched turned to success for Bud. This success spurred Bud to start thinking of expansion. He was considering purchasing a little-known Kansas City-based magazine called Bon Appetit. His signals in this area motivated Paige, who immediately started jockeying for position to take over the reins of that magazine as well. Our staff working lunches took on a new dimension.

Quenelles Anyone? Bon Appetit

One day Paige, Sam, Andrea, Kelley and I went to lunch at the posh L'Ermitage. Paige ordered quenelles.

"What is a quenelle?" I mused, smart enough not to say it out loud. I ordered something more recognizable, a cold lobster salad with green beans and homemade aioli.

Paige's order arrived and she asked if we would like to taste a quenelle. I jumped at the chance. This little poached dumpling with finely ground meat tasted like a cloud.

Paige tasted it and said, "It's a little heavy."

"Oh my, I have a lot to learn about food," I thought.

Lunches were a learning experience on many levels. The venue changed regularly but occasionally we dined at the landmark Bistro in Beverly Hills. After being seated, it was great fun to people watch. Betsy Bloomingdale and Nancy Reagan were regulars making their way in the door and upstairs to the private dining room.

Andrea and I shared a love of cooking and we each had a copy of Julia Child's new book, *The Art of French Cooking*. We made quiches and shared recipes and quiche tins. This was the start of gourmet cooking in the US and yes, real men ate quiche then. Cooking was and continues to be one of my passions.

Paige called me in after two years at the magazine and said, "Laurie, I'm promoting you to Features Editor. You'll do all the art and antiques articles in the magazine."

I was overjoyed and overcome with fear. I was not an expert.

"You'll be working with John L. for antiques and David S. for art on all the features," she continued. Fortunately, both were top-notch experts in those areas.

A learning extravaganza! I loved art and antiques. My goal had been to become an editor. Paige announced my promotion in an internal newsletter sent to all contributing editors and correspondents, which at this point spanned three continents.

I was in charge of soliciting all the photographs for special features and then choosing them with the art and antiques specialists that consulted for the magazine. I sent periodic newsletters out to our correspondents and contributing editors who were phenomenal in rounding up some of the best examples.

I was awash in art and loved it, but there was a great deal that I didn't know. I was now assigned to deal with incoming features and continued to be the liaison for contributing editors, which encompassed a broad swath.

I was enamored of my new art area and dug in right away. The AD offices were directly across the street from the Los Angeles County Museum of Art where I began to spend more time in the library researching art and antiques - my promotion from Assistant Editor to Features Editor meant that I was in charge of those particular features in each issue. I regularly pored over all the current design magazines and the art magazines such as Art in America, Art and Antiques, and ArtNews, in addition to current popular magazines. I was determined to stay on top of all the new and emerging trends.

I took a class in copyright law at UCLA to ensure that I was compliant with legal dictates and befriended the professor, an attorney, Mike E., who specialized in this area. He came on board as a consultant to the magazine.

More and more copyrights were coming to the fore, and I needed to ensure that both the magazine and I were covered.

Since the magazine was bimonthly then, we worked months in advance. Doing Christmas articles in July was not uncommon. But advance preparation was paired with intensive critiquing.

It was great fun for me watching issues unfold as we planned. Sam, Andrea, and I would gather in Paige's office for an editorial meeting. Typically, six months before the magazine's publish date, we would review the interiors and plan a balanced article menu. Then art and antiques features would be reviewed. Sam frequently wrote one or more articles per issue. He was a great writer/interviewer. Andrea was fast at work writing, editing, and proofreading the articles. A host of freelancers also contributed and sometimes the contributing editors or scout editors, such as Jack Loring, then director of PR for Tiffany's in New York, or architect/furniture designer legend T. H. Robsjohn-Gibbings, "Gibby" in Greece would write pieces.

Art Daily Daily I had a fascinating array of art and information that crossed my desk. Perhaps some are familiar with these and more. I certainly wasn't to start but became so in short order. I dived in to learn as much as I could. Here's a sample:

Brief Glossary Barbizon paintings - school of French landscape painters Louis Comfort Tiffany - American designer and artist

Chippendale - 18th century now popular furniture created by Thomas Chippendale II Follies - an ornamental small building French creil - glazed pottery from France Faïence - European earthenware made in the 16th to 18th centuries; examples: Delft, majolica

Majolica a type of faïence Delft - Faïence Palladian architecture architectural style of Andrea Palladio who reinterpreted classics Canterbury magazine rack Louis XIV, XV and XVI - baroque, rococo, and neoclassic styles of furniture respectively Oriental kilem, flat woven rug/carpet kerman carpets traditional classic Persian carpet coromandel screens 17th century Chinese themed screens sulfides cameo incrustations Fabergé eggs - fabulous egg creations encrusted with jewels created by Peter Carl Fabergé Art Deco - style first shown in 1925 with hard geometric shapes and bright colors Marquetry - finishes inlaid with differing materials Pongee - raw silk Pointillism - painting style with tiny dots or points of paint Plinths the block base of a column or pedestal ormolu - gilded finishes pied-à-terre - small place for occasional or weekend use Hepplewhite a type of 18th century furniture Imari - porcelain with blue, red, yellow, and green on white Japanning - lacquerwork that originated in the Orient but was later created in Europe Jardinière - decorative plant or flower container or stand bombé chests - having a bulge in the front or sides Francesco Scavullo - famous fashion photographer Ansel Adams famous landscape photographer, known for his black and white work Alfred Stieglitz - famous American photographers Edward J. Steichen renowned American photographer and painter Inigo Jones important English architect Thomas Church - California based landscape architect "This would be a good issue to include follies," Paige would say.

"Follies - what are they?" I mused to myself. Yes, I know follies are whims or things like that, but Paige wasn't talking about that. This was one of many areas that I dived into with abandon. These small buildings were perfect replicas of other buildings but were strictly decorative.

In the articles on photography, I discovered a wealth of depth and art in photographs by Ansel Adams, Edward Weston, Alfred Stieglitz, Edward Steichen, and others. The term chiaroscuro refers to light and shadow or black and white. Most all of these photographers were known for shooting in black and white and their photographs were incredibly powerful. Their art touched me and took me to another place.

Occasionally we had lunches at Ma Maison in West Hollywood owned by Patrick Terrail. He had a flamboyance that was revered at the time. When esteemed top chefs from New York came to Los Angeles to visit, he ordered McDonald's and served them hamburgers for lunch. He was the talk of the town for a time. Ma Maison was the neighborhood lunch spot.

A Different Gemini Across from Patrick Terrail's Ma Maison restaurant, where we ate occasionally, was Gemini G.E.L. During this time, I managed to befriend Sid Felson, one of the founders/ owners of Gemini G.E.L. I would frequently visit Sid and lunch at Ma Maison with him.

Gracious and welcoming, Sid would introduce me to the current artist in residence at the time -Ellsworth Kelly, Sam Francis, Robert

Rauschenberg, Jasper Johns, Ed Ruscha, or others. Sid had a full staff to help push, pull, or whatever was the case for the current pièce de résistance. The artist in residence would come in, plan, or execute an artwork and then the Gemini staff would make sure that it was executed to perfection, whether print or whatever medium.

I would arrive and was told to go in. Sid would be working with the artist in residence and after a nod from Sid, and a mouthed, "Hi," I would stand and observe. He would finish up and then the tall, thin and remarkably down-to-earth chap, would announce, "I'm going to lunch."

Witty and art smart, he had an understated humor. The current project was always fascinating since I never knew what media I would see when I entered. Frequently, Sid would give me a book or brochure about the artist or current work. I have a small, prized collection of them. I knew that what was going on there was cutting edge but had no idea that Gemini G.E.L. would become an institution immortalized by the National Gallery of Art with its complete Catalogue Raisonné on file there.

Years later, as the National Gallery of Art, in Washington, D.C., explains, "Gemini G.E.L. (Graphic Editions Limited) a publishing workshop in Los Angeles, has been at the forefront of these exciting developments in contemporary art. Their groundbreaking creations include prints in lithography, etching, woodcut, and screen-print, often used in combination, as well as sculpture in diverse media."

While art captured my attention, it wasn't my only focus at the time. I studied the writing styles of all the writers who were assigned and submitted stories. One writer that Paige took under her wing was a brilliant chap named Joel Reisner. I hadn't known him long enough to know the details of his life, but his face showed deep angst. Pleasant and likeable, Joel would submit his writings and I marveled at the ease with which he put words on paper. Medium height with dark hair and a slightly rough voice and a deep laugh, this thirtyish young man was incredibly witty and his wit was evident in his writing, even if just in brief magazine pieces. He took readers through a verbal symphony with all the nuances and crescendos in between.

One afternoon Paige came out of her office with a serious look and said, “I just had a call. Joel committed suicide.”

I was shocked and saddened. The torment that I had sensed surfaced and captured him.

Eventually Andrea left the magazine to tend to her young baby and child. I was sad to see her leave. She was real, a breath of fresh air and great fun to work with. I missed her in our postmortem meetings, analyzing and tearing apart the magazine to see how we could make it better the next time and then plan future issues.

We analyzed and critiqued every facet of the publication, graphics, photography, writing, captions, and content/pacing. Several of us spent hours every issue eliminating widows, a single dangling word at the beginning of a line in a caption, and orphans, three or four words at the beginning of a line.

This may sound glib, but it was no mean feat trying to ensure that a two-line caption accurately described some priceless or near priceless piece of art while ensuring that the copy didn’t extend beyond two or three lines or the designated length for the caption. These intricate lines were complicated by the fact that these captions typically incorporated such design delicacies as “...the pongee silk upholstery is accented by the French creil panel, and the marquetry box inlaid with mother-of-pearl on the other....”

All of the editorial staff kept a keen eye on what Paige did and said and what was going on. Paige was not exempt from eccentricities. She came into work one morning and announced that she would never go anywhere without her walking stick.

“Ok,” I thought, “an element of style? Could be cumbersome.”

Walking stick came and went. Obviously, she agreed.

One day Paige, Kelley, Sam, and I headed to Hollywood. Paige said, "I'm going to buy a crystal ball."

"Hmmm," I thought, "a crystal ball?"

Paige and Kelley each found one and bought them. Sam and I mused quietly.

Since I was one of the original staff members and I got along with most all of the staffers, I was the unofficial designee to introduce the new staffers to the old. It became somewhat comical since each time, I would hesitate, hem and haw when I came to a random person each time different. I knew these people well but each time, I would momentarily forget the name of one longtime staffer. Fortunately, people laughed instead of taking umbrage.

I worked feverishly in the office and hoped that I was proving my mettle. Septembers, for some reason, seemed to be my travel months.

The Grand Tour

In September 1977, Paige called me into her office and said, "I'd like you to go to New York. There your assignment is to meet and talk to all of our advertisers, the top art and antiques dealers in the city. Also, I want you to meet with our people there: Valentine Lawford, Jack Loring, and Lester Grundy and plan out some future issues."

She could probably hear an audible gasp. What an assignment!

"You'll stay at the Regency Hotel, Jacques Camus is a friend of mine so if you need anything, just contact him. Oh, and then, I'd like you to fly on a press junket to Italy, via Alitalia. Meet with our photographer/scout Robert Emmett Bright and check out a count's estate for the magazine."

My breath left.

I said, "Yes, of course," with an ear-to-ear grin on my face.

I loved these trips which fed my wanderlust. I think my earlier trips were my training. My later trips resulted in some nice features for the magazine. Perhaps more significantly, it was years later that I realized that I was the only one sent on these excursions. Why? I'm not sure. Maybe Paige thought since I regularly sent missives to the contributing editors that I was the likely choice to meet them personally or that I was an easy ambassador in the field, and Kelley and Sam were indispensable at home. Either way, I was grateful.

I readied my passport, clothes and found a white chemise knit dress that I thought would be perfect for New York in September since weather reports quoted forty to sixty degrees. I stepped off the plane and into ninety degree-weather with ninety percent humidity. Ugh.

On the plane, I had noticed this handsome gentleman sitting in first class who appeared magically at the curb as we all scurried for taxis.

He looked over at me and said, "You'd better grab this cab, or you'll be waiting here all day."

I was grateful, hopped into the cab and sped off to the Regency. Lo, there he was upon my arrival. He smiled and I returned with a nod. Little did I know that he would play a part when I left Architectural Digest.

I stopped at the concierge and asked how far away and how long it would take me to get to my list of galleries. He smiled and showed me a map. This gallery was around the corner, this one down the street and this only several blocks - all within walking distance. I was stunned. Obviously, I wasn't in Los Angeles anymore. My next day was planned out from morning to night with meetings.

Meeting and greeting new people were a joy for me because I had always been outgoing. As I entered the galleries, I saw the most exquisite art and antiques. I met with the owners/managers and extended greetings from Paige, Bud, Bill, and the magazine.

The antiques and art were breathtaking and real. All the galleries were within walking distance from the hotel. Only a few appointments were a taxi ride away and I quickly refined my taxi hail.

I had read about La Grenouille Restaurant in Women's Wear Daily and W and was fascinated by the appearance of this eatery daily in the who's who and who's where coverage. The paparazzi were always standing guard there to capture whoever. I made luncheon reservations at the restaurant. I can't remember if I dined alone or with someone because of the entertainment. This French bistro was brimming with the well-known. Tom Brokaw table hopped all through my lunch. First, he sat at one table and chatted, and then he walked across and sat down next to Ethel Kennedy and talked for a long while.

La Grenouille, or frog in French, was rather like a fairy tale for me. Someone kissed the frog and voila, a restaurant filled with the rich, powerful, and celebrated.

One evening I was invited to dinner at Lester Grundy's apartment. A beautifully designed apartment with a crystal-clear high-rise view of New York at night greeted me as I entered the door. Lester had been a former editor of House Beautiful. I had long followed the name and now I met the man. He was charming. We sat down in the living room and started talking design as I kept peeking out the window at the New York night skyline. After planning out a number of strategies, I went into the bedroom to retrieve my purse readying to return to the hotel. His little dachshund dog had used it as a chew toy, so only half the carrying strap remained after dinner. Oh, well.

When I returned to the hotel there was a note in my box. "Please join me for drinks in the bar, tomorrow at 5 P.M." signed Dave. I was fascinated, excited and cautious. After a full day of appointments, I returned to the Regency and stopped in to visit Paige's friend, the hotel manager, Jacques C. He had an exquisite French accent, salt and pepper gray hair, and was impeccably dressed and most gracious.

He asked how my accommodations were and if I had any messages. I mentioned the note from Dave.

"He's not supposed to be able to do that," he said. "Let me pull his file." He called for his file and began to read: "Lives in Laguna. He is married and has five children. He is the president of the Pacific Design Center in Los Angeles."

I thanked Jacques for his time and the information and off I went.

Amused and bemused, I figured I had nothing to lose and would meet Dave for drinks in the Regency Bar. I headed for the bar at the appointed time and voila, there was the handsome chap from the airplane/airport sitting in a booth across from the bar. Six feet tall and impeccably dressed, he stood up and greeted me.

I sat down and we started to talk. All the while I was on alert for his story, and would he tell the truth? He did. Eventually, he stated that he was married and had several children and lived in Laguna. He also told me he was the president of the Pacific Design Center.

I relaxed a little and we started to chat. He quickly sized me up and said, "If you come down here at night and order a drink, don't sit at the bar."

"Why?" I inquired.

"At night, the highest priced call girls in New York hang out at the bar here," he explained.

Having only read about such things, I just about fell out of the booth to look at the bar. My mind shifted and I was transported to a bawdy novel.

He laughed and said, "And they let you come to New York alone? If I arranged for you to take a horse-drawn carriage around Central Park with a friend, would you go?"

"I'd love to," I replied. "But I'm booked solidly with appointments during my time here. Thanks though."

We laughed, talked about New York and our jobs. Off we went to our rooms because it was getting late and I had a dinner engagement. I called the office, changed clothes, and returned to the lobby to hail a taxi.

"Soho," I asserted. My taxi moxie was improving daily. The taxicab driver took off and I soaked in all the sights of New York. We arrived and I hopped out onto the sidewalk and immediately turned around to see a demonstration. A street-wide line of people with other lines behind were demonstrating about something.

Fearing mob mentality, I quickly escaped into the loft building in which Jack Loring, our New York Contributing Editor lived. I entered the huge freight elevator and pushed the button for the fourth floor. Up I went. The doors opened and I was in Jack Loring's loft, a beautiful huge space with contemporary furniture and pieces that seemed to go on forever.

I quickly asked Jack what was going on with the demonstrations.

"Oh," he said, "I wouldn't worry about it. Little Italy is across the street. There is no crime here. If even so much as a little old lady's purse is stolen, a dead body shows up on the roof across the street. There is no crime."

Reassured, I moved on.

Jack was tall, blond, dashingly good looking, bright and remarkably savvy in many ways.

Others arrived and I was wowed immediately. People whose names I had only read about were right there and were chatting over an elegant dinner. Mary Ellen Mark the photographer, and Robert Hughes, art editor for Time magazine, were there and Jack's roommate emerged and greeted everyone.

Dinner was a delight with wonderful gourmet fare, clever conversation to match and a sling of art innuendoes.

It was getting late, and the guests bid us adieu and Jack looked at me and said, "Shall we get down to work?"

I quickly tried to rouse myself. We talked and planned features and stories for about six months. By then it was almost three in the morning.

I took a break for a drink of water and walked across the loft to the kitchen. I flipped on the light and an army of cockroaches scattered. I gulped and looked for the washed glass that might have escaped their contamination in the dish rack. I returned to the living room area and said with true Sagittarian bluntness, "Jack, did you know you have cockroaches in the kitchen?"

"Oh, that's nothing," he replied. "For a while we had a huge rat perched in the corner of the high ceiling. Every time we walked in, he threw crumbs at us."

I mentally moved on.

After multiple yawns, we agreed that we had accomplished a great deal and he called a taxi which I hopped in and sped back to the hotel for some sleep.

Another day I was to have lunch in the hotel with our Contributing Editor, Valentine Lawford. At the appointed early hour, I headed downstairs to the restaurant and there was Valentine, classically dressed, perfectly coifed, and groomed. He was the ultimate vision of a gentleman.

"Laurie?" he asked.

"Valentine?" I responded.

Immediately, I felt at ease with this older dark-haired man whose minimal height belied his stature. We were seated and began talking.

"New York is such an exciting city," I said.

"Yes, my dear, but it is very different without money," he replied sagely. "It is very different when you are here daily." I remembered these words for a long time, and they made a difference in my life later when I pondered the possibility of moving to New York to further my career in journalism.

Little did I know at the time that this former high-ranking diplomat in Churchill's London office from 1944 to 1945, interpreter for Winston Churchill and Charles de Gaulle, was an accomplished writer and was also the partner of Horst, the famed portrait and fashion photographer whose work I followed and admired. From Rita Hayworth to Suzy Parker, Horst P. Horst's work appeared in French Vogue in 1931. In the 1960s, he turned his sights to interiors, later documented in a book, Horst: Interiors. Under the auspices of Diana Vreeland, then editor of Vogue, Horst shot some of the most famous and stunning fashion and fanciful photos of the time. His unique style captured and typified a culture.

Valentine was, as I described him in a correspondent memo, a: "Distinguished writer, former member of the British Diplomatic Service, interpreter for Winston Churchill and General De Gaulle."

Lunch was an experience and his words, delivered so kindly and with such a polished flair, stayed with me.

The next day I readied to hop a plane at JFK airport for Rome. I packed up and descended to the lobby to the concierge and asked for a taxi. I stood at the curb and the taxi arrived.

"JFK, please," I asked. "Oh, and please go via Harlem." I had always been wildly curious about Harlem after reading about it so many times in so many books. I looked around and intently absorbed every sight as we headed toward the airport. Harlem was a stunning place to me, so rich in history. I looked at the buildings, the people and wondered what stories, what achievements, what heroes were emerging even then.

I arrived in Rome and took a cab to the Excelsior Hotel. Dr. Sam had counseled me on where to stay. The Excelsior was a classic luxury old-world Roman hotel.

I arrived wide-eyed and marveling at the art, architecture, and décor. Every few blocks there was a piazza and sculpture, sometimes with fountains. I checked in at the front desk and the clerk informed me that despite phone calls and letters, there was no reservation for me. I gulped and hoped this was not a portent of things to come.

"It is ok," he said. "I have a room for you."

Instantly, my angst eased. The porter scooped up my luggage and escorted me to my room. I scouted out all the decorative and architectural details of this vintage 1906 hotel.

"Bathroom, where's the bathroom," I mused. Finally, I opened what looked like a closet door and voila, there was the water closet. Behind door number two was a bathtub, half of which was filled in. A long tube with a sprayer, which was flexible and came off the wall, hung from a hook just above the open part of the tub. A European shower... interesting, I thought.

The first morning I pulled on the tapestry and the impeccably outfitted floor butler appeared.

"Yes, Mam," he said. "How can I help you?"

"I'd like a piece of toast, a cup of coffee and a glass of orange juice," I replied.

"Do you want Italian coffee or American coffee?" he asked.

"I'm in Italy so please make it Italian coffee," I responded.

He appeared shortly with a tray of orange juice, toast, and a demitasse of espresso. I was charged and ready for the day.

The next day I requested the same from the floor butler but this time American coffee. The floor butler appeared with a tray with toast, orange juice and the largest cup imaginable of the same espresso. I was super charged that day and went flying out of the hotel door.

During my free time, I visited the Spanish Steps, the Vatican, and a host of exclusive shops.

Later, I had a scheduled meeting with our photographer, Robert Emmett Bright. How charming yet real he was. How nice to put a face with a name after receiving letters and phone calls from him for years. We talked about possible features and sources for art and antiques pieces, and he gifted me with a photograph of the moon just behind the Vatican tower. The photo was stunning and after having worked on a number of photography magazine articles, my appreciation had grown immensely.

This was a working trip. I dined with Helen Barnes, one of our correspondents and writers there. On a charming square, the restaurant had an inviting alfresco patio where we sat and worked until late at night. She offered much input on day-to-day concerns and ideas for future features.

I met up with another correspondent, Adrian Cook, who spirited me to Count San Miniato's lakeside home on Lake Bracciano. It was large and quite nice but wouldn't translate in photographs. The house gardens, designed by famed landscape architect Russell Page, were breathtaking. Emmett would be dispatched to take record shots.

When I arrived home, I wrote a five-page memo to P.R. (Paige) from LL on October 4, 1976 about jeweled fantasies, Chinese export porcelain, samples of Wiernerwekstaette, the galleries I visited and more. I then wrote a column for A.D. on the Milan furniture show.

Previously Paige had met Robert Hughes during one New York trip and asked him to write one of our art pieces. The piece arrived and she handed it to me.

"You edit this, but I'd like to see it when you're done," She advised. "Oh," she said, "Don't let anything intimidate you. Treat it as any other manuscript."

Daunting for sure. Here was a manuscript by someone I admired greatly. I quickly put this out of my mind and set to work. In several hours, I put it on Paige's desk.

She walked out shortly and handed it back for processing saying, "Well, done. You've actually made it better."

I met Robert Hughes at Jack Loring's. He was impressive and very knowledgeable. I was cowed editing this piece, so I was elated that I had passed this test.

I beamed with a smile that wouldn't stop and breathed a huge sigh of relief.

Day-to-Day Life at AD Unpredictable except for Bud's "Good morning" greeting to all he passed... Paige decided to trade in her Jaguar for a new model Cadillac...economical decision...Executives given an office decorating budget ...results: ho hum except for Paige's showcase space, with sisal matting flooring, beige flannel upholstered walls and poufy camel-colored flannel banquettes... A press proof headline that said "Friend to Greto Garbo et al," which caused a scramble to correct it before press...UCLA Extension courses in graphic design to ensure we knew the parameters of what we were asking for... Pre-computer days so magazine headlines still set in hot type - hot metal poured into molds and then pressed on paper... Party at Wallis Annenberg's palatial house north of Sunset Boulevard with Greek Tourist Bureau director. Casual meant flowing chiffon and three-foot-tall ice sculptures. .... Welcoming and gracious, Wallis Annenberg, daughter of T.V. Guide and Racing Form mogul Walter Annenberg...A ringside seat as Bon Appetit developed...as we created pet names for covers, "mahogany chicken" shellacked to ensure rich brown color and the phallic coeur de la crème with enough gelatin to stabilize it during a hurricane...architectural tours of Los Angeles for our contributing editor, former GQ editor. Hours of Frank Lloyd Wright, Greene and Greene and more as he "oohed" and "ahhed"

Lunch at the Bistro in Beverly Hills required a men's jacket. Borrow a jacket? Trip to hotel to scoop it and all was fine with the Bistro!

Working at AD had quite a few perks, not the least of which were trip gifts from Paige: Bone combs from Haiti, antique vintage 1930s Underwood typewriter... A social strata and scene developed, risky at best, at the Greenhouse Restaurant downstairs... A frequent business lunch and after-work drink destination, as staffers recounted and defused the day.

Things were changing at the magazine. The staff had grown, especially with a new magazine, Bon Appetit. Some people got along, and some didn't. I kept my head down and kept going. In our little corner of the offices, there was never a dull moment.

Chuck R. was designing the magazine. A talented radio program writer and designer, Charles brought a whole new touch to the magazine. It was at this time that Bud and Paige decided to bring in a "big gun" designer too. Milton Zolotow was brought in as a consultant to redesign the magazine and provide template formats for certain sections. In essence, it was a facelift, an updating that revitalized the look and the impact of the magazine outside of the designs that it carried. Pages were treated and presented as art, framing the interiors and photography. Milt provided a template for future designers.

About this time too, a new apprentice designer, fresh from Great Britain came on the scene - Marian H. In her twenties, as I was, we developed a friendly camaraderie instantly - one that lasted decades.

Blonde, five feet six inches, she was attractive and quick to speak when motivated. One day while on a field trip to a "high design" printing plant populated with many gays, she looked over at me and said, "Say, can I pants a fag?"

I recoiled instantly and motioned to her to step aside with me so we could talk.

"Marian, I don't think that that is quite the right thing to say here," I said. Before I could add anything, she fired, "That just means can I bum a cigarette?"

"Oh," I said sheepishly, unknowing of British idioms.

At about this time, Bud hired a chap named Bill B. as chief financial officer. There was a brief moment when Paige was to answer to Bill. At which point, she marched into Bud's office and asserted, "I will not report to him. If I do, I'll march across the street to Prudential and type letters."

That was the end of that. Bud was not about to go against Paige, his lucky rabbit's foot, or golden goose, because everything that Paige touched turned to gold for Bud. Paige had already propelled Architectural Digest well beyond its origins as a true architectural journal, beyond the reaches of House Beautiful and Home and Garden, both powerhouses in the interior design world at the time. And this new fledgling magazine, Bon Appetit, which Bud bought from a small company, had already leapt forward challenging Gourmet under Paige's reign. Paige, however, had a firm vision.

"This magazine is not for those who sit at home and do nothing. This is for the busy, active woman and couples who enjoy good food and company," she explained.

Bon Appetit was working and working well. It was very difficult for us to keep editing copy at 10:30 A.M. as wonderful aromas of food came wafting down the halls in pre-New York, pre-test kitchen days.

With a raft of designers hoping to get into the pages of AD, there was always a steady entertaining tide of interior designers who flowed in and out of our office. One very talented designer was Jack. We would receive beautiful transparencies of homes designed by Jack, who not only designed them but also photographed them. No mean feat, really. Many were shot at night to keep photographic light more even.

We received one such stunning interior and laid out the four by five transparencies on the light table. Transparencies were selected to be sent out to have the electrical sockets and other undesirables hand painted out. But upon closer observation, these had some added intrigue. There were shadows on the walls. Paige called Jack to check on these images. She emerged from her office and calmly told us.

"Oh," she said, "Jack photographed the house when his friends were there. They were partying in the nude."

Creative, sensitive, avant-garde. Sure. But, nude?

Paige canceled Jack's article. Shortly after a large box of flowers arrived at AD for Paige. She opened them and there was an audible gasp. The box was filled with wilted, dead, long-stemmed white roses all crawling with bugs. That was the end of Jack at A.D.

Paige worked tirelessly to expand the scope of the magazine – in all facets but particularly in design, celebrity, and social stature. After all, voyeurism was a basic tenet of the magazine, and fortunately a trait enjoyed by many. Stars and starlets in the seventies were big sellers.

One afternoon Paige came into my office, sat down, and said that she would really like to feature Bette Davis's home in Connecticut.

"What do you say to your matinee idol?" she asked.

"Paige," I responded, "You are equally important, and I've seen you talk to all manner of folks. This shouldn't be hard. I'll dial the number."

I did and we all listened to Paige's eloquent conversation. Bette Davis said that she would think about it. She did and Paige was ultimately successful.

Matinee idols figured elsewhere too. Paige's first T.V. appearance on a talk show was an experience. We helped her prep and prime for the occasion and the occasion was, of course, appearing as herself and the AD editor. Still, she was appearing with Linda Carter who was a pro. Paige's time on air was taped and, just like the magazine, we poured over it with her to critique what could be done better or differently.

Paige called me into her corner office one day and told me that she would like me to go to Washington, D.C.

W, *Women's Wear Daily*, *Town & Country* and all manner of magazines were on our regular reading rounds. We'd check off our name on the routing slip and send the publication on. I had read a great deal about Washington, D.C., the social and art scenes there. I was chomping at the bit to go.

Sam suggested that I stay at the Madison Hotel, just blocks from the White House and the Capitol building, and very near the

Washington Post offices. Opened in 1963, the Madison was and is a luxury hotel. Even President and Mrs. John Kennedy attended the opening. The furnishings matched its verve and historic traditions.

After I checked into the hotel, I was anxious to hit the streets and walk. The doorman carefully guided me.

"Turn left and walk all you want," he said. "The other way can be a bit dangerous and rough."

"Thank you," I said and off I walked to the left.

Instantly I spied the Washington Post building and thought of Watergate and the Senate investigators who appeared at the magazine's office in Los Angeles. The buildings were all old and classic, but remarkably pristine and kept up. The atmosphere in Washington, D.C. is like no other city I've visited. All have a rich sense of themselves, but Washington is remarkably insulated. It's as though there is no other city on earth, much less in the U.S.

A year before, Sam had invited me to dinner at his place where I met another old friend of his, John, a tall, distinguished gentleman. John hailed from Washington, .and worked in one of the highest civil service positions without being elected. During a decidedly elegant dinner of rack of lamb, flageolets, dessert cheeses and grapes served with sterling silver grape shears, Sam, John and I laughed and talked into the evening. I enjoyed hearing John's articulate and insightful quips about Washington. Now I had a chance to see for myself. Sam had arranged for me to have a second dinner with John while I was in Washington.

I dined with John who was thoroughly entertaining as was his sense of humor. He suggested that the next day, I visit one of the coffee shops not far from here.

"There," he said, "you will see Washington lobbyists at work. It's a sight to see."

Indeed, my memories of the trip are few but watching the Washington work corps prepping for the day, the week, or the month, talking as fast as they could intently over coffee before the workday, is an image that has stayed in my mind.

I met with some magazine contacts there and each time I sped off to a meeting asked the taxi driver to take me via the Washington Monument, for example, so that I wouldn't miss anything. I spent several hours at the Renwick Gallery of the National Museum of American Art and other museums. I turned one corner and saw one of Seurat's pointillism paintings. I was captivated. I stood in front of it for almost a half hour, walking up close and backing away to see the full depth and image. Breathtaking!

My most important meeting in Washington was yet to come and the intervening years have caused the meeting contents to fade, but not the excitement. I was to meet with Clement Conger, sometimes referred to as the "Grand Acquisitor," the curator of the White House collection. A tall, soft-spoken courtly gentleman, Mr. Conger greeted me warmly, answered all my questions, most of which were open-ended so I could learn as much as possible. Memories of what we talked about have faded with time but the magazine did a stunning article on his collection so we must have talked about something of import.

The diplomatic rooms at the State Department and the state rooms at the White House were his domain. Mr. Conger amassed the American Collection. He is credited with raising millions of dollars for the State Department and the White House collection.

This was my last trip for the magazine. Sam made sure that it was memorable for me on many levels. Beyond my fourth-grade civics class, I had a vista of government and culture that were inimitable. Washington, D.C. is a city steeped in history and tradition. As I flew home, I couldn't help but think how fortunate I was to have glimpsed a fraction of this firsthand.

Reflections Paige told us that she attended Cal-State Los Angeles and that she had no family. In the five years that I was there, she never once had a call from family. This fact saddened me. She did meet my mother one day, and I marveled that Paige was cordial and seemed almost intimidated. I puzzled over that meeting then and continue to do so now.

There was great irony in all the gorgeous homes that I saw over a period of five years, yet there was only one that I could have lived in comfortably. That home belonged to Angelo Donghia, a remarkable New York designer and a Parsons School of Design prodigy. His designs were comfortable, contemporary, classic yet creative. He used dark-lacquered walls in contrast to white over-scaled furniture, the sum of which was so inviting. Some say that Donghia's designs are reminiscent of those of the iconic forty's French designer Jean-Michel Frank. Sadly, Angelo lost his battle with AIDS not long after.

Paige had become more engrossed in her Rolodexes, one for business and one for social engagements. She had delegated more, and Sam and I were chaffing under the changes - actually not the changes but the people directing who lacked Paige's finesse and humanity. I loved my tenure at AD, but I was itching to fly with my own wings and irritated at certain staffer's barking orders.

I went into Paige's office one morning and said, "Paige, I so appreciate all that you have done for me."

She interrupted with a look of surprise on her face "You're leaving, aren't you?"

"Yes, Paige," I said.

On April 12, 1977, Paige sent out a memo to all staff members:

"I truly regret to announce that Laurie Lewis will be leaving us in approximately two weeks to head public relations at the Pacific Design Center.

I know everyone will miss her as much as I will. (And I will!)"

Moving to the Pacific Design Center as Director of Communications gave me time to scout out other magazines while still staying in communications and design. And, yes, this was a result of my trip to New York and the man, Dave, whom I kept running into until I finally had drinks with him.

Paige had taught me so much and enabled me to have another college education in culture. She taught me tact, patience and how to speak softly, yet be resolute. Those traits I value despite the fact that in looking back over some post-AD years and experiences, I realize that people underestimated me because I spoke softly. She channeled my competitiveness, honed my curiosity, and provided me with a lifetime of Cinderella experiences.

Years later after the magazine had been sold and Paige was still at the helm, an almost unheard of feat in publishing, I wrote her a note. I wanted to thank her while I could still get in touch with her.

Months later I received a bread-and-butter letter: "I remember you well, think of you often and wish you well." I could only chuckle. I knew the form well.

Chapter 6: A Nine-Month Nightmare

Laura, my college roommate, had dated him and moved on. Tall with a slight frame, Ryan and I started dating. This double-boarded gastroenterologist and internist - he had taken extra classes and training, signifying that he was more than qualified to practice in these two areas -was studious and ever so conscientious. He spent hours making rounds, spending time with and counseling his patients.

I was working at AD and frequently invited him to the evening gallery openings or other events. I discovered that he had been married before and had two children. I would accompany him on the weekends when he had his children and, of course, my soft spot for children starred.

Ryan was bright, good looking, and engaging. He cut a dashing figure with a slight frame. He had a simple but straightforward sense of humor and an infectious laugh.

He would call on the phone and say, "Hi, simply hi."

We attended gallery openings and doctor parties, the latter tended to be strait-laced. We spent a weekend in San Francisco and dined at a wonderful chic restaurant. He was not as free-spirited as I was, but I was falling for him.

After dating Ryan off and on for over a year, he asked me to marry him. I accepted. We married amid family fanfare and had a lovely ceremony. We married at the Catholic church, where both my mother and I attended grammar school, and then held the reception in my parents' backyard. Southern California family and close friends attended. Interestingly, my parents were uncharacteristically quiet about the liaison.

Later my mother would simply say, "Leopards don't change their spots."

With no plans for a honeymoon, we took off for Palms Springs, which he knew I loved. The day after we married, Ryan bought a condominium in the desert.

He looked at me and said, "I'm not putting you on the deed. My first wife took almost everything from me. I'm not going to let that happen again."

Shocked and hurt, I wondered if this was normal or was this just a negative reaction to his first marriage dissolving? But I said nothing.

I gave up my apartment in Beverly Hills and moved into his condominium in Westwood. The condo overlooked Century City to the east, so the mornings brought bright sunlight. From noon on, the apartment was dark. Dark spaces have always negatively affected my senses and my outlook.

We played an occasional game of tennis, but he was much more comfortable reading medical journals, which I sometimes scanned out of curiosity. We attended some business parties at which he sometimes joked and talked, and other times, he stayed stone silent not talking to anyone, much to my amazement and surprise.

Ryan's relationship with other doctors at his hospital was tentative at best. He had no best friend, only acquaintances and no close ones.

Ryan had bimonthly weekend visitation with his children, a five-year-old boy and a nine-year-old girl. I worked on family dinners to try to provide a normal family atmosphere. I conferred with his first wife, the children's mother, to make sure that I was backing her up for continuity in the children's' lives.

One night I excused myself from the dinner table to use the bathroom. When I returned, the older girl was gone. I quickly asked what happened, and Ryan told me he sent her outside after she said something he disagreed with. I was appalled and immediately ran after her to ensure her safety. I found her huddled on a front step, scared and crying. I brought her inside and told Ryan that a young child should not be sent out in the dark alone, and it wouldn't happen when I was around. He was angry and reactive.

Ryan knew that I wanted children. When I did not become pregnant quickly, he suggested one of his two brothers impregnate me. I was repulsed. I recoiled.

Ryan started to suffer from major mood swings which became more and more pronounced. At one point, he had a melt-down, sat in the corner crying in his bathrobe and did not go into work. I called the psychiatrist at his hospital who said he could do nothing until Ryan acted. Ryan saw the psychiatrist, who said that I was to blame for his "nervous breakdown" or at least that's what Ryan told me. I saw the psychiatrist too in the hope of helping him. Ryan was clinically diagnosed with endogenous depression, a major depressive disorder. This was news to me since there were no indications of this before we married, or I was too naïve to see the signs.

His depression started exhibiting itself in various ways. Ryan would alternate between screaming at me for local phone calls I made which appeared on the phone bill, and saying I was his love. This was interesting since I was self-supporting save for the mortgage, which he paid. I lived in a bifurcated world, never knowing which way his psychological wind was blowing.

I left the Pacific Design Center, where I worked after AD, and rejoined the publishing world. First, I took an assignment at the *Daily*

News to head a weekly magazine for their affluent subscribers. I quickly discovered challenges at work. Adding to the writing team, I brought in a staff writer from Newsweek and another crack writer who had written for the *National Enquirer*, plus a variety of other publications. I inherited a staff photographer and two newspaper staff writers, one of whom was an acolyte of Isaac Asimov, hardly a match for what was supposed to be an upscale magazine. The other newspaper staffer was Paige's stepson. To complicate matters further, at the time, the *Daily News* was chockfull of dysfunctional administrators, each clawing for stature and power. This presented quite a multi-tiered chess game as I tried to steer clear of the fallout. But I pushed through these challenges. Work was still much calmer than home.

I came home from work one night and realized that the apartment refrigerator in the Pullman kitchen was beginning to die, not keeping food cold. Some food actually spoiled.

When Ryan arrived home, I told him about the refrigerator and he said, "No, we don't need a refrigerator."

With the help of my friend and staff photographer, David L., I went out and purchased a refrigerator, nothing elaborates, but it worked. When it was delivered, Ryan blew up, ranting and raving about this new appliance. Things deteriorated from there. He became surly and screamed at me even more that night.

My upbringing was calm and more "Ozzie and Harriet." My parents had an occasional spat - my mother fought emotionally, and my father fought logically - but it was fleeting. There was no screaming and arguments were usually over some trivial issue.

I finally moved into the second bedroom to get some sleep, since Ryan would scream at me sometimes multiple times a night for inane reasons. He came into the second bedroom and did the same. Several times I spent the night in a motel. Going to work was a relief. Life was predictable there. There was no mood pendulum swinging, just the normal machinations of people working together or trying.

Ryan was jealous and resentful of everyone I encountered. My saving grace was that my job required me to "work a room," meet and greet attendees at events or those under consideration for articles. Otherwise, I think he would have tried to restrict me even more.

I had been raised as and lived my life as a free spirit, outgoing and liking people. I don't think Ryan knew what to do with me. I was a handful, soft-spoken but head strong. But I knew that control is not love.

Ryan started buying windbreakers in volume. Soon he had fifty or more windbreakers. More importantly, he also was abusing prescription drugs. I had never encountered these types of behavior before. He was the doctor, and I had only a vague knowledge of what medications he was taking.

I decided I couldn't live like this anymore. By this time, my migraine frequency increased and I developed a nervous stomach from stress. My mother and David L. brought a rental van over one night so I could move out. Ryan waxed poetic and professed how much he loved me. He played every manipulative emotional gambit. I backed down.

We saw a marriage counselor for a short time and then Ryan quit. I continued in therapy to try to ground myself. Both the then current therapist (who moved to Hawaii) and one later said that I should have been in a padded room after what I had been through.

Events and life got worse. One night he started to raise his hand to hit me.

With probably a false sense of bravado from my Olympic training, I shouted, "If you put a hand on me, I will knock you through that wall behind you."

Ryan backed down and retreated to the bedroom, but when he emerged, he had a gun pointed at me. I looked with horror at the gun and was numb. I didn't even know there was a gun in the house. My anger flashed. What right did he have to try to hit me? I stood my ground. Foolhardy at best, in retrospect.

Was I scared? Yes, Ryan was reactive, unpredictable. He was floundering and didn't know what to do. This was a scene right out of the Albert Camus novel The Stranger, senseless yet the threat of violence was real.

I was in shock. My philosophy had always been marriage should be nonviolent, if one laid a hand on the other, one walked out the door. A gun was a different dimension altogether. I walked out the door.

In fact, I ran to my car and drove to David L.'s house. I was so stunned that I parked on the lawn, left the car door open and the motor running. He turned off the car and listened as I talked nonstop for several hours as I tried to ground myself, to make sense of what had just happened. How had this man morphed into a monster?

I spent the night in a motel. In days, I was out of the condo. I took a small apartment in Beverly Hills and filed for divorce. Ryan's grandmother, who lived with her daughter and Ryan's father, called to wish me well. Then she hung up abruptly. She didn't want Ryan's dad to hear our conversation because, she explained, that he would make things difficult for her. His mother called to tell me she was "independent" too. I was so saddened by how cowed and browbeaten both of these women were.

Ryan didn't want a divorce, so he had an attorney friend send fifty-page interrogatories to my attorney, running up my bill.

Finally, my attorney called me and said, "Look, you are not fighting over money or anything. You've already quitclaimed all of his properties to him. (Ryan owned multiple condos and land in the high desert.) Stop for a while and see if he won't calm down and agree to a divorce. He's just running up your bill."

I agreed since the attorney bill would and did take me years to pay off. The nine-month marriage was now technically extending.

After a few months, I was offered a plum position in San Francisco as editor of a national magazine called *Goodlife*. This targeted glossy lifestyle magazine covering food, fashion, interior design, and cultural highlights was distributed in Atlanta, Philadelphia, Los Angeles, Dallas, Houston, Washington, D.C., San Diego, and San Francisco. I jumped at the chance and moved to San Francisco.

One night, not long after I moved, Ryan called me and said that he would pay for the attorney bill. I breathed a sigh of relief. "The divorce would finally happen," I thought.

The next day I received a call from Ryan's brother. He explained that Ryan, who was thirty-eight, had had a massive stroke. I was stunned.

I asked to be laid off and returned to Los Angeles. I had taken a vow for better or worse and this was worse. I watched over Ryan's care at the hospital and his transfer to Rancho Los Amigos Hospital in Downey, a rehab center for extreme cases. I stayed in his Westwood condo.

Ryan had a carotid stroke, a major event, affecting one entire brain hemisphere. He was paralyzed on one side of his body. He had global aphasia and could say only one word, *Amen*, ironic to me since he had a hefty vocabulary of four-letter-words, some of which I had never heard before. That word Amen meant I'm thirsty, hungry or whatever. His understanding of spoken receptive language was garbled. The occupational therapists were teaching him to feed himself and had him tracing the alphabet to reacquaint him with letters and words.

Ryan's father, a former professional gambler, and an industrial realtor, visited one day during one of these sessions.

He took one look, grabbed the exercise away from Ryan saying, "This is beneath my son the doctor."

I became angered at his father's ignorant reaction, which was hurting his son.

"I have never met anyone with such a big mouth and a small brain," I blurted out.

Needless to say, my usual approach, speak softly and carry a big stick, which I had learned from Paige, was eclipsed.

Later his father called me and said that he was going to seek conservatorship. I sighed. Another attorney? How could I afford it? I resolved to go to court and voice my mind. I did attend the court hearing and as soon as Ryan's father's attorney voiced the petition, the judge granted it with the bang of a gavel. In just a few minutes, all was a fait accompli. No questions asked, no other circumstances considered.

His father came to me and said, "You will live in the condo and travel. I will give you money. But you will report to me."

I retorted, "I don't answer to my parents that way. I'm certainly not going to answer to you."

I was done. I took nothing from his father, but I did take Ryan out to lunch after he was discharged to his father's house. We went to a quiet, charming wheelchair accessible restaurant in Rancho Bernardo, since he was wheelchair bound at the time. I was unsure what Ryan understood and what he didn't. The staff at the hospital had counseled me on how things would affect Ryan. Not only was he cognitively impaired, he had typical post-stroke symptoms like increased lability, lack of emotional control, and a host of other effects. I did not want to decimate him. I wanted to establish separation.

Ryan's comprehension was marginal at that time. His understanding of what was going on was minimal. It saddened me to see him like this. The combination of dealing with his father and Ryan in this state, was overwhelming. His speech was halting, and he relied on key words. He indicated to me that his father was irritated because his vocabulary had increased from the one word, Amen, to a host of other words, including four-letter words. Dysfunction loomed large.

I wondered about the future. His father was in his eighties and not in the best of health. Ryan did have two brothers, one a ne'er-do-well struggling through life, and another was a successful musician who could step in if needed.

His father made up my mind - I was not going to answer to this churlish man. I wanted as little to do with him as possible. In addition, my family was strongly encouraging me to get out.

I was shaken and shattered. I had never set my sights on something, given 100% or more, and had it fail. This was a seminal moment for me. From the early years in school to achieve academically or in sports, to making club teams in volleyball, to becoming an editor, I was driven to make it work. Even giving 150%, I could not have made this work. Nothing could have made this work. I was defeated, lost at that moment.

I moved into a small apartment in Westwood across from the park. The nightmare was over.

Chapter 7: How to Be Married

If my first foray into marriage, a nine-month tumultuous upheaval, was typical, I could eliminate any thought of such a liaison from my life altogether. Eventually, with help from my good friend Geoff and an intensive work schedule, I reverted to my humor-loving self in my late twenties. My opening gambit was to enjoy my friends and move full speed ahead at work.

Geoff and I had started a food group for couples and singles. Quite a crew we put together, all avowed foodies - an exercise company CEO, various computer gurus, a magazine editor, a cruise ship hostess, a CPA, a clinical chemist, a physical therapist and more. The host cooked the entrée while attendees brought or made side dishes, and all had to supply recipes and beer or wine authentic to the cuisine.

It was at one of those dinners that I met up with the much talked about John Havel.

Swedish fare starred that night. John brought liver, which I affectionately named "liver loaf," although it was probably more of a pâté.

"Do you like liver?" I asked.

"No, "he replied, "but I knew that I could fix it. My usual is fried baloney or take-out pizza."

There was hope for him. I detest liver!

John was six foot three, balding, with blue eyes and a ready smile. He had an easy-going demeanor; a ready repartee and he could work the room with ease.

John had a long lineage at Saint John's Hospital. His father was one of the first radiologists at the hospital. After college, John trained as a radiology technologist and returned to work at Saint John's for his entire career (except when it was closed for nine months post 1994 earthquake). Geoff worked in IT, Information Technology, at the hospital, and they played on the hospital softball team and partied together.

John and Geoff would come to my apartment for dinner occasionally and we would talk until the wee hours of the morning, solving the problems of the world. Soon John started coming alone and we started to date.

Our adventures were usually funny but always memorable. I had won a hundred dollars in the lottery, a fluke, and told John I would take him to dinner with the winnings. That night I planned a special treat - a pedicab to take us to dinner in Westwood Village, which was only a few blocks away from my apartment. The young collegiate pedicab driver showed up on time, and John and I hopped in. Neither of us was small, and it was a slight grade to the Village and then up hill to the restaurant. The poor pedicab cycler pedaled and began to sweat only two blocks from my apartment. This was a full-on workout for him across Wilshire Boulevard and into the maze of Westwood streets. I began to feel sorry for him. We offered to walk the rest of the way, but the driver would not hear it. Finally, we arrived and breathed a sigh of relief for the cycler.

On a typical evening, John would come over and we would talk, eat, watch T.V. and just enjoy each other's company.

As he left, I would always say, "Call me when you get home."

It was a short hop, about ten minutes, from my apartment in Westwood to his in Santa Monica. One night he left and no call. I was worried; even if John caught every traffic light, he should be home. Finally, he called and told me what happened.

"I was halfway home and looked over on Santa Monica Boulevard and two young guys were beating up another young man. I left my car in the middle of the street and ran over. They fled and the other kid went his way," he said.

"Eek! That's dangerous...." I launched into my "be careful" speech. His very size scared the kids away without a punch thrown.

A big guy, John was a football fan extraordinaire, college mainly. He once tried out for the Dallas Cowboys but was told he was too small.

John could be mischievous and impish, which I loved. One night as we teased each other, he picked me up and threw me over his shoulder. I was in awe since I am five-foot-eleven inches tall. He soon let me down and we continued the verbal good-natured sparring.

Humor and gentleness were his signatures. Early on in our relationship we were dancing at a wedding. I had attended an all-girls high school and during ballroom dancing lessons, I always had the role of the male, since I was tall.

After dancing for a time, John looked at me and asked, "Can I lead for a while?"

I was surprised, and didn't even realize that I was leading, but I was enchanted by his gentle sense of humor.

We were still platonic friends. Then one Saturday, we drove up the coast for dinner at Alice's Restaurant on the Malibu pier. The ocean breeze cooled the evening, and we walked the pier waiting for our table. He stopped and kissed me. It was an unforgettable, earth-shattering kiss that sent me into paroxysms of joy. My defenses were lessening.

Sunday night, as he was leaving, he kissed me goodnight and I was electrified.

I grabbed his hand and said, "You're not leaving."

Over a period of months, my defensive walls were gone. Spending time with him made me happy and whole. By this time, we had become best friends. I was fast in love with him but getting a commitment at age thirty-eight, well that was different.

I was miserable when I wasn't with him. I loved his humor and gentleness. He could always make me laugh regardless of how serious the conversation was. He was upbeat, so positive. My psyche fed off that positivity. Always a positive person, I realized a new level when I was with him.

John and I decided to go to Santa Barbara for a mini-vacation weekend. We booked a quaint bed and breakfast. I sacrificed a private shower for an ocean view. Not a good choice. John kept teasing me about the fictional meeting we would have with John and Mary, porch mates, who would become life-long friends and the time we would have.

After stopping for dinner at the Chart House, we arrived at the B&B. It was a charming old cottage-style house, nicely furnished. Our room upstairs had a queen bed, a toilet and sink, and a porch that extended the length of two guest rooms and, of course, an ocean view! We hopped in bed and well, two of us in a queen bed was tight. I didn't get much sleep that night.

John awakened me at nine in the morning and told me that I had missed breakfast. Nine was the cut-off time. No problem, I could scoop something up along the way. We set out for the day's adventures. We drove around the town and stopped at El Encanto, a charming Spanish-style hotel. We had a leisurely lunch and then took off for more exploring before stopping at the B&B before dinner. We went to our room and walked out to the porch, and there was another couple. The chap stood and introduced himself as John and she was

Mary. I had the hardest time not laughing out loud. We shook hands, exchanged greetings, and fell into the lounge chairs.

After showering, we went down to the great room to meet the other guests and enjoy a glass of wine. The owners asked if we would be staying for dinner. We had made reservations elsewhere only to find out that the B&B had received a James Beard-like award for food. Guests chatted and then someone commented on how quiet the B&B was.

The owner volunteered, "You really can't hear anything except for the room right above us."

I shot a look at John and looked down at the floor. That was our room!

We ventured out for the evening with dinner reservations nearby and wound up at the Santa Barbara Biltmore. Stately! We stopped in the ballroom/bar and danced for a while. We were sitting at a table with a couple who had danced there for exercise for twenty years. Each had pedometers on their ankles so they could measure a mile. She, who had a nylon leopard design long dress on resembling a nightgown, referred to her husband as "the doctor." He had been the former public health doctor for the City of Santa Barbara. Genuinely nice people but two characters that were forever seared into our memories.

We returned to the B&B and climbed into bed. I was exhausted from not sleeping the night before and was out immediately. John had no trouble falling asleep.

About 1 A.M., someone knocked on our door and screamed, "Fire!"

Both of us hit the deck and looked out the window. A car in the adjacent garage had caught fire and there was fear that it would spread to the B&B.

After watching for a time, I said, "Wake me if it gets worse." And went back to bed.

John was awake most of the night listening to the firemen dragging the hoses, tick, tick, tick, over the concrete.

Morning came and we both missed breakfast, and set off for a leisurely drive home to Santa Monica. We were both exhausted. I dropped him off at about 2 P.M., sped home and soaked in a bathtub for hours, since my trade had only allowed me a shower. John took an hours-long nap. It was a memorable weekend.

It was fall and Thanksgiving was approaching. He invited me to his brother's house for the holiday. Thanksgiving is the Havel family holiday. The whole family comes, flying in from back East or driving from Northern California. This is the time that they gather and enjoy each other, and the family works very hard to keep that closeness and connection. Nieces and nephews, family cousins all gather either in Southern California or in Northern California depending upon where Notre Dame University football team is playing. One year the team played in Hawaii, so did we.

I had met John's brother and sister-in-law but not his parents, and the two other brothers. I was a wreck, wary of meeting his other family. I awakened on Thanksgiving morning with a crushing migraine. Hours of medication later, I dressed and trekked over there. His brother Nick sat and talked to me for a long while, putting me at ease. I met his oldest brother Tom and his parents Elizabeth and Tom as well. Each was friendlier and more welcoming than the last. I survived my migraine, enjoyed the day, and found that for his family, sauerkraut was a traditional Thanksgiving dish. I learned to love it.

Despite dating for a while, I had not passed John's ultimate test meeting David Saxby, his life-long friend. It was puzzling to me that John was so reticent to introduce us.

I met David and, in true blunt form, said, "You know John is worried that we won't get along."

Dave smiled.

Dave and his wife Elise, and I got along famously. Dave was strong-minded, and so I think John feared that we would clash.

John worked with many headstrong women at the hospital. He had no problem interfacing with them and certainly was not threatened by them or me. I could talk with him, express opinions freely, confide in him and he in me, or we could be comfortably quiet.

It was about this time that our friend Patti, a cruise hostess, promoted a Caribbean cruise for a group of us - about twelve of us. She asked me to be her guest. John and a host of others signed on immediately. I was thrilled, hoping that this romantic setting would spur John to propose.

The bon voyage dinner in Fort Lauderdale, allowed us to get together in small groups. Patti, John, and I walked along the water and chose a restaurant. John, always the adventurous one, ordered alligator.

"Tastes like chicken," he offered.

He was up early and delivered a much appreciated newspaper and a cup of coffee to me in bed the next morning.

Dinners on board were a multi-course adventure in food. If not full, there was always the midnight buffet, which some frequented for dessert.

John loved gambling so he was very interested in the casino. The casino staff was patient and helpful thankfully. John and I ended up at different tables. I won $100 and was thrilled. He was surprised and amused because he knew I was not experienced or that fast at Blackjack. He won more than that the second night and shared.

There was an onboard costume contest one night, among the 700 passengers. Hands down, John won, and for good reason! He dressed as a hula girl with a grass skirt, coconut bra and wig - quite a sight for this 250-pound guy. The runner-up was a bride whose dress was fashioned from toilet paper so there was a strong element of creativity. Observers kept offering her a drink of water.

We visited the Bahamas, Cancun, Jamaica, the Virgin Islands, St. Croix, and the Cayman Islands. The culture, charm and food at each destination were enchanting. We went snorkeling on one daily excursion. John brought his hospital scrubs for me to wear to avoid sunburn during the half-day excursion on the boat. They were a little large, but much appreciated for my slightly burned fair skin.

We docked in Jamaica and John, Patti and I had a two-block walk to the resort where we would spend the day. A host of barkers greeted tourists. One approached the three of us. Later John told us, he was trying to sell him a prostitute. How I missed that I still don't know.

We took sunset cruises, and I was still hopeful that he would propose. I sent a humorous postcard to my office saying, "Have toured Nassau and snorkeled today in St. Croix. Six more days and 4 ports. Tonight, only a barbecue on deck and dancing under stars. Weather's horrible, food worse, people unfriendly, send money! Hugs." I was having the time of my life!

Work and life went on. John and I continued. But there was no proposal.

One night, after we returned home, when he was over, I said, "You know you want to get married and have a family and so do I, so if we are not going to do it together, we should split up and find someone else."

He did not say much, but I didn't see him for three heart-wrenching days. He went over to talk to his brother, Richard, for advice. I will always be grateful to his brother!

The third night, he showed up at my apartment, knelt down and proposed! My heart soared! Checkmate!

Even the beginning of our marriage was a grand ride.

I had been married for nine months in my late twenties. John came from a very Catholic family, as did I, so annulment was the only solution. No mean feat. Sometimes this took years. I filed for an annulment in my parish. There were no time guarantees.

Then one-day John's older brother Tom called me and said he wanted me to see his priest friend who had served at the Vatican. He could help me expedite my annulment, Tom said. But first, he wanted to review my answers on the questionnaire. I dived in and read the questions and answers to his brother, a priest and a psychiatrist. As such, he is a great listener and very rarely has voice inflections indicating approval or disapproval. Unnerving to say the least since the annulment questions leave nothing to the imagination. Where did you have sex? How often? What type? And on and on.

I hung up the phone and said to John, "Well, there goes that relationship!"

John and I spent countless enjoyable hours together. Finally, he said, "We're getting married!"

"John, don't go against your mother. We'll wait." I said.

His matriarchal mother was staunchly Catholic and a very conservative one at that. He wouldn't have it.

John, the traditionalist, insisted on asking my father for my hand in marriage. At age thirty-eight, I was a child of the sixties and seventies and a staunch feminist. I used to verbally spar with my father over the issues. My father and mother loved John. I wondered how my father would respond.

My dad hemmed and hawed and then said, "She is an adult. It's her decision, but, of course, you have our blessing." Perfect.

We slept in the spare guest bedroom at my folks with the door open. Seems overplayed now.

We shopped for rings, and he picked a simple gold band. I too thought that a good choice for me. He would have none of it.

I finally asked, "You won't be happy without diamonds, right?"

He wanted diamonds. Finally, we found a simple band with modified pavé diamonds.

His brother, Richard, and Geoff planned a bachelor party for John at Geoff's apartment in Santa Monica. I went out to dinner with girlfriends. We drove by after dinner but saw nothing.

Geoff called me later and said, "Tarp the apartment!" They had been plying John with alcohol.

I thought it exceptional that they had a female stripper named Lily to entertain the guys. They actually shaved his hairy chest with an "L" how thoughtful!

I planned a secular wedding at Stratton's, a charming restaurant in Westwood Village, part of the Geffen Theater complex, with a lovely Spanish-style fountain in the courtyard and a traditional interior with a walk-in fireplace. We chose September 10th, his mother's birthday, as the date.

All of our family members and close friends were in attendance. It was a day that both John and I relished. One of the songs aptly played was Time of My Life. It was for me. Afterwards we changed clothes and went over to his brother's house since his family was there. Family was and continues to be so important.

Soon after I called my mother and said happily, "Mom, he didn't change!" I was reveling in the fact that this was nothing like my previous experience.

"He's not supposed to, Laurie," said my mom.

Not missing a beat as I hung up, John said, "Do you want me to?"

I railed in protest, "No!"

During my tenure as editor of a lifestyle magazine, I had been on a press junket to Las Hadas in Manzanillo, Mexico, the resort created by Bolivian tin king, Antenor Patino. The movie "10" was filmed there. Swim-up bars and tropical magic seemed like a good choice, I thought. John was game so we booked it for a couple of days after the wedding, so we had time to see and visit with family and recuperate.

We jetted to Manzanillo from LAX, fortunately not a long flight. We deplaned and were greeted by armed federales in the airport. We both took double-takes and wondered what was going on. Everyone was calm and orderly, so we proceeded to grab a taxi to take us to the resort.

We hopped in the front seat of a taxi van. There was another couple in the back seat. The roads were narrow, and it was rainy. John, the protector, used his arm as a human seat belt for me the entire trip - no seatbelts - and the driver could have been driving in the Long Beach Grand Prix. Our eyes were riveted to the road.

"Where are you taking me?" he asked.

I gulped and watched as the couple in the back seat exited the van for another hotel along the way.

Picture the Palos Verdes Peninsula in California. That was the size of Las Hadas - five restaurants, hotel rooms, timeshare homes on the point, a beach that was cradled in the half circle cove on the south side of the peninsula. We ascended the road to the main lobby, and all calmed and we both relaxed. The driver stopped and a hotel associate greeted us, took our luggage, and asked if we would like a glass of wine. Much better!

We spent a glorious week dining at fiestas, fancy restaurants, sipping Corona with lime as we watched windsurfers tack back and forth in the bay, napping and well just enjoying ourselves.

One afternoon we were soaking in the sun by the palatially large pool which had an island in the center populated with iguanas. Every day at about 4 P.M., one of the hotel staff walked out with a tray of fruit and flowers. Instantly all the iguanas came running poolside or swimming across the pool to get dinner. One guest in the pool looked at the onslaught of iguanas swimming toward her and started to scream. No one quite knew what to do or say. Iguanas swim in a back-and-forth tacking mode. The female guest happened to be in the same back and forth tacking pattern as one iguana. She thought the iguana was after her, and she screamed louder and louder and then stopped swimming and stood still mid pool. The iguana had no interest in her. The animal zigged and zagged around her going for the staffer and the food. She immediately realized that fact, stopped screaming and developed a rather red glow of embarrassment.

Another day we walked along the beach and saw a local with a beautifully colored trained Macaw bird. People on the beach were enchanted. The local looked away and the bird worked his way up my clothing to sit on my shoulder. This avian decided he wanted my earrings and started for them with his beak. I called to John who raised his arm in a backhand position.

The local yelled, "Don't bap the bird!" He rescued the feathery creature, my earrings, and my earlobes.

We returned with much less fanfare, no armed federales thankfully, and settled into our lives together in a two-bedroom, two-bathroom apartment in Santa Monica. The apartment was a scant block from the hospital where John worked. There was a fireplace in the living room, with a small patio bordering the living room, and a Pullman kitchen opposite.

A few days after we were home, John looked at me and said, "If I knew marriage was like this, I would have done it a long time ago," he said.

I couldn't help but smile and my heart warmed. I felt the same. Typical of John, he cut to the heart of matters so simply.

A short time later, I received word that my annulment was final. We planned a second wedding, very low key on Thanksgiving at the priest's chapel at Saint Paul the Apostle in Westwood. John's brother Tom, the Marinist priest and psychiatrist, married us. We finished and went over to his brother's house to celebrate Thanksgiving with his family.

Each family member had Thanksgiving jobs. John's task was to mash the potatoes, which for thirty or so people, were in a huge stock pot. Tom was then the official family carver of the turkey for Thanksgiving. While he was a psychiatrist, the turkey was carved to surgical perfection with pieces in graduated sizes carefully arranged on the plate.

I couldn't stand it and finally asked, "How do you carve it so perfectly?"

"Easy," he said, "I eat all the odd-sized pieces."

I felt much better.

My good friend Ann, who attended both weddings, called not long afterwards and said, "Laurie, I have a great idea for the third wedding a circus theme."

All I could do was laugh. We did keep getting married.

I sent photo postcards of John frequently to his parents, scribbling descriptions of John's escapades on the back.

John's dad died of a heart attack just a few months after we were married. I'm terribly sorry that I didn't get to know him better. I'm sure that John was very like his father, and I knew John's kindness, understanding and compassion. Dr. Thomas E. Havel, John's dad, took care of my mother at one point, advising her that "We can't keep taking chunks of your breast out." Fortunately, all was benign and my mother in her no-nonsense form said, "If necessary, we'll keep at it."

The family trekked back to Minnesota in winter for his dad's funeral. Mom led a tour of the cemetery noting family connections.

Who was John?

Even after four years of dating and then marrying John, I was still getting to know him. Who was he?

He was a tall, athletic man with extraordinary physical strength, who could hold his own with any man. Yet, he was the confidante of many women and men, friends and family who sought out and enjoyed his counsel. He could transform any situation, serious to light, into a new and upbeat, sometimes humor-filled perspective. Whether performing a vintage SNL Blues Brothers dance at a party with his brother, Richard, or welcoming extended family to gatherings, he was a bright light.

People across multiple circles of friends talked about Havel, who dressed in button-down Brooks Brothers shirts and khaki pants when not clad in shorts and polo shirt. This wasn't gossip but entertaining badinage: Havel did this or that, or Havel said this or that. Self-effacing, John was often seen wearing lampshades, baskets, or a chef's toque on his head or whatever was germane at the time.

His humanity and compassion were obvious. He had the uncanny ability to cajole, tease and draw out people – friends, strangers, waiters, or passersby. He could talk to anyone and put them at ease in a conversation, frequently with humor. He loved helping, counseling, and celebrating people, whether he knew them or not. He treated all the same regardless of social stature. He had such a soft heart, whether listening to the life story of the person in line behind us at the zoo, counseling a friend with HIV, or caring for aging sick neighbors. I loved that about him.

John's winning ways were universal. Early on I called my mother and said I was peeved with John.

"What? You're upset with our John?" she asked.

"Mother, you are supposed to be on my side," I said. "He put a small section of fence up against the garage and spray painted it. Now the garage has the outline of the fence."

Neighbor Tom came over to check this out, shook his head and tried not to laugh. We lived with the outline on the garage for years, till we repainted. I chuckled daily as I saw it out the kitchen window.

Just after we married, I put individual Sonnets from the Portuguese by Elizabeth Barrett Browning on his pillow. They seemed so appropriate to me. I quickly discovered that that type of poetry was not his expression. The poetry of people was his strongest suit. After people, he loved animals, nature and the great outdoors.

He was as much at home in the saddle as sitting in the theater. So, it fit that soon after we married, John decided to go on the annual horseback trip to Yellowstone with Geoff and a few other friends. He and Geoff were part of a group of "citified cowboys" who packed in with seasoned cowboy and rider, Ralph, and his wife, Candy, who would cook up lavish trail meals of cowboy comfort food.

He tried to talk me into joining but leaning over mid-summer at 5 P.M. to grab snow off the ground to chill my drink, was just not for me. Always cold, I would have been just thawing out at about that time.

He readily joined a food group that sought to sample authentic cuisines, despite his scant cooking knowledge which increased exponentially as he became a cook, baker, and grill master. He jumped at the chance to try something new. This adventurous world traveler ordered salted squid guts at an authentic Japanese restaurant and sampled alligator off a Florida menu.

John's sensitivity was always front and center. We were watching T.V. one evening, a - touching story which crescendoed emotionally. I looked over at John who had pursed his lips and squinted his eyes his I'm going to cry look. He and I were both crying.

Christmas traditions developed quickly and lasted. We picked up a tree at a local lot and John would put the lights on. I, who had collected ornaments for decades, hung bulbs and small iconic decorations on the always full tree. John would put on Nat King Cole's "The Christmas Song (Chestnuts Roasting on an Open Fire.") Almost immediately his lip quivered and his eyes squinted.

I asked why he was tearing up and he said, "Because I had such wonderful Christmases growing up."

Another common denominator between us.

His patience and gentleness were well-known and appreciated. At work, he was a beacon of knowledge for newbies and a prized resource for seasoned doctors, techs, and others especially after being at the hospital for decades. He had a soft spot for children and babies, and frequently they were brought to John to do their x-rays. He developed lasting friendships with many he worked with over forty-six years.

Before we married, John told his coworkers that he met someone and planned on marrying. Almost immediately, they threw a wedding shower with a generous buffet and gifts. They were checking me out, and one of them even told me how protective they were of John. Odd to be on the receiving end of that. I was bemused and actually pleased, even though I wasn't sure I had passed muster. Over time, I think I passed.

Seeing the reaction, he had on others was enlightening.

There was irony in the fact that John, who spent a lifetime at a hospital, was needle phobic. Hospital phlebotomists planned to lay him out for the then required blood test for a marriage license. He had a tendency to faint when he saw his own blood. I, on the other hand, donated regularly since I'm a universal donor. He always looked away.

At home, the mere mention of a worry or problem elicited heartfelt suggestions and possible solutions from him. The same held true if I mentioned a quandary that a member of my family had. He would immediately set to work on a broad array of remedies.

As a husband and father he was unparalleled. He very patiently and kindly broke down any and all emotional barriers I had. He was impish, playful and a first-class tease. A glint in his blue eyes always gave him away.

Discussing ideas, politics or everyday items was enlightening. His insights were unique and expansive. Quiet was also welcome and comfortable.

Fiercely loyal to friends and family, he loved running into paramedic David Saxby at the hospital or roving the countryside of New Zealand with him and his then-pregnant wife Elise. On long phone calls, John shared family, child rearing, health concerns and fun for decades with Dave.

Family was a touchstone for John who relished gatherings and encouraged nieces and nephews and great nieces and nephews. One nephew, as a child named his plush animal protector, John the Seal. That plush toy still sits in his bedroom as an adult, a tribute to John.

He loved ribs, hot dogs, Taylor Swift songs, daffodils and laughing.

It was no surprise to me that this chap, who caught my eye, captured my heart, and was so much more than I imagined, was a talked-about and celebrated friend to many.

The Humbling Exhilaration of Parenting John and I loved his apartment in Santa Monica, just a block from Saint John's Hospital. But if we were thinking of starting a family, it was time to buy a house. We drew a circle on the map with Saint John's Hospital at the center. Since my work fluctuated from downtown Los Angeles to Camarillo, we pinpointed Encino, just over the hill from the Westside. The area had post -WWII houses built in 1948, and at that time most were rentals. Would they stay that way? Would gentrification set in? It was a gamble.

We found a house in Encino with a nice flow which I thought had great potential, but it had dark cabinets, dirty dishes in the kitchen sink and had been closed up for a year.

The house was about 1,500 square feet with a covered patio directly opposite the front door. It had three bedrooms, two baths and scant closet space. Still the master bedroom with an en suite bath was sizable, and the bathroom was nicely done with a large bathtub framed by a tiled shelf. The kitchen too had spacious counters which excited me since I had been used to cooking for six plus people with two feet of counter space on either side of the sink. A challenge to be sure!

We put an offer in on the house and held our breath. The offer was accepted and immediately, I had butterflies in the pit of my stomach.

"What have I done?" I thought. "Was this a major mistake? Was it a dog?"

We had a team of cleaners work a week before we set foot in the house. Then a team of friends, Geoff, and his girlfriend Michelle, came over and helped paint and lighten it up. My misgivings were fading.

We befriended the chap next door, another Tom, who was a crusty curmudgeon with a heart of pure gold. He and the neighbor on the corner, (Leonard) Axel, would rout John on Saturday mornings to have a neighborhood lawn mowing party. We settled in and our learning curve on tending a house rose steadily.

Tom had tended the front lawn for a year when the house was vacant. The backyard was a different story.

John took one look at the backyard and said, "Let's put a rope around the backyard and charge admission for Desert Storm."

There was lots of work to be done.

It was John's birthday. I decided to do a birthday party amidst the boxes and cleaning supplies. Richard and Arlene, Geoff and his mother Claire, and friends Ann, Lynn and Mike trekked over to celebrate.

John was given a tee-shirt with his nickname "Mongo" headlining. In addition to being a Java script interface or global database, the word means "big," and was one of John's monikers. He identified as "Big John."

Once moved in, we developed deep relationships with neighbors in the early days.

Tom and Martha, who were our parents' ages, mentioned that they were going to celebrate their fiftieth wedding anniversary, I contacted their relatives to see if I could arrange fifty cards for them. Better yet, each of their siblings said they would travel out to California from parts all over the country. John and I planned a big party at our house for Tom and Martha and their relatives. It was great fun for us and a great surprise for Tom and Martha. We met the family and put on a festive dinner.

Axel, the widower who lived on the corner, was fast friends with Tom and they both adopted John.

Mail carriers Lilly and Mike lived across the street and had three children in a blended marriage.

As we all sat outside in front of our house, our two neighbors Joyce and Barb, Magi and Yossi from up the street, a lady drove by and said, "You're having too much fun!"

John, being friendly John, immediately responded, "Come join us!"

Deb, who lived just a couple blocks away, did and became a lifelong friend.

We settled in, had friends for dinner and worked in the yard. We were happy and learning so much about each other. I learned that John loved art and antiques after antiquing with neighbor Susie Holmquist as a young man. He showed an openness to ballet and loved stage plays and musicals.

A Character Sketch

GMB: Geoff was a good friend, like a brother before and during our entire marriage. At about this time, he moved in with us. For eleven years of living with us during the week as he ran his computer consultancy business in Los Angeles (he returned to Arizona on the weekends), Geoffrey Michael Burks imparted his humor and insights.

Geoff took over the front bedroom, my office, which actually worked well since he usually returned home from work late in the evening, and I did all my work in the afternoon. He loved cooking and sometimes would come home early to cook for us. He loved hot spices too and more than once he "spiced" us out with Mexican pork stew and other creations.

"Assistant Havel, here," he answered the phone. There was typically a pause as the caller regrouped to figure out if he/she had called the right number.

Many years before when John was on a doctor-supervised starvation diet, he would go over to Geoff's apartment and peer over his shoulder.

"Is that chicken? What does it taste like?" John would ask.

Geoff teased him about it for decades.

GMB was a groomsman at our wedding. He leaned over to John and handed him a five- dollar bill.

"Here's the money I owe you," Geoff said.

John turned immediately and handed it to me, saying, "See, I haven't had any money since I got married."

Shortly after, Geoff called to ask how married life was.

John didn't skip a beat. "It's great but she steals the covers during the night," he volunteered.

The next week we received Geoff's wedding present, a king-sized blue blanket for the bed.

With a master's degree in history and an MBA, he worked in computers as an analyst, programmer, or manager of information systems. It all made perfect sense to me since he had several degrees, none of which covered computers. On the weekends, he flew home to Phoenix to his mother's condominium which he inherited.

Before we were married, gum trouble prompted John's dentist to suggest surgery. Pebbly concrete steps led to John's second-floor apartment. I knew that John had a history of fainting with no warning. Immediately my worries started about him falling down the stairs after the surgery. I enlisted Geoff's advice.

"What do I do if he faints on the way up the stairs?" I asked.

"Step aside," he said.

He then listed a host of folks at the hospital who sustained injuries trying to catch people who were falling or passing out.

Fortunately, John made it up the stairs without incident after the surgery. I breathed a big sigh of relief.

When our daughter was a newborn and developed her first cold, Geoff held her, John paced and I ran off to get a humidifier. Geoff watched and learned as she grew.

When Abbie was a wee tyke, we gifted her with a foot-powered plastic car. She loved it and cried when we had to separate her from the huge toy and put her to bed.

Geoff just shook his head and said, "She'll do the same thing when she's sixteen."

One day, Geoff watched Abbie rock out to a Beach Boys song Barbara Ann. That was the moment he dubbed her "Baboo," a nickname that lasted for years.

Geoff took a nine-year hiatus from living with us when Abbie was about three years old. He retreated to a military friend's house since he was deathly allergic to cats and Annie Kitty had graced our household. We stayed in close touch.

We worked on starting a family to no avail. I thought it was just stress from my work. Time proved otherwise. We consulted a doctor and, after tests, decided to embark on in Vitro Fertilization.

"Hi, hightech mom," said my brotherinlaw Nick on the phone. The term gave me pause, but then I retraced my steps for the last few months only to agree.

"It's phenomenal what they can do, and what they know now," I responded.

"Yes, and others of us don't understand the emotional upheaval and other elements of stress that enter into it," said Nicky insightfully.

By this time, John had picked up the phone and he and his brother were discussing one of the many release forms we had signed. John volunteered to copy the forms and send it up to Northern California to Nick, a urologist who was on his hospital and ethics committee.

"Yes," I thought, we just went through the entire thing that appeared not long ago on the news where exhusband and exwife were in court contesting the disposition and possession of fertilized human embryos. Our release form covered all that and much more.

John and I, both forty years old and married a scant year and a half, were just about to embark on the final stages of in Vitro Fertilization or IVF as it is more commonly referred to in the hospitals and doctors' offices.

It was June. I had surgery the previous December to remove scar tissue from a past unknown infection, and to remove a fibroid (benign) tumor. John and I had been working up to this moment.

Looking back, I was in a rush right after the surgery thinking that time had run out and we had to move right away. Where oh where though would we come up with the $7,000 to have IVF? These were hard costs, I mused in retrospect. Pretesting raised the sum another $3,000.

John and I had spent months raising the money he working overtime at the hospital as a radiologic technician and I working at my public relations/advertising agency and freelance magazine writing. The evenings when we both met at home after work with one or both of us fidgeting under the stress, seemed almost forgotten now. Even the disappointing incident last month, when I ovulated but not to the doctor's liking, thus postponing the entire effort for one more cycle, was a fastfading memory. While John and I had examined the situation inside out and backwards, we dreaded the possible disapproval of family and friends one fear that never materialized.

I heard John on the phone say to Nick, "Yes, there's an eight percent chance of success."

What an astounding almost foolhardy statistic to take on, I thought, but both John and I loved children. He had coached

Derek's and other little league teams for years. John immediately went over cuddled newborns when we were with friends. I too had a longstanding love of children and had stocked the house with all manner of children's toys just in case of a visit or we were babysitting. I had saved items for years in the hopes of having a little one to pass them onto.

Secretly, I was curious. John was a big man, six feet three inches tall and 260 pounds. He had played football in high school and college. I was five feet eleven inches and a former Olympian. Would the child be athletic? A storyteller like John? We irreverently referred to the child as Moose or Moosette, since in our minds there was no way, this hopedfor little tike could be petite.

Months of pretesting for us both had been completed. Each of us had the mandatory HIV (AIDS) blood test. John had his sperm tested for number, motility, and normalcy. His sperm count was high, quite suitable to impregnate a major city suburb.

A hospital insider, John continued to be impressed with the service at the huge UCLA hospital/medical center and described some of his episodes such as giving his first specimen at the nearby medical center. He was there first and very early so he could get back to work. Of course, the staff knew why he was there so no need to stand on ceremony. John was squeamish about nothing save needles and quite literally about needles. So, he quickly launched into conversation with the staffers about how the test was done etc. and other elements of IVF. He entered the specimen room, which was outfitted with a blue sofa, suggestive magazines, and a videotape, soon to emerge with his plastic specimen cup ready to turn in and a printed list of mental tips such as be sure that the lid is off before you start. He faced several other men, sheepishly sitting in the waiting room who looked at him with dread. Later John had the "hamster test," which in story form he embellished to include little hamsters scampering across the floor, when in actuality the test required a semen specimen which in a later lab procedure is analyzed for its ability to penetrate hamster ova.

Finally, all seemed in order.

On the designated day, I was to inject myself with Luperon. Fortunately, John and I had a shot lesson at the doctor's office. My Luperon needle was small, but the following day John was to inject me with Pergonal, with an impressive twenty-two-gauge needle, approximately 3 inches long. Aside from his needle phobia, the idea of physically hurting someone was foreign to John.

While lunching with Ann, my business partner, that day, I said, "I wouldn't be surprised if John came home today with a nurse to give the shot."

She laughed and agreed.

He almost did and confessed that he thought about it. He already had nurse volunteers at his hospital lined up to give me the injection if I came into the hospital. He called twice that day, bemoaning, dreading the shot.

When he arrived home, he was clammy, sweaty, and promptly announced that he would keep his lab coat on to bolster his confidence. I asked him to pinch hard and insert the needle quickly. He did both. A fine job!

The next day, however, I realized that pinching hard may not be the answer. John was a big man with many hidden strengths and obvious physical strength as well. I awoke with a fiveinch bruise. If I was to undergo four more weeks of shots all in the upper outer quadrant of my hips, I was running out of square footage fast.

John refined his technique and became the best shot giver ever. The bruises ended too. Early on in this sixweek process, John reminded me that we were working with only an eight percent chance of success.

"Yes, but I do everything passionately," I responded. "And if I'm going to do this, I'm going for success. If it doesn't work, I'll be crushed."

Days passed quickly and we geared up for the next phase of monitoring. Ultrasound exams were to be performed on the fifth and seventh Pergonal days and then daily thereafter.

One of two IVF nurses, Sue, patiently answered our unending questions and introduced us to several doctors.

"A terrific response" they reassured me. Sue said, "You have the ovaries of a 30 yearold."

John and I were ecstatic.

Monday morning, we repeated the scenario but this time in the doctor's office in Santa Monica. She too seemed pleased with the response.

Tuesday morning, I was again en route to the medical center since my doctor was again off appearing on a popular morning television show discussing infertility.

It was more than a little difficult for both John and me to return to work daily and concentrate. He kept telling me that we were going a step at a time.

Wednesday morning it was back to Santa Monica. The doctor had called to advise me that the retrieval would be Friday.

By this time, I was revved up on hormones and there was no chance that I could assume a handsonhips posture. They were much too sore.

Thursday the doctor sat us down and reviewed four different consent forms for the IVF procedure. She had slipped several to me the day before so John and I could review them. One of which asked detailed questions on the disposition of the fertilized eggs if not all were re-implanted. Who would take custody if we both die? If one of us dies? If we divorce? Did we want them discarded or donated? Heady conversations ensued.

Friday morning came and we reported to the medical center admissions office at 6:01 am. Twenty minutes later, Sue, the IVF nurse, already gowned for surgery came down calling out our last name. I signed one last hospital release form. John was asked to finish the remainder and I was whisked off to a room on the second floor, the OB/GYN IVF section. Sue told me to take a Valium, which I did, and slip into the hospital gown. So far so good. Sue had a cassette tape one of my then favorites of George Winston for me to listen to while she proceeded to ply me with Demerol and antibiotics.

"Great drugs," I said as my body warmed all over. My doctor and several others said hello. I was out.

I awoke feeling great pressure on my abdomen. Sue was holding my hands, or I was squeezing the life out of hers, I can't remember which. They were probing for the last two follicles.

"Done," the doctor said. "We retrieved twelve."

I slept for another couple of hours and John walked the grounds. I dozed in and out for several hours and then finally awoke at about twelve noon. This was Friday and the first of fourteen days of progesterone injections.

After some juice and milk, I determined I would pass on lunch. The nurse gave me meds for nausea due to the drugs.

"Ready?" I said.

"Sure, Hun," said John.

I shifted into the wheelchair transport and we set off for the parking lot and home. Halfway there, driving down Ohio Avenue, I said, "John pull over."

Thankfully, he didn't even ask why. I was sick.

I slept the rest of the day and part of the next as I lounged around the house. John attended a party for nephew Derek who had just graduated from Loyola High School, but he was home soon.

We chatted and I kept thinking that the worst was over. John started teasing me about being sick, one of my least favorite things.

He had me laughing and had diffused my seriousness in no time.

We had a call from the hospital to alert us to the fact that it would be Sunday before the transfer at 8:30 a.m. when we would learn how many of the nine cleaved or divided properly. A trial-run transfer using a catheter only had already been performed in the doctor's office to ensure that all would go smoothly, and it had.

Sunday morning came and both John and I were thankful that the appointed hour was 8:30 instead of the previous 6:30 a.m. Again, we went through admissions and were taken upstairs to room two seventeen. I slipped into my hospital gown and was told to relax, and that they would start in about twenty minutes. John and I watched T.V. Barbara, the second IVF nurse, came in and directed me into a wheelchair.

She had a fresh batch of heated blankets. Nirvana. I always get cold when I am nervous and while I wasn't as reticent about today as last Friday, I was still fearful and emotionally charged.

We had been told that John could be with me for everything but the retrieval since there was a lack of room. John was right alongside me.

The room was only about ten by ten feet, all white and bare except for the table, a chair for John, and a small but powerful light, about three inches in diameter. The doctor had told us that they were unsure how light and sound affected embryos, so the light was purposely low and everyone spoke in hushed tones.

Shortly, my doctor appeared via a door in the back of the room. She was gowned and masked as if for surgery. Right behind her came several other doctors, an embryologist and a huge incubator that contained a highpowered microscope. The doctor motioned to John to come over and take a look at the six fertilized eggs which were about to be re-implanted.

Strangely, I was probably as far away from the action as possible, and everyone was whispering. I was struggling to hear but lip reading was no use since all but John and I were masked.

Eventually, I was told a "stitch" would be taken, a small incision was made to facilitate the transfer or insertion. I held onto John's hand tightly.

It was over. The doctor asked me to roll over onto my stomach. I was shifted to a gurney and taken back to the room, where I was given two Valium and asked to sleep for three hours. No one was allowed to remain with me, so John kissed me and headed out.

Three hours later, he reappeared, and I was wheeled to the car. I was to go home and remain in bed, getting up only to go to the bathroom and raising my head only when necessary to eat. John stayed home with me until Thursday.

By Tuesday night not showering had become a major discomfort for me. I teasingly asked John if lice appeared spontaneously on your skin or if you had to be near someone with them. He just rolled his eyes and shook his head. Wednesday, I was allowed to shower. Baths were not allowed for weeks.

Now, the wait. I was to maintain a very lowkey activity level and no stress for the next two weeks. I could though go to the market, for example, at the end of that first week.

Thursday, I developed a dull pain in my lower right side. This pain seemed to tense or tighten somewhat each day.

"Well, nothing's perfect," I thought.

But Monday I awoke, and I had bled during the night. I naturally alerted the doctor right away. By Monday night, I had buried my head in John's shoulder sobbing uncontrollably.

"I tried. I quit smoking. I stayed in bed. No wine. Only one cup of coffee a day," I blurted out.

John was wrenched emotionally as well but still he was strong, calming, and hopeful.

By Tuesday, I had to face reality. The signs were not good. Meanwhile the pain was increasing, not unlike a blood pressure cuff as it tightens. The doctor said the pain was not typical for IVF patients and started studying its origins. By Wednesday, the pain was intense. I called the doctor in tears and went in.

"Please can't we call this a push," I begged. "Let me go home and take a strong pain pill and a hot bath to relieve the pain." I continued to bleed.

The doctor very adeptly redirected my anxieties and asked that I come in to see her the following day. John gave me another progesterone shot, and I held my sides. That night I walked the floor with the pain and then cried myself to sleep.

The next day I set off for the doctor, calmer but still worn down by the pain.

The doctor took one look at me, confirmed the bleeding and said, "We're going to call it for bleeding. Discontinue the shots. Go home and take a pain pill if needed," she counseled. "There's been just too much bleeding to support a pregnancy."

Dashed hopes were tempered with anticipation for the relief of this pain. Once home, I called John at work and relayed the doctor's message. Later, when John came home from work, he asked for a complete recap of the conversation I'd had with the doctor. I told him we had an appointment with her for a postoperative consult next week.

He looked at me plaintively and asked, "Are we doing a pregnancy test Monday as planned?"

"No," I replied.

"Do you want me to shoot you up with water just for old time's sake?" he said in jest trying desperately to recoup some good news, some hope from this definitive conversation. No matter how heavy my heart, he could always bring a smile to my face.

I was reminded of John's early caveat of an eight percent chance of success. Now we had shifted. Perhaps it may not work, I admitted, but I did not want to wallow in a large dose of selfdefeat and pity. John and I had adopted a mustwork attitude and now were facing the emotional pain of IVF not working.

The physical discomfort lessened somewhat each day, but both the pain and the bleeding continued well into the next week. John and I alternately buoyed each other up from bouts of lows.

It was his strength, strong sense of humor and endless compassion that kept me going. Now we both had to decide what next. Do we try this again? What other options are there? Did we abandon hope of pregnancy and adopt? More questions and only a very few answers.

We sat across the desk from the doctor, listening intently to hear why our recent in Vitro Fertilization attempt had not taken. I was still bleeding and swimming in an emotional sea brought on by the many hormones administered during the last weeks. John, who had lived every emotional minute with me, was equally low.

"What do you suggest now?" I asked the doctor.

"The surest way for you to be parents is to adopt," she said candidly.

We went home and mulled over the options. Another ten thousand dollars for a second or possibly a third IVF try might still end up with us baby-less. And it was a struggle to muster up the money for the first try which we had been forewarned carried a low percentage of success because I was forty.

We took some time off to let the emotional crescendo pass, six months, while we both put ourselves back together and until I finally started to feel real again. Right before Christmas, we agreed that it was time to look into adoption. We made an appointment to speak with an attorney who specialized in family law and adoption. After apprising us of the costs involved, typically twelve to fifteen thousand dollars, we asked a number of questions regarding special needs or older tots who may be part of a family group available for adoption, and she very graciously volunteered that she would love to work with us but that adoption was not her main specialty and that our needs may be better served by talking to the people at the adoption agency.

In March, we attended the Pathways to Parenthood three-part class the agency offered. It was an eye-opener as psychological profiles of babies and children from birth to five years old were presented along with the attendant or inherent problems. They explained how to advertise and where it was legal, and how to screen calls from a prospective birthmother, the preferred term rather than "real" mother. The effects of adoption on the child both in early and later years were covered, as well as the fact that many adoptees' have an incontrovertible need to know about his or her birthparent or birthparents.

Also covered were costs involved and the profile of older children that are available through the county, many of whom are or have been abused by their birthparents or spent time in foster care or are born with drug addiction and the consequential problems. The agency related that it is an approximate sobering five-year wait if the adoptive couples wait for the agency to find the baby. Nonetheless, the underlying emphasis was on open adoption in which the birthmother or birth parents selected the adoptive parents, and the almost limitless types of communication that have been effectively tried. No longer was adoption kept quiet. Many adoptive parents would send photos of the baby through infancy on through childhood to the birthmother. Some actually had face-to-face meetings when the child was older while others had them regularly. This was certainly a whole new world from the secretive world of adoption that many had experienced.

We immediately assessed our capabilities financially and emotionally and decided that we were not equipped to handle a special needs child, one with severe physical or emotional handicaps. But what about sibling groups? John was very wary of the emotional problems that seemed to be almost unavoidable in older children, despite the fact that I was strongly behind adopting siblings, say an older tot of two years old and an infant. It wasn't to be since John felt so strongly against this situation and wanted to start with everything possible to optimize the adoption rather than invoke the high probability of problems in older children. I learned that as easy going as John was day to day, when it was important and he felt strongly about something, he was unmovable. An infant was our choice.

We paid our fees to the agency and signed up for another series of classes and a home study. We were fingerprinted and cleared to ensure that we were neither child abusers nor felons. We were interviewed regarding our finances, living quarters but most importantly our philosophies. We then had an adoption résumé printed up, and I sent it to everyone we knew and a host of obstetrician/gynecologists' offices locally. John talked to some of the doctors at his hospital.

We found very quickly that this was a tough sell. It became obvious very soon that either we started advertising in the states in which it was legal or needed to tap into a network.

There was an agency in another state that, for a fee of twenty-four thousand dollars, would find the birthmother and take care of everything. This was expensive and going through an attorney was almost as expensive. We received some recommendations and contacted one attorney well-known for adoptions locally. We called him and received his newsletter and a list of fees but were never able to speak with him in person. This was a very personal situation for us, and some legal support was welcome even during the search.

Then someone gave us the name of an attorney in Beverly Hills who not only handles the legal aspects but finds the birthmother. His fees were commensurate with the others, save for a higher orientation or first meeting session. We called and met with him and liked him tremendously. He was warm, reassuring and introduced us to a birthmother who had stopped into the office briefly. She was lovely. At last, we had met a birthmother and had some point of reference. Even more importantly, the attorney was supportive and so reassuring to the birthmother. She seemed genuinely comfortable with him. John and I told him that we wanted to proceed, that we found him most personable and likable and were impressed with his rapport. His staff too was friendly and accommodating.

The attorney guaranteed us a birthmother in less time than the normal gestational nine months. John and I were thrilled but still wary of raising our hopes. We departed, went home, and started preparing for the Christmas holidays.

The attorney's Beverly Hills office was part of an office suite in a space identified as ISC or the International Surrogacy Center. Truly the attorney was located amidst a hub of "baby" activity and, as he informed us, was contacted by birthmothers and adoptive parents both far and near.

One evening in early January, John and I were watching the early evening news when the phone rang. I answered and immediately my heart raced and adrenaline pumped.

"Hello, Laurie, this is Durand," said the attorney. John immediately asked and I told him who it was.

"Well I know this is sooner than I promised but I met with a birthmother today and I think you two would be a good match for her," he said. "Can you be in my office tomorrow morning at 9:30?"

"Of course, we'll be there," I chimed. "And thank you."I hung up the phone and stared glassy eyed at John.

He looked at me and said, "I'm going to be a papa," as he burst out in tears.

One look at him and I followed suit. After a few moments, my composure returned, and I reminded myself that the birthmother had to "like" us or approve of us. John continued tears streaming down his cheeks.

We were up bright and early the next morning. We arrived at the attorney's office a little after 9 am. We were ushered into a conference room and asked to view several videotapes. The attorney appeared on the screen and proceeded to state ground rules: with a limited amount of time avoid small talk, be honest and take the birthmother's feelings into consideration, understanding that she was just as nervous and apprehensive as we were.

The video ended and John and I sat nervously smiling at each other in anticipation. The door inched opened and in walked the attorney to usher us down the hall to his office. He quickly forewarned us that the birthmother was teary and anxious since the birthfather was ill and unable to join her. She was frightened.

We walked into the attorney's office and his phone description the night before had been accurate. This Irish pixie, twenty-four years old, was about 5'4' tall, with light brown hair and green eyes. She had on a brightly colored maternity smock, and big tears were trickling down her cheeks. The attorney began with a brief round of introductions, and then in a manner most reassuring to all of us, gently led the conversation to the point. This pregnant young woman intended to give her baby up for adoption, and we wanted to adopt a baby.

The attorney's silence had opened the floor inviting us to join in. John sat mute for the moment, so I chimed, "If it's any consolation, we did our crying last night."

We started to talk as openly as possible about the facts. John opened up and became more his gregarious self as his nervousness subsided.

After perhaps thirty minutes, the attorney suggested he take the birthmother to another location in the office for a break. John and I breathed deeply.

"What do you think, Hon?" he asked.

"I'd say it's a go. What about you?" I responded.

He nodded in agreement. We both stood up and walked over to the windows to unwind and look out at the city vistas below.

The attorney and the young woman reentered. We all sat down. The attorney asked if we wanted to proceed. John and I nodded and smiled.

"Yes," we responded. the attorney turned and focused on Lorena.

"Yes," she replied.

Tears welled up in my eyes. The attorney took a snapshot of the three of us and suggested we adjourn for lunch. John and I offered to take the birthmother to lunch. We rode down the elevator to the ground floor and walked to the restaurant talking nonstop all the way. With precious little time face-to-face now, there was a lot of ground to cover.

We had wanted an agency adoption for the very simple reason that, after counseling, the birthmother relinquishes the baby to the agency. The agency immediately places the child with the adoptive parents and the adoption is final. In a private adoption such as this through an attorney, the birthmother signs an intention to relinquish when the child is born. This remains in effect for six months at which time it becomes final. The attorney had suggested that we have the agency take the relinquishment if that worked out.

Over lunch, Lorena said that she had no problem talking with the agency people, but she had been snubbed by the agency people in the northern part of the state and so would prefer to deal with those in the southern part of the state.

We returned to the attorney's office and after a brief exchange of information, it became apparent that Lorena should depart for the airport immediately to avoid missing her flight. Lorena had asked us, and we agreed to visit her soon to meet the birthfather. The burden of travel wouldn't fall totally on us, she volunteered. They would travel south. She departed and John and I retired to the reception area to sign contracts and write out twelve thousand dollars in checks.

John and I returned home emotionally spent. Days later Lorena 's health history arrived in the mail from the attorney's office. We pored over it carefully, wondering how much she knew of her family health/genetic history just as we had discovered small gaps (nothing serious though) in each of ours. The attorney's office had prescreened the form and noted nothing of major import. We reviewed the form and tripped over one entry that said "flat feet/deformity." She had checked yes.

Later I talked with Lorena and inquired.

"Yes, I had club feet. They were broken and reset, and everything was fine. My nephew also was born with club feet. My daughter was fine though," she explained.

Lorena always offered full explanations. She had given a child up for adoption before.

We received a call from the attorney's assistant a few days later advising us that Lorena didn't have a phone because there was a large outstanding phone bill and deposit due. Lorena would have to take that money out of her monthly living expenses before a phone could be hooked up.

The attorney set up a fund for Lorena which we funded. The attorney was the go-between when questions arose about tapping into this fund.

John and I flew to Santa Rosa a month later to see Lorena and meet the birth father, David. We met and took them out to dinner. All was calm and friendly until David looked up and said, "I am not used to selling my child."

I froze not anticipating this confrontation. John, in true John form, looked in his eyes and in his most soothing voice said, "We don't want to buy your baby. We want to adopt and love a child."

This instantly defused David. I was so proud of John.

We flew back and months elapsed. There were riots in Los Angeles after the Rodney King incident. We hunkered down and entertained at home rather than venturing out. Lynn and Mike, who lived only blocks away, came for dinner. It was a talk fest.

Just before dinner, Mike looked up at the outside south wall of our patio and said, "I wonder what is behind that wall."

He and John shot looks of agreement and got mallets out. Before we knew it, large amounts of stucco and wire mesh from the wall were stacked on the area outside the patio and the patio was open on two sides.

The next morning, we had a call from the attorney that Lorena was in labor. We flew up to Santa Rosa again. After a twenty-four-hour labor, Scarlett Cobalt Prescott Greenberg, later renamed Abigail Elizabeth Havel, was born through Caesarean section. I was in the delivery room with Lorena as the baby was born. I held Lorena's hand and, of course, every time she squeezed by hand, an alarm sounded from the blood pressure cuff. She later told me that she thought she was dying each time the alarm went off. I assured her otherwise.

We arrived at the hospital the next day and John spotted a group of first graders visiting the nursery. Excited, he dashed in, scooped up the baby in the nursery and greeted the tykes on his knees to be on their level. I kept thinking germs. He finally came to the same conclusion and quickly retreated back into the nursery.

Being a papa was one of the greatest joys of his life. From the moment she was born, Abbie was his intense focus. He wanted everything for her that he had and more.

At lunch, John and I discussed names. I had been leaning toward Kilty, my Irish-Swedish mother's maiden name, but one look at the baby and I backed down. It just didn't fit. John initially said he liked the name Mary. His sister and my sister were named Mary. In fact, Nick and Pat named their youngest son John Robert Havel after John. Both families had mirror names.

Finally, he said, "I like Abigail, and we can call her Abbie."

We agreed.

In an adoption, the first birth certificate carries the name of the birthmother and birthfather. When the adoption is finalized, another birth certificate is issued with the name chosen by the adoptive parents.

David, the birth father, disappeared just before the birth. not to appear until a week later.

We stayed with Lorena in the hospital for a week and began to get to know her and bond with baby Abbie.

She seemed to trust us. We were probably the most stabile figures in her life. I felt motherly toward her she could have been my daughter.

From the moment Abbie was born, I knew that there was a possibility that Lori could renege and take Abbie back. Still in my heart, I knew that it would go through. And thankfully, it did.

After a week, Lori was being discharged and we headed home to start a new life adventure with baby Abbie.

John was laden down with baby car seat, bags, and paraphernalia.

Just before we boarded the plane, he looked at me and said, "I could never understand why parents with small children were allowed to board first."

He went ahead of me, and I watched as he unintentionally banged into almost every passenger seated on the aisle.

We finally arrived home intact and while we had the nursery ready it seemed cavernous compared to this wee baby. We talked to Mom Elizabeth on the phone, and she suggested that we take a dresser drawer and outfit it with a baby blanket and place the baby in there. We did and our Persian cat Kerman jumped right in.

"Well. that won't work," I thought.

John slept on the floor outside her room for the first week to ensure that she was ok.

Since Abbie was born on May 5, Cinco de Mayo, John irreverently but affectionately referred to her as our "Taco Baby." I learned to cook authentic Mexican food and we had some spirited birthday parties on that special date.

We both relished our roles as parents, we were devoted to Abbie.

About a week after we returned home, Mom Elizabeth called, "Hasn't changed your life at all, has it?"

John and I both laughed at the understatement!

When the adoption was legal, signed, sealed, and done six months later, Mom called and said, "We can finally sleep now and relax!"

I was so touched.

Abbie Girl

John and I doted on Abbie Girl. We rejoiced in the humbling exhilaration and love of parenting. She was the third dimension of our life.

When she was young, I told John that it was his job to teach her a sense of humor. He was the good humor man with a sense of people and humor that was never mean-spirited. Rather he was always uplifting.

Abbie was a good study and soon I began to call her Silly Goose, and later just Goose. She rankled at the name, and I had to drop it. I thought it was a supreme compliment. She punned and chuckled at jokes and funny situations with an infectious laugh.

We did the obligatory but sometimes torturous Chuck E. Cheeses birthday parties when she was young. We celebrated her Cinco de Mayo birthdays at home and other fun destinations. When she was older, we started a tradition of dining at Benihana's which she loved. She was always a "foodie."

As a young tyke sitting in the shopping cart at the market, she would reach out and grab vegetables as I bagged other veggies. I had to keep a running tally to check out.

One day she stood in the middle of the aisle and loudly said, "Mom, tonight I'd like bucatini for dinner."

Bucatini is nothing more than fat spaghetti but other shoppers in the aisle stared and glared at me. She was adventurous with food and loved trying new things and other cuisines.

One of her favorite excursions was and is still going to the Korean market with my sister-in-law, Gwi Soon. In fact, I had to drive Abbie solo to the Korean market when she was older so that she could revisit some of her favorite foods introduced to her by her aunt.

Once I received a basket of food as a gift and in it was a can of fiddlehead ferns. She pestered me for days until I opened it, and she could try them.

As a wee tyke, Abbie was very sensitive to noise. As we all watched a football game and roared at a touchdown, she recoiled at the noise. She recovered her calm with some cajoling from us, but it was troubling.

One day she watched as Notre Dame University football team made a touchdown and threw her arms up and exclaimed, "Touch Up!" Made perfect sense to me. How logical.

I made sure that many Christmas and birthday gifts for her were directed at motor skills development. Hers lagged somewhat but eventually with slides and bicycles and other such impetus, she caught up. As a teen, she took karate lessons and kept moving up in belts of achievement.

John and I spent a lot of time with her, and she enjoyed visiting Richard and Arlene. She was shy and retiring, sometimes hiding in her room, when family and others came over to our house. It was puzzling.

John and I had both attended the same parochial elementary school, but we were not in the same class. Both of us were religious and attended mass semi-regularly. When our sister-in-law Pat, Nick's wife, helped us get Abbie into the local parochial school for first grade. We were ecstatic.

In short order, we realized there were issues. Abbie would come running and jump into my arms when I arrived to pick her up. Finally, the principal called us in and told us that she exhibited inappropriate behaviors, and we should consider getting her tested.

We took deep breaths and resolved to find the right "tester." Shortly after, we pulled her out of that school and put her in a small private school with small classes where the teachers worked very hard with all the students. Somehow my religious zeal tempered after the parochial school incident with Abbie.

As Abbie grew into her teen years, she and Lori, her birthmother, would talk on the phone. One day Abbie was stubborn, disrespectful, and acting out with me. I told her that that was unacceptable, and I would turn her phone off until her behavior improved. I did and happened to disconnect her from Lori. Lori called me. I apologized for cutting her off. I had no idea Abbie was on the phone with her.

I explained Abbie's behavior and Lori said, "I would have done the same thing."

I encouraged Lori to get more education. She did become an LVN, but life was not kind to her. Lori had had a rather unsettling childhood and youth, with multiple foster mothers and a father who showed up once when she was in the hospital on oxygen, and tried to light a match in the room. She had little reason to trust people.

We stayed in touch with Lori for years via phone. I became a distant surrogate mother whom she called when she had problems or was down. We even had lunch with her when Abbie was two years old. She sent a book on adoption to me before Abbie was born and later sent a beautiful Disney book for Abbie.

Lori married a chap in Alabama when Abbie was a young teen. She had adopted his daughter and then they had a child of their own.

I could hear him bellowing, screaming, and yelling as I was on the phone with her and would say, "If you have to hang up, I understand."

At one point, Lori told Abbie that she was going to come out to California to visit relatives and wanted to visit her. Abbie was thrilled and couldn't wait. I sat Abbie down and tried to explain that Lori's life was not like ours. Lori may or may not come out to California.

Abbie's ramped-up excitement about Lori coming out turned to anger when Lori was a no-show.

"I'm never going to talk to her again," said Abbie

I was sad since I knew that Abbie didn't fully understand.

Shortly after, I talked with Lori who was hospitalized with congestive heart failure. I gasped and wished her well. Then we didn't hear from her. We found out that she either had a heart attack while driving and struck a tree or struck a tree and had a heart attack. Abbie tracked down and does talk to some of her half-sisters and brother.

We'd never heard of it. And then there were so many vague symptoms and a dizzying number of differences. One child may exhibit this symptom and not that. We were awash trying to connect all the dots and the meaning of A.D.H.D. We felt as though we were the only ones grappling with this. We identified some of our daughter's symptoms, but how is it treated? What's the best for her? What now? What do we do? To whom do you turn? There were no quick answers.

When our daughter was in first grade at a small parochial school, we had been greeted with repeated complaints: Your daughter hasn't done this. Your daughter has done that inappropriately.

No doubt each day was agony for her, and it was trying for us as well. We knew that she was not as mature as the other children in her class. Asking her to get her pajamas on and brush her teeth each night was an adventure. Inevitably she would forget before she reached her bedroom door, or she would become so distracted that the request was forgotten. She was terribly impulsive. Getting her to sleep took extraordinary measures and patience.

My sister-in-law, Pat, who raised four great children, said, "You just stare them down." She went into Abbie's bedroom and sat, trying to calm Abbie.

After two hours, she came out and said, "I give up."

The principal and teacher at the parochial school requested that we have her tested. We agreed. There was no mention of the suspected diagnosis other than our daughter Abbie exhibited inappropriate behavior.

"Where would you suggest?" I asked, thinking that they had had experience. The response was they weren't sure, but we might try one of the large learning/tutoring franchises. Those choices didn't seem to us to be the best avenue.

John and I married in our late thirties and adopted Abbie several years later. We both loved children and were thoroughly committed. Further, John, like others in his family, was found at a young age to be dyslexic. This in a time when little was known about dyslexia. His father, a radiologist and general practitioner and his mother, a nurse, made sure that he received all the help he needed to continue through school and college and was prepared for life. There was no question that we would follow through to provide the same for Abbie.

One of my good friends, Sally, had worked in special education so I asked for advice. One of her old friends was a psychologist who was on staff at Cedars-Sinai (and formerly served on staff at UCLA) in Los Angeles. She did just this type of testing, but it required multiple sessions.

After four testing sessions, we met with the psychologist to be told verbally and in a lengthy written report that our daughter has A.D.H.D., Attention Deficit Hyperactivity Disorder. The psychologist administered the Beery Developmental Test of Visual Motor Integration, the Wechsler Individual Achievement Test (academic functioning), Wepman Auditory Discrimination Test, the Wechsler Intelligence Scale for Children, and others. We called our pediatrician and asked for her advice. The pediatrician discussed the possible use of medications and wrote out a prescription for Ritalin. She then referred us to a child psychiatrist. We called Tom, John's brother, to ask his advice on the medication. He seemed to concur that a trial run of Ritalin for a time wouldn't be all bad. Abbie suffered roller-coaster mood swings with the medication. It broke my heart.

We knew there were challenges that she faced, but now these had a name. Not too much was known then. We were heartbroken to think that she had to face these issues. How could we make it easier? What could we do? I dived into every book and online site that I could find on A.D.H.D.

Meanwhile we enrolled Abbie in another small private school with a staff that was more than willing to work with her. We saw the child psychiatrist for almost six months with very little change in Abbie's behavior patterns or our understanding of what was going on despite tapping into the internet to find whatever we could on A.D.H.D. Rather, we walked away thinking that perhaps we were inferior parents. After all, according to the psychiatrist, Abbie was old enough to do certain things and there was no reason she was not doing them. She even suggested we wire Abbie's pants to sound an alarm if she wet during the night. With Abbie's sensitivity to sound, this struck us as inhumane.

I finally took Abbie off the medication. The psychiatrist never mentioned that A.D.H.D. children frequently exhibit immaturity far behind their chronological age.

The psychiatrist finally referred us to an educational psychologist. This was the beginning for us. The educational psychologist Dr. A. worked with Abbie and us on techniques to help her stop wetting and, to help her and us prepare her for the social steps she was about to take but typically well behind the other children. Dr. A even visited

Abbie's school to work with the teachers and staff on how best to work with Abbie at school.

During one office visit meeting, Dr. A suggested that we may want to contact the D Medical Clinic. There was a pediatrician there who had worked with A.D.H.D. and children with autism for more than 25 years. Still the medical community was just learning about A.D.H.D. and autism.

Another doctor, I thought and to what purpose?

None had provided much insight so far except for Dr. A. After a time, we did contact the D Medical Clinic and made an appointment. Armed with the first testing evaluation, Abbie and then John and I met with Dr. B (one of the principals of D Medical Clinic, who was a clinical professor of Pediatrics at the U.S.C. School of Medicine in Los Angeles) who talked at length with Abbie and then us. He described all the tests that would be administered to determine exactly what Abbie's attentional challenges were. In a series of visits, she would receive: a comprehensive neurological evaluation; Pediatric Early Elementary Examination; a psychological evaluation for self-esteem and emotional fallout of the A.D.H.D.; A neuro-developmental test to evaluate learning style; a Test of Variables of Attention (TOVA), and a neuro-physiologic analysis.

One test, videotaped as Dr. B., described the ways she assimilated information most readily - the ways that were easiest for her to learn. On a scale of one to ten, she was an eight in terms of severity of her A.D.H.D., he advised. This was an eye-opener for me. Not only that, but she had a ten-second audio delay. Imagine sitting in a classroom with a teacher prattling away, as Abbie was desperately trying to catch up to ten to twenty words ago.

The doctor sat down with us, discussed her diagnosis quite positively, and gave us a written summary. The brains of A.D.H.D. children work differently, he explained. They process brain chemicals differently. She is very bright but A.D.H.D. symptoms don't make these children good candidates for sitting in a classroom. This can cause a downward spiral of self-esteem and under-achievement.

I relayed that Abbie had heard Beethoven's Ninth Symphony at school, and once at home, she proceeded to sing me good night in the melody of Beethoven's Ninth Symphony.

She needs to "live" in the world of music or her other loves as often as possible, he advised, to provide a sense of achievement and boost her self-esteem. Children with A.D.H.D. need a great deal of praise. The difficulty we faced nightly getting her to go to sleep could be managed and he gave us the tools and an over-the-counter remedy, melatonin. It was a miracle.

Each child is different. All A.D.H.D. children don't fall into the same neat category, he advised. Different children exhibit different symptoms.

Immediately we felt relieved. These were real-time solutions and help with everyday challenges we faced. Not only that but we were given a folder with multiple articles and medical clips on A.D.H.D. Dr. B's waiting room was full of fliers, ADDitude magazine and others, and literature - a wealth of information and online sources. Indeed, I checked the diagnostic guidelines for A.D.H.D. (available through the American Psychiatric Association or in the Diagnostic and Statistical Manual of Mental Disorders), which describe the criteria. Abbie exhibited a good many of the symptoms with regularity.

I knew that Abbie was impulsive but as I started to read some of this material, I marveled and had the feeling that John and I weren't alone. One young boy with A.D.H.D. was convinced that if he put enough Jell-O® in the pool, that he could walk on water. Oh, the clean up! Another child thought that it would be a challenge to roller-skate in the house over dust bunnies sprayed with hair spray. Flammable? Sure!

We found out that A.D.H.D. is included in the IDEA (Individuals with Disabilities Education Act) and Section 504 of the Americans with Disabilities Rehabilitation Act. At the time, that didn't mean much to us, but it certainly did later when we enrolled her in public school. One flyer described various aspects and the classic signs of A.D.H.D.. Another emphatically stated that saying, "Try harder" to an A.D.H.D. child is like saying to a paraplegic: "If you try harder, you can walk." We began to get a well-rounded view of A.D.H.D., including other treatment philosophies/modalities, but still we had much to learn.

Dr. B talked to us about possibly putting Abbie on medication. Immediately I bristled.

"I am not a fan of medication," I spouted.

He very deftly explained how much more is being learned about the chemistry of the brain. He delved into the explanation of frontal lobes, how individual brains process dopamine and that in A.D.H.D. children this process seems to be different. He was careful to emphasize that each child reacts to medication differently and that he had seen significant improvement in some children.

"Ritalin?" I asked.

There is another newer drug that is taken once a day Concerta, with no mood swings, he explained. Rather the child's mood climbs and retreats like the arc of a bell curve. Abbie tried it and her concentration did seem to improve. We called it her thinking/concentration pill. Indeed, under Dr. B's supervision, we tried several different combinations of drugs in an attempt to find the best balance for Abbie. None seemed really strong.

Abbie's private school announced that there would be no fourth grade or higher in May. We scrambled to find another school for our third grader and enrolled her in the neighborhood public school.

We were reluctant since both John and I were the product of private schools.

Abbie started the fourth grade at the neighborhood school, and we held our breath. Now we had to learn the ways, means and legalities of public schools. I had already written the principal requesting an IEP (Individual Education Program) in the hope of getting Abbie in a small class. Further, I had contacted and received information from the Team of Advocates for Special Kids in our state. This non-profit organization offers classes to parents to learn what is available and how to take advantage of it.

Prior to the IEP, we had submitted our test results for consideration and the school district psychologist asked to test Abbie, which, of course, we did. The day of our IEP arrived, and we had asked Dr. A to attend with us as our advocate.

We were pleased with the IEP. If there was a need to put Abbie in a smaller specialized class, that option was available but mainstreaming her was probably better for her, and we agreed. She would be taken out of the classroom for specialized instruction in math (this because processing conceptual/abstract information is frequently difficult for children with A.D.H.D.), and her math was borderline. Her reading was strong but organizing it and repeating it was difficult, so certain language exercises would be specialized for her. She would also receive speech therapy for a slight lisp, and the occupational therapist would work on her penmanship.

One therapist asked, "Should I bring it up?"

She mentioned that Abbie had exhibited some signs of Asperger Syndrome, a form of autism, a new moniker for me.

The only resistance that we experienced then was that the school psychologist wanted to keep Abbie in the third grade. For Abbie's self-esteem and because she could do the fourth-grade work, we decided against this. As we left the IEP, Dr. A said that had we kept Abbie back, she would have met grade-level criteria and wouldn't be eligible for the special programs and help. My antennae went up and I knew that we would have to be alert and watchful.

Abbie thrived. She loved her teachers and made great progress. We also learned a host of tricks to help her from the very dedicated special education staff. She was frequently overwhelmed by a full page of math problems. We simply folded all but one row under so that she only saw and worked on one row at a time. This seemed to take the pressure off of her. Turning a lined paper sideways offered space keepers, and helped her to keep division problems in the correct line of tens, hundreds etc. We switched subjects if her frustration level mounted too fast. Later we come back to it when she was calmer.

We tried the newest, the first in twenty years, recently approved drug for A.D.H.D. Strattera which is a non-stimulant. Abbie could not tolerate the drug because it upset her stomach every time she took it. We tried Focalin and that too agitated her to an extreme. She is off medication now and doing well.

Another recommended psychiatrist saw her for a time and wanted to try multiple different psychogenic drugs to see if one of the group would help her. Most provided little or no help.

One night at about 5 P.M., she was laying in her bedroom and asked me to stay with her.

I said, "A group of us are outside. Come sit with us."

"No, I'm dizzy," she said.

I quickly checked the medication she was on. Thankfully, it was a new bottle and I immediately realized that seven pills were missing.

When I asked her why she took seven, her answer mirrored her impulsivity, "If one was good, I thought seven would be better."

We shot over to the emergency room at the local hospital where they put her on suicide watch. John and I spent the night there keeping watch with the medical staff. Fortunately, she weathered this event without any serious effects.

Getting her to take so much as an Advil is now a trial. And she is shot shy. She knows the power of medicine.

We were bolstered at the time by reports on studies indicating that A.D.H.D. children who have been medicated are less likely to become recreational drug abusers when older – perhaps because they experience the power of medications firsthand. Some dispute this.

We weathered middle school and puberty and struggled with high school. Abbie is and was a delightful girl, headstrong sometimes, gentle and caring but was extremely naive. She was still several years behind her peers in maturity although her socialization skills improved immensely. She had a gaggle of girlfriends and, gulp, she discovered boys.

High school was a challenge, but Abbie mastered it and graduated. I succumbed to tutors when it came to math. Math has never been my forte, and I was totally unknowing of how they taught it, I so could not boost Abbie's understanding.

We were optimistic. We were able to get intervention long before the third and fourth grades when some A.D.H.D. children are already behind academically and suffering from a severe loss of self-esteem. Abbie was bright and did well in school but still lagged behind in math and organizing skills.

Mid-high school, we discovered a clinical therapist, a clinical psychologist who saved us again. In addition to helping us learn to leverage behaviors against rewards and motivations, she encouraged us to get Abbie tested by Regional Center. This is a private nonprofit center, one of twenty-one in the state of California, that contract with the California Department of Developmental Services. Regional Centers offer services to people with carefully defined developmental disabilities. This would be a safety net for Abbie since once in, she would remain in the system for life.

We took Abbie for testing. We met with the testing psychologist and several others days later who told us that Abbie was diagnosed with PDD-NOS, pervasive developmental disorder, no other source. Ah ha! I thought. A.D.H.D. has its symptoms but Abbie's reactions exceeded those of ADHD. That explains the behaviors, the sensitivity to loud noises, lack of eye contract as a small child, why medications rarely made a difference with her, and a host of other things. She was on the autism spectrum - another comorbidity, complication. PDD-NOS was a milder set of symptoms, but nonetheless on the spectrum. The psychologists said that Abbie wasn't severe enough to be admitted as a Regional Center client. I sat quietly and the subject of depression came up.

"How do you know she doesn't just suffer from depression?" asked one of the psychologists.

"Well according to the *Oasis Guide to Asperger Syndrome,* which had just come on the market and was considered a bible written by parents and doctors, it is a normal, reaction for youths to react this way when they realize that there is a deficit," I said, continuing to cite the book.

When finished with the verbal volley, the team of psychologists admitted her as a client to Regional Center. John and I breathed a sigh of relief.

Should something happen to us, she would be provided for. John lamented that what she faced affected people skills. Communication skills were innate to him, his base of relating to others. Saddened, I started immediately thinking how to counter these obstacles. I, too, had little difficulty talking to and relating to others. What hurdles would she have to overcome? But if there was a way, we would find it. No easy fixes nor prediction of the future. John and I worried nonstop about her future. I took it day-to-day. John worried about everything all at once.

In retrospect, the hours that we worked with her to look us in the eye and with so many other things, paid off. This was many more dots to connect than just A.D.H.D.

Abbie had life coaches and a coach to teach her how to ride the bus and other activities, all from the Regional Center, for which I was most grateful. Having your mother take you through your paces, leaves a great deal to be desired. I took all-day seminars in autism and read every Temple Grandin book I could get my hands on. (Grandin, a noted scientist, designed a large percentage of livestock apparatus nationwide, and she has written extensively on autism as a person with autism.)

In high school, Abbie met the twins Tom and Zack. Both were bright, nice and on the spectrum. Abbie started seeing Tom. I must say I learned a lot. First, the twins spoke in voices several octaves lower than normal unless they were on stage performing, in which case they spoke normally. On one trip to the grocery store, one of them boomed, "I found the cookies." Almost everyone in the vicinity turned around to see where this deep Darth Vadar-like voice was coming from. Just a normal trip to the market.

Reading social cues correctly is a big hurdle for those on the spectrum. Another time, I was nearby as Abbie and one of the twins began to bicker. Curious, I listened as one misinterpreted a statement as snarky and reacted and then vice-versa. The original comment was innocuous. It was eye-opening for me.

Impulsivity is usually high, and their emotional thermostats doesn't always stop at the normal spot. They can become incensed and angry and keep on going, far beyond what one might consider normal.

Abbie attended junior college but was not motivated and certainly didn't anticipate how education can benefit your life. She attended with a laissez-faire attitude and then started looking for work. She spent much time dithering around and meeting a girlfriend.

After spending some time in Texas after her 21st birthday, she returned and spent time with Andy to whom she became engaged. After more than a year, that fizzled. She rekindled her desire to go to school. She did and did well, worked hard and enjoyed it. Then Covid hit. That tamped down her enthusiasm for school. From in person to computer screen, was not a good transition for her.

Just like every other child, children with A.D.H.D. and who are on the spectrum grow up. At age twenty-nine, Abbie moved to Alabama/Florida. She had met someone online but rather than jumping in blind, she visited in the summer. Then in October, she drove herself cross country as her father and I held our breath. She had arranged an apartment and a job which we applauded.

It was a steep learning curve from there on! She paid her rent for three months in advance and checked into a pawn shop to buy a refrigerator. That refrigerator was guaranteed for two weeks. It broke down in the third week. I could go on with the adventures that she faced - and that we faced but via long distance. She is married now to Danny, a terrific chap, supportive and loving.

Whether then or now, there are no cookie-cutter answers.

She has learned to manage her life and faced life's challenges with aplomb. My admiration for her has only grown. She has retained her stubbornness and is not one to give up. She attacks life head on for success or dusts herself off and continues when faced with difficulties.

The Marriage of Two Unusual Laughs

I had always been known for a loud laugh, much like my mother's laugh. John too had a distinctive laugh, a deep resonant contagious laugh. No matter the circumstance, he could always bring a smile to my face or make me laugh. Laughter is life elevated.

Early in our marriage, whenever I became owly or cranky, John would look at me and gently say, "Would you like to go outside and cut the lawn with your teeth?" Or occasionally he would ask, "Would you like to clean the front porch with a toothbrush?"

I knew immediately that I was shrewish to the maximum.

John, the consummate gift giver, would always come up with clever personal gifts after a little thought. Once I relayed that my sister, Christina, had been offered a job by a masonry company after they saw the rock wall that she built.

He said, "I know what to send her for Christmas - a hard hat and a beer!"

Buying for him was a bear, since he would rarely admit to wanting anything.

Once in a while he would say, "I'd like to get a barbecue smoker."

Those times were few and far between. I would save and file away any whims he expressed during the year for his birthday or the holidays.

One Christmas, he opened a gift and I was puzzled.

"That's beautiful," I said. "Who gave it to you?"

"Oh, I saw this and bought it for myself and had it wrapped! he said.

I laughed and shook my head.

When we were first married, I had a tendency to sleep in on weekends. John was up at dawn's early light and had the T.V. on. One weekend, he watched an infomercial on car wax and became smitten with this wax that defied fire and all manner of car damaging elements. He was so pleased to tell me all about it when I stumbled out of the bedroom.

"And it comes with this great shammy!" he said.

I laughed and shook my head. When it arrived, he realized that there was a great deal of hype in the infomercial.

But then the tables turned. He would turn on Time-Life programs with sixties music. One night they played almost all of my favorites from that time.

John encouraged me to buy it, and finally said, "You don't know how to spend money."

That was it. I ordered it on the spot. We both enjoyed the CDs, and I squirmed from the regret of spending money.

He looked at me and to assuage my guilt, said, "It's only money!"

Since John went to work early so he usually went to bed before I did.

On those rare occasions when it rained, he would look out at the driveway which was only half covered in rain droplets before a deluge.

"Ah, they said fifty percent chance of rain," he said as the rest of us laughed. At night, neighbors used to tease John, "Oh, it's time for bed. He's just taken his socks off."

That was the cue.

One night I heard him moaning and groaning and ran into the bedroom. He was having a nightmare. I hopped on the bed, kneeling next to him, and tried to awaken him.

"John, it's ok, you're having a bad dream!" I said loudly.

I saw him fidget, cock his arm in his fear position to backhand whomever and protect himself. I was destined to be "bapped" off the bed.

I thought, "Oh dear, here it comes and he won't even realize what he's doing while he's asleep."

Fortunately, he woke up and I breathed a sigh of relief for him, his nightmare and me!

In the early days, John and I hosted dinner parties with fully set table and multiple courses. After the guests left, John and I would start on the dishes.

It was not uncommon for John to say, "Did you miss a dish? You used every dish in the kitchen."

John would turn on music, usually loud music, come up behind me and spirit me away from the sink to dance with him, celebrating the evening and then a hug from him. A "John hug" was unlike any other, enveloping me like a cocoon. I felt safe, secure, and happy.

John's Hospital Persona

John's hospital persona was no different from his home persona.

John had a special attachment and fondness for Saint John's Hospital in Santa Monica, later Providence Saint John's Hospital. He worked there during high school when his father was a radiologist there. He grew up in Santa Monica and used to see David Saxby, a Santa Monica paramedic, in the ER. There were many draws. John was an almost-native Santa Monican brought there soon after birth from Omaha.

After training as a radiology technologist, John worked at Saint John's in the mid-seventies. There was a tight-knit group that worked together at the time: Jean, Peggy, Tom, Sue, Patty, Lisa and later

Christina and others. They stayed in touch for decades. As time went on, people changed and Gary, Pat Pat (I never did learn why they called her Pat Pat) and Shalima became central figures. John finally stopped answering the home phone, "Radiology," but it took years.

John took newbies under his wing and trained many. He enjoyed that. He loved people, patients, and everyone in between. And they loved him. He was hospital employee of the year once and was known simply as "Big John." In fact, years later after he retired, I was talking with an x-ray tech who mentioned she had worked at Saint John's.

"My husband worked there for decades," I volunteered.

She asked his name.

"Big John," I said.

She knew instantly who he was.

This was John's domain for forty-six years. I knew it peripherally as he knew my work. I knew of stories in the emergency room when a mother came in with her husband and children and she suffered a broken wrist. Angst and distress were written on her face. John simply teased her before taking the x-ray to put her at ease.

"You'll do anything to get out of doing dishes," he said.

She smiled and seemed to relax.

At work when asked how his weekend was, he would tell his co-workers, "I donned my cowboy boots, thong and cowboy hat and went outside to weed. My wife closed the blinds. It was not a pretty sight."

They were wise to him and so learned to take such stories with a grain of salt.

Yet one time, he said, "Well we sat out in front with the one-legged man, the two lesbians and the mail people."

The one-legged man was Axel, an amputee whom John and I were terribly fond of and actually cared for in the final days of his life. The two lesbians were our dear friends from across the street along with neighbors a few doors down. One of John's coworkers rode by with her husband on bicycles and stopped to say hi.

The next morning, she went into work and announced, "He's telling the truth!"

That set off a whole new wave of mystery about his stories.

One day he went to the cafeteria and sat down at a table that he knew was populated with extremely religious folks. He had watched a religious history show the evening before that espoused some provocative theories.

"Did you know that Jesus was married to Mary Magdalene?" he asked. He sat back, ate his lunch, and listened to the firestorm of faith that he had ignited.

I never quite knew what he told his friends at work. I could only imagine when I had occasion to go to the hospital. I was quiet, for sure, until I tested the waters.

One year when Abbie was a wee tyke, John was the hospital Santa Claus. I couldn't wait to get to the hospital to see him dressed as jolly old St. Nick and take photos of him. I asked around and discovered he was in the rehab center across the street. This was a detox/rehab center and frequently had celebrities in residence. In the door I walked with camera in hand. Three nurses almost jumped me figuring I was paparazzo trying to snap a photo of the celebrity currently in residence. I humbly slipped out and waited for John to emerge. He was masterful as Santa, and his personality too was perfect!

He did suggest that I bring Abbie to sit on Santa's lap when she was about two years old.

"She will recognize you, your voice and mannerisms," I said. He finally agreed that she was too young to unmask the mystery of Santa.

Saint John's afforded John some interesting experiences as well. Numerous celebrities and dignitaries were treated at the hospital over time.

One night he came home, and I could tell he had a story to tell.

"One of the members of the Saudi royal family, the Saudi Queen Mother, is in the hospital," he relayed. "Saudi security wanted the entire floor to protect the patient! Apparently, the Saudi point person walked into the office and placed a suitcase of cash on the desk. That was it! The floor was theirs."

Another time, he called me and let me know that he had been screened in one of the anterooms of a VIP suite. It was Elizabeth Taylor who was sick with some unknown infection. Once screened, hospital personnel were not allowed out. They sat there waiting, as an infectious disease doctor came in to see what the malady was.

This was high AIDS time so any deviation from normal was highly suspect.

I tried to call John later since it was hours after his usual time to come home, but there was no answer. When he finally arrived home, I peppered him with questions: What was the infection? Were you gowned and masked? What precautions did they take to protect you and other staffers?

I don't know that I ever found out what the malady was but quite a few staffers were held over just in case they were needed. For John it was just another day at the hospital.

Years later when I took him in for a test at the hospital, we were sitting in the waiting room and John was surrounded by x-ray techs who had come to say hi. One of the hospital guards came through. He greeted John immediately with enthusiasm. He told all the techs that John was great and recounted how he had helped him when he started work there. John was kind to all.

Often, he would call me from work saying, "Laurie, how do you spell this word?" I relished helping him. John had severe dyslexia which hampered him as a youth, but he learned to read thanks to Sister Benedict and I was fine with being a secretary. He loved sitting down with the sports section of the paper on Sunday mornings. He would regale me with the outstanding or unusual statistics of height, weight, speed, etc. for college football players.

At his retirement party August 10, 2018, I sat and watched as a steady stream of doctors, nurses, techs, his bosses, and staff came in to bid him good-by. He posed for photos with all in front of a sign that said, "The Legend Retires."

John was captured photographically over the years at the hospital and, in fact, his photo immediately following the 1994 Northridge earthquake, still hangs in the hospital entry hall today, just a few panels down the way from his father's photograph from the sixties.

Travel was a recurrent theme in our marriage. John was adamant that we join the family for vacations. I enjoyed it too since it was always an upbeat adventure.

Both John and I had traveled. He had traveled to Europe to Italy and Spain with his parents, with Dave and Elise Saxby to New Zealand and numerous places in the U.S. I had traveled to Hawaii en route to Japan for the World Games, Canada for the Pan American Games, Mexico for the 1968 Olympics, Holland on a press junket, Italy on business and assorted U.S. and Canadian cities to see friends and on business.

When the family said they were going to a dude ranch in Wyoming, John was ecstatic. Abbie was about eight years old and loved horses as did John. They say you haven't ridden until you've fallen off well, I've ridden. I just wasn't as courageous as they.

Abbie, with a pink cowboy hat, rode a horse named "Brownie." She still fondly remembers that horse and time. We and the brothers and their families attended ranch-style breakfasts on the trail, threw axes at haystacks, and rode horses. John felt ill on the day of the big ride. I asked what happened. He said that he was nervous over me not liking horseback riding. I was stunned and assured him I was fine. He spent one day in bed as Abbie and I were guided up the mountain to the Great Divide.

Abbie lost her hat on a tree branch, and I was helpless to circle back and retrieve it. Fortunately, one of the guides did. Abbie's horse kept nudging my horse which finally kicked at her horse. My horse skills were not polished or sharp.

Finally, we arrived at the crest. I looked back and gulped.

"We still have to go down," I thought with dread.

Green pastures accented with lightening felled trees greeted us. It was beautiful and calm as we rode around.

Time to return. We tacked our way down the mountain which wasn't quite as scary as I had anticipated. We arrived and I breathed a sigh of relief. Abbie had not one iota of fear or reticence.

On the last evening we attended a rodeo. What an experience! I kept telling John that the riders didn't make enough money to pay medical expenses as we watched a few take rough, tumble, threatening spills. All the attendees from the ranch immediately adjourned to a nearby saloon. Conversation centered on one of the daughters of the ranch owner who had a role in a current movie *Coyote Ugly*.

Park City, Utah was a favored destination for years since Richard and Arlene had a condominium there and had generously invited us up. We hiked and played summer and winter. Abbie played with her cousins, Stephanie and Alex's two girls, Alicia, and Julia, one slightly older and one slightly younger than Abbie. They would play and hike around the lake giggling all the time.

Later John's entire family, the four brothers and their families, and the next generation would rent condos and we had a warm, festive family gathering. John and I joined Richard, Nick, and Tom and their grown children and their children. We cooked at one condo or another, shared dinners and there was always a contingent to join in if horseback riding or another activity was on the docket. Relaxed and enjoyable times with family were special.

Park City is both a down-to-earth little town and a sophisticated draw, with nearby Sundance, ski slopes and other spots. The family would all gather to find a place on the town main street to watch the 4th of July parade. School children marched or were driven down the street while local ski shop instructors, ski patrol and hospitality businesses and all manner of townspeople followed. It was heartwarming to watch and applaud.

The four brothers worked hard to keep the family together and support each other and the nieces/nephews. A diverse family with urban designers, teachers, doctors, lawyers, architects, radiology techs and more, the family is not judgmental. Rather they are welcoming, ushering in new spouses and their families with open arms. Always open to new ideas and ever ready to good naturedly tease someone, this was quite a group. There were family challenges and crises, and as they happened, the brothers pulled together to support each other and their children. I realized where many of John's kind traits came from.

The brothers were dedicated to family. Before John and I were married, UCLA had a volleyball ceremony to retire my jersey/numbers and others. I decided to throw a party afterwards and invited John's local family. After the ceremony, I started introducing his family and to my surprise there was brother/Father Tom in a turtleneck. He cued me and I introduced him as Tom, no formal titles. He joined the others and came back to my apartment where I had a potpourri of food and appetizers ready to serve.

I was in the kitchen and Tom entered. John had always put his brother Tom on a pedestal. After all, Tom left home for the seminary when John and Richard were young.

I looked at him and said, "You know your brother has you on a pedestal and is more than a little intimidated by you."

Tom spent the next few years working to get to know John better and to let John know him on vacations and get-togethers. I was most impressed and grateful.

Hawaii was on our agenda twice Maui first in 1991. Yes, Notre Dame was playing football there so, of course, we had to go root for them. We stayed at a lovely condominium complex on the ocean. There were amusing geckos everywhere, inside and out. Mom Elizabeth joined us on what would be one of her last trips. This was also a celebration of Nick and Pat's twenty-fifth wedding anniversary. We had driving adventures and toured historical Maui.

In 1993, Abbie was a wee one when we went for a family vacation in Kauai. Richard the logistics wizard, managed to arrange all the airplane flights from Northern and Southern California to meet in Oahu so that we could all fly together to Kauai. Abbie played with (our goddaughter) Alicia and Julia after hula lessons in the morning and romped in the surf that afternoon. By evening, she barely had enough energy to smile for a family photo. We rotated dinners in each family's condo. If someone wanted to go horseback riding on the beach or another activity, there was always a contingent to join in.

John had a video camera and shot footage throughout the trip. I discovered these treasures including Abbie's hula lessons with her cousins, Alicia and Julia, thirty years later!

In October of 2018, we were invited to Colorado Springs for a fiftieth Anniversary Reunion of 1968 Olympic athletes. John and Abbie came as my guests. We signed volleyballs and flags for gifts, did spoof videos, had a gala group dinner Saturday, and took a spate of photos as we reconnected. There were speakers Saturday morning, including the 1968 iconic logo designer, Lance Wyman.

Abbie connected with quite a few athletes, and John and I had a chance to catch up with my Olympics roomie, Miki. Saturday, we toured the sports facilities for Olympians - most impressive! Saturday afternoon we had a choice of tours. John, Abbie, and I chose the Air Force Academy. We saw the athletic facilities, talked to cadets and each other, and toured the chapel then in the throes of renovation. John elected to Phihang back since his knees were not in good shape. Abbie and I toured the Buddhist and Catholic chapels and other sights. It saddened me that we had traveled so far, and John had missed out on sights that he so would have enjoyed.

Local travel was on the agenda as well. We made the rounds of weddings near and far. Family weddings were always on our list. We were invited to my cousin's wedding in Modesto, California, so we booked the flight and found that it was a small plane. John and I crouched down and walked like Cossack dancers to get to our seats. Fortunately, it was a quick flight.

We reveled seeing my five cousins, my Uncle Bill and meeting Julie, the beautiful bride. It was a quick turn around and we saw all in the lobby Sunday morning. Tom and Julie gave away demitasse sets and coffee, an apt gesture since Tom was and is in the coffee business. As we passed and said our good-byes and best wishes, Tom admonished us not to pack the coffee in the suitcase. I had.

"How bad can it be?" I thought. The suitcase, all my clothes wreaked of coffee. Never again.

One night to celebrate David Saxby's birthday, John and I joined Dave and Elise and decided to reserve seats on what they said was the only Murder Mystery Dinner Train Theater in Southern California the Fillmore Express.

Did I say express? Well, yes, it is a railroad, the Fillmore & Western Railway, but it did not travel far and wide and certainly not at top speeds during dinner rides all the better to leisurely take in the scenery, show and dinner.

As we talked, laughed, and dined on pre-selected entrées ordered, a cast of characters charmed and engaged the diners. Gloria Swansong, Cesar Deville (pronounced Davillie), and a troupe of six or seven other actor/singers, traveled from one dining car to the next unraveling their murder mystery.

Stepping back in time, this mystery was set in the 1930s and the actors were elaborately made up, pancaked and costumed. Perhaps one of the most entertaining aspects of the show was the cool repartee and one-liners the actors used on diners who verbally joined in the performance as our shyness and reserve slowly dissolved. One pert actress, playing a cigarette girl, had an unmistakable Judy Holiday voice, while several other actors in camp costumes sang so beautifully, there was rapt attention and silence during their performances. We were all captivated.

Two hours later we were in Santa Paula. Right across the street is the Glen Tavern Inn, reputed to be haunted, where several diners had made reservations to stay that night.

Curious, I quizzed the train conductor at the stop regarding this "haunted" hotel."Nothing to worry about," he said, "unless you're staying in room 103 or on the third floor where Harry Houdini stayed."

The forty-one-room Glen Tavern Inn is a stately old three-story Tudor-Craftsman building that was named a national landmark and placed on the Register of National Historic places in 1981. Built in 1911, the hotel is said to be the "most haunted" structure in Ventura

County. A number of guests and staff have reported strange goings-on while in the hotel. The third floor is reputed to have been a gambling salon and a house of ill repute when it was first built, and Santa Paula was in its oil town heydays. In the early days of Hollywood, John Wayne, Harry Houdini, and Carol Lombard are said to have stayed there.

In addition to solving the murder, the question of the evening was which of the two singing actors are married and own the business? It was an enigmatic but memorable night.

Even local jaunts were an adventure. One weekend, Lynn and Mike, John and I planned dinner in Chinatown. We all had a hum for Chinese food so what better destination? We arrived, parked and walked the streets to our appointed restaurant, gawking at the Peking ducks hanging in the windows and taking in the sights. Dinner was lovely except that we managed to order every dish with peanuts. We laughed and separated the peanuts.

After dinner we started walking up the street and decided to stop in at bar to have a nightcap. We entered and immediately in front of us was a grand ballroom. We peeked in and there was a traditional Chinese wedding. Curious, we kept watching from the door. The bride, groom, family and friends had finished dinner and were standing around seemingly timid about starting up the party.

John, being John, wanted them to start partying. He entered, introduced himself respectfully and began dancing with the bride. All soon joined in. John wished the smiling bride and groom a happy life and exited to us at the door. Lynn, Mike and I just laughed wondering what Chinese cultural mores had been crossed.

We went upstairs to the bar and listened to a Chinese impressionist sing Frank Sinatra songs while we sipped and laughed.

Over the years, friendships cemented and melded. We were going to meet John and Kathy also members of the cooking group, close friends of mine- whom John also knew. I used to visit them every Sunday. They were fabulous chefs.

I would stand behind them asking, "What are you doing and why?" as I understudied their cooking techniques.

I probably drove them crazy but I learned so much! They thought nothing of doing a seven-course Japanese dinner for Japanese guests, and many other impressive culinary feats.

John and I decided to ride with Judy and Roy in their car to Orange County for the get-together. John knew Judy from the lab at the hospital. Her husband Roy and I were in the same business and so we would meet for lunch occasionally, compare notes and laugh uproariously. They were also in the food group and Judy tutored John on making timbales for one food group session.

Roy was a BMW enthusiast and even traveled to Europe for driver training.

We sat in the back of his BMW and poor John sat for an hour with his head bowed onto his chest, neck cocked since the car was a little small for him. Neither of us took cars for granted after that, always testing for height and width limits.

My sister, brother and I wanted to throw a fiftieth anniversary party for my folks. John and I thought it would be fun to host the party at one of the nearby Temecula wineries. We set out to check them out - wineries, and wineries that practice méthode champenoise (wineries that make champagne requiring a second fermentation in the bottle) and check out the possibilities. We reveled in the vineyards, tasting rooms and stores as we scooped up souvenirs from our time. Ultimately, we decided to hold the celebration at my sister's large house in Temecula, but exploring the wineries was worth it.

Family friends and those with decades long attachments to my parents attended. There were many strong memories among these great friends assembled to celebrate.

We enjoyed Christmas days at my sister's home in Temecula, and Christmas Eves at nephew Derek and Alison's. We visited and fished in June Lake with the Saxbys and waterskied on the Sacramento Delta with family. We flew to Boise for Stephanie and Alex's wedding and to Philadelphia just after 9/11 for Derek and Alison's wedding.

We hosted a wedding rehearsal dinner for nephew Tom and Cristina and relished dinner at their apartment. We traveled to Lake Geneva in Wisconsin for nephew John's wedding to Maureen. We trekked north for Liz and David's wedding and later when nephew Patrick and Theresa married in Golden Gate Park in Shakespeare Garden, a most romantic and picturesque setting in San Francisco.

Later we drove to Napa Sonoma for nephew Peter's wedding, which was held in a dramatic wine cave. Unfortunately, my videos reflect a wine cave and barely anyone or anything is discernible in the dark photos.

More recently we drove to Palm Desert for the wedding of my nephew, one of my sister's six children, Eric to Danyelle. It was very near my mother's house so we had a regular family gathering.

We would drive to Palm Desert to visit my parents several times a year. Once they suggested we play golf with them on their executive nine-hole course. Both of us were game. John paired with my Dad and I paired with Mom. Fortunately, they guided us with choice of club and plied us with hints and tips along the way.

John was very close to his brother, Richard, his wife, Arlene, their daughter, Stephanie, and their son, Derek, since he was a regular at their house as the kids were growing up. John and Richard were the closest in age. We visited them regularly for family events too. Uncle John, as he was known to nieces and nephews in both our families, used to wrestle with Derek regularly as he was growing up. Derek's friends called him Uncle John and John knew them well. He had coached many of them when they were younger.

John and I enjoyed parties, and early in our marriage, thought it would be fun to throw an anniversary surprise party for Richard and Arlene, who had been so supportive of us. Stephanie colluded with us, coordinated, and made sure the house was guest ready. Arlene had made restaurant reservations for that night for Richard and her. John and I showed up just before their departure time. The doorbell rang and some of their friends stopped by. It kept ringing and more people arrived. Arlene's anxiety level ticked up with the arrival of each guest, thinking they would miss their reservation. Finally, we told them to cancel the reservation. This was all a pre-planned party, with Stephanie's help. John and I had prepared dinner, everything was ready in our car. What fun!

Arlene used to say that John was the brother she never had. They would talk on the phone updating and confiding in each other regularly. Later, nephew Tom, was frequently over too. John and I were and are fortunate to have such great family and friends.

I wasn't the only one charmed by John's humor. One Saturday, I was scheduled to take a class. John decided to team up with Ann and take two-year-old Abbie to the mall to entertain her. John popped little Abbie on his shoulders and the three walked into Victoria's Secret.

John immediately proclaimed, "I'm here to buy my daughter a bra!"

Ann said there was a pregnant silence in the store before giggles and guffaws broke out.

Tom and Martha next door doted on Abbie and soon became Grandpa Tom and Grandma Martha. We would hand her over the back fence so they could spoil her with ice cream and all manner of things. Occasionally John used to take baby Abbie next door to Martha when she was fussy or wouldn't go to sleep. Martha would hold her and voila, Abbie calmed down.

We had a great group of neighbors, a core of ten who gathered nightly on our front porch. Frequently we fixed dinner for them after the laughing fest, counseling session we had in front of the house. Abbie was little and still needed much attention but John and I managed. In the winter, we put Geoff's fire pit out front and Magi and Yossi would toss foil-wrapped potatoes in for appetizers.

One Saturday, this spirited group opted for a school-inspired field trip when the metro line first became active near us. Axel in his wheelchair, Sharon and her girlfriend, Debbie, John, Abbie, and all boarded the bus, traveled to the North Hollywood hub and then on south to the Aquarium of the Pacific in Long Beach. We trekked through Watts and a host of areas that we were unfamiliar with. One young man on board seemed to fancy twelve-year-old Abbie. John and I kept a careful eye on both of them.

We arrived about noon, enjoyed lunch, and then toured the Aquarium, a fantasy of fish. Amidst our hoots and hollers at the sharks, eels, and assorted sea life, we enjoyed the sights and each other cementing our friendships. We returned to the station and home. The field trip was a success!

It was nothing for us to have the whole group for dinner and then play a raucous dice game of "Right, Left, Center." What made it fun was there was no skill involved. It was simply a matter of luck, so you could be behind and win the whole pot.

But our group couldn't stay together forever. Some were older and sadly died, and others moved away. The complexion of the neighborhood changed. Lovely folks, but not the same camaraderie.

My brother Scott, his wife Gwi and his two boys Bekdoo and Marcus, frequently came down to visit at Christmas. Scott could get all worked up watching T.V..

After one of Scott's rants, John would lean over, look at him directly and calmly say, "Scott, it's only a T.V. show."

Scott calmed down.

John could enrich any moment. One night pre-Christmas, when nephews Bekdoo and Marcus were middle-school age, we took them to Candy Cane Lane to see the Christmas lights. While inching in the car line, we came to a house with thousands of lights, a floating rug with Aladdin atop, Christmas music and many Disney characters. John hopped out of the car with Abbie, stood in the driveway and greeted those in the car caravan as though he owned the house. The boys laughed uncontrollably.

Day-to-day life did have its ups and downs. One night, John said, "I have a rash on my stomach." I looked and sure enough.

"You need to go see the dermatologist," I said.

He did and came home with a handful of prescriptions. Three weeks later, I too developed a rash on my stomach. I went to the dermatologist and returned with a handful of prescriptions. None of them worked on either of us. The rash spread and became much more uncomfortable, especially at night when I wanted to jump out of my skin. We both returned to the dermatologist who said we were being eaten alive by mites, but that it wasn't scabies. We had the house sprayed. We had the bedroom carpet removed and wood flooring installed. The siege continued with no let up. John had developed quarter-sized lesions on his legs. My back was red and inflamed. After eight weeks, we went to see my internist Dr. S. who referred us to a dermatologist nearby in Santa Monica.

Dr. L. examined both of us, taking scrapings off our hands. He had two of his colleagues come in and check our rashes.

Dr. L. said, "Yes, we can help you. You have scabies and one of the worst cases, we've seen."

No doubt John picked it up somewhere in the hospital, probably the emergency room.

What followed was head to toe application of a neurotoxin to the scabies for five successive days. We returned to the doctor and reported following all of his directives: no sitting on upholstered furniture since the scabies can live in upholstery. We sheathed our mattresses in casings that kept bad bugs in and others out.

We were still uncomfortable since the neurotoxin had irritated our skin. We celebrated Thanksgiving at home together that year for fear of infecting others. All was fine but I reinfected twice. Again, top of head-to-toe application of the ointment. I was puzzled - why me? Then it dawned on me. Eight weeks of driving my car with sheepskin covers resulted in the scabies living in the covers. I immediately cut them out and threw them away. Success!

B.C., before child, we visited John's mother, who we called Mom, as often as we could. Talking to her on the phone, we became concerned, at one point in time, that maybe she wasn't eating too well. We had great fun visiting with her in Vacaville, just north of San Francisco, and planning the menu of her choice. John and I would go shopping during the day and then we would cook.

Just as we were leaving that last visit, Mom called me aside and told me she had a severe pain in her chest days before. I gasped and asked her to please visit the doctor. She agreed. I hopped in the car and told John first thing. We knew that she had heart problems which had reared up before.

The Imprimatur of a Matriarch

"Your mother-in-law was truly a matriarch, the only one I've ever known," said our friend Lynn as she delivered sandwiches for lunch. She had come over to sit with me after I received the news.

Five years after we married, the phone rang. Abbie hiked on my hip, I answered, "Hello, Nick." Nick was John's brother who lived in Vallejo, California, near Mom Elizabeth.

"Uh, oh," I thought. Nick doesn't usually call during the day.

"Laurie, I have some bad news. Mom died last night," he said.

I hung up the phone and sobbed uncontrollably. This couldn't be.We had just talked to my 84-year-old mother-in-law two days earlier, and she sounded fine.

John was at work, so I called him at the hospital.

"John, I have some bad news for you. I just had a call from Nick," I said.

"Yes," he said. I relayed the somber message.

Shortly after, John walked in the apartment door, took one look at me, and cried. I got up from feeding the baby and hugged him. We cried, hugged, and cried together. Perfunctorily we went through the motions of packing and were off to meet Richard and Arlene at the airport.

The mere thought of an airport always signaled excitement for me, the anticipation of a gateway to the world. No excitement was present this time, instead there was a gnawing dread. Perhaps if I didn't go, Mom wouldn't be dead.

John adored his mother. As an elementary student, he had been diagnosed with dyslexia. Both his parents were determined to make sure that he received whatever help he needed to overcome this. Mom enrolled him in Marianne Frostig Center of Educational Therapy, which was located in Pasadena, quite a distance from Santa Monica. Mom showed him what busses he needed to take to get there. His first bus ride was a success, but Mom was in her car following right behind the bus to make sure.

We arrived in Oakland early evening, stopped in Vallejo at John's brother Nick's house and joined Nick and his wife, Pat, and Father Tom and drove to our hotel just eight miles out of Vacaville.

The next morning John and his brothers went to set up funeral arrangements, and then all headed back to Mom's to start an inventory and to make other arrangements.

The family was together, except for John's sister, Mary Beth, who was en route. As each sibling encountered another, each broke down and cried. It was a personal mourning time, made even more poignant by the fact that we were standing in Mom's apartment, surrounded by her things, her scent, and her familiar indomitable spirit.

Mary Beth, her husband and two little children had arrived finally from Washington state.

Richard and Nick, the trustees, explained the facts of the will. So typical of Mom and her fairness, all the items were placed in a pot. If no one desired an item, it would be put in the pot and others would have first choice or if unwanted, the item would be sold, and the money replaced in the pot and divided up among the five children.

The next morning, we again returned to Mom's home. Jobs were divvied up, and later the family started poring over old photos.

I knew Mom's humor, her staunch support of her family, her steadfast faith. Numerous anecdotes came to mind. As John and I prepared for a trip once with the family, I went for a haircut and requested a modified wedge. Before I could say a word, the beautician buzz cut one side of my head. Did I tell her not to do the other side? When I arrived and saw Mom Elizabeth, she took one look and asked, "What order of nuns are you joining?"

I could only laugh.

I flashed back to John telling me about being summoned to the Brother's office, the disciplinarian, at his Catholic high school.

The Brother just looked at John, shook his head and said, "Another Havel!"

John, 6' 3" high school football player, had patted a cute young nun's rear - anathema at that time and in that setting. I could only imagine his mother's reaction.

When together, the brothers started to reminisce. One brother, as an older teen, managed to seriously disengage the car during a date. The result, the car would go forward only. Totally unknowing, the next morning Mom loaded the small children into the car to go to mass, put the car in reverse and drove right through the front of the garage.

"Ooops! Out and into the other car," she exclaimed, "We're not going to be late for mass."

The garage was an ongoing topic of family teasing. That night, thirty or so years later, when the family assembled at her house, Nick confessed. The look of amazement and amusement on family faces was priceless.

Her humor was universal and equally applied.

"Children are much easier to raise after they're forty," Mom had quipped. Her Midwest no-nonsense Nebraska roots were evident.

Once while observing five Havels around the grill, our friend Ann asked Mom Elizabeth how many Havels it took to barbecue.

She shot a glance toward the grill and quickly responded, "Five of them or one of me!"

While her humor was ever good-natured and always entertaining, she was quick to defend and support her family and equally quick to not-so-gently reprimand, if appropriate.

The next morning, all of us drove off to the mortuary in Vacaville for a private family viewing, a public viewing, and a memorial service. Now it was time for me to face Mom's death.

The families made their way up to the open casket, where they knelt and prayed. The sheer terror of having to read during the memorial service was my one saving grace in helping me to regain my composure.

Drawing from past experience and his ordination as a priest, Tom began, "When I was ordained, my hands were anointed and then wrapped in a white cloth. The custom then, it was the priest's mother's privilege, or rather mine, to have his mother's hands wrapped in the same white cloth upon her death." He continued, "I learned more from my mother about faith than from all my schooling. If I have failed my faith in anyway, I have failed my mother."

He wove various poignant thoughts and feelings together in a moving tapestry of tribute.

"This is a family affair. I will not be the only one speaking," he explained. Nick rose and stepped to the podium. "I have driven up the freeway to see Mom always with a sense of anticipation. For she was not only my mother but a good friend, and I would look forward to talking with her as I drove the fifteen or so miles from Vallejo," he reminisced.

Nick too pulled in snippets from a lifetime of experience, and the strong influence that this matriarch exerted. All was told with love.

Next Richard rose and made his way up to the front of the group and said that his prepared talk wasn't right.

"Family and the strong sense of family that Mom instilled in me are a factor in my daily life," he began. "Each day I look at my wife and children and hope that I have done as well as she...."

Mary Beth then stepped up to the podium and said, "I have chosen a different lifestyle, many times in conflict with mother but...."She continued to speak of the tremendous impression, the imprimatur that was uniquely her mother's, that she too lived with day to day.

Father Tom interceded. "There is another son, John, who is perhaps the only one who didn't inherit the Havel sin of talking too much," he explained. "We know him as the gentle giant, a continuing symbol of Mom's love and devotion."

The memorial service ended, and the family adjourned to Retirement Gardens, Mom's retirement residence for a post-service reception/luncheon. John and I were driving Mom's car. There in the back window was a paperback entitled *"on the shores of paradise."* She was a voracious reader of all types of books, investment literature, classy trash, as she liked to call some popular novels, and a host of periodicals. I couldn't help but find that book prophetic.

No sooner did John and I enter the church with the baby than one lady approached us saying, "This must be Abigail Elizabeth. You know I've followed her since she was born."

One friend had written a spirited note to the family on a stick-it pad, saying she had talked with Elizabeth just Wednesday evening, and that Elizabeth had explained that she wasn't coming to dinner because she wanted to watch Joe Montana and the football game. This only confirmed my suspicion that football was a religious experience in the Havel family.

We arrived home later that day and Geoffrey went to pick up Chinese food for dinner. We unpacked and repacked readying for the next day's flight to Minneapolis, near the town of the family's roots and the foundation of so many memories.

At the airport the next morning, John bought a small globe keychain and gave it to Abbie proclaiming, "I bought her the world!"

The next morning, we drove several hours to Montgomery, Minnesota where the funeral mass and burial would take place. Montgomery was a quaint, small town that had suffered the ravages of time and technology. The main street had some boarded-up buildings while others such as the bakery and bars remained. Tom, the oldest, reminisced about spending summers there helping his uncle.

Father Tom said mass, and then ascended the pulpit.

"My faith and who I am, I owe to my mother," he began, immediately evoking thoughts of all of Mom's wonderful qualities.

After mass, we walked out slowly, somberly, pensively. We entered the cars and drove the few blocks to the cemetery where Tom officiated again.

We drove Tom back to the church to change and then on to the hotel. Tom asked to leave the town passing by the cemetery. The gravesite was quiet, peaceful. All was in order. There was no sign of a service an hour before. There, amidst the rolling green hills surrounding the cemetery, trees swayed in the breeze. The sun had come out and we left together. Mom's funeral said so much about the Havels.

My In-Between Years

John and Abbie years were jam-packed. While attending to the family, I continued to work. I had taken Churchill's interpreter Valentine Lawford's advice to heart when we lunched - New York was exciting but everyday life was very different. While moving to New York to explore other publications was enticing, the thought of living in that city with only a modicum of money was off-putting. And publishing was not known for high editorial salaries unless you were at the top of the magazine and at top magazines. I decided to stay on the left coast. Besides, I had lived in San Francisco for a year doing *Goodlife*, after which time, I longed to take out the trash and walk barefoot across a lawn. Strictly urban areas were fun but I was more for urban sprawl.

I had interviewed for west coast Editor for *Family Circle* and later for *Sunset* Magazine but to no avail.

I had worked on staff at *Goodlife* Magazine, *Society West*, The *Daily News*, and *Los Angeles Home and Garden* Magazine until I married John. I stayed home with Abbie until she was a three, and then worked part-time as contributing editor for the *Small Business Times* (published by *LA Business Journal*). At the time, if a new publisher or editor was hired, it was common for one or the other to bring in their team, so hopping from magazine to magazine was typical. All the while I freelanced for a host of upscale, travel and lifestyle magazines. I wanted to be near family and friends.

I took a job with a public relations/advertising firm that specialized in commercial real estate. The vice president, Ann (former food editor of the Dallas Times Herald), hired me over another applicant who played the saxophone. We joke frequently about her hiring me over the saxophone player. I am glad that she did. We remain life-long friends.

But real estate? I knew little, if anything, about the topic. My first press release was on a commercial project, and I froze when I saw "glulam truss walls." I was in over my head, or so I thought until I looked them up - these are simply large warehouse walls. After that, I was fine, whether writing about high-rises downtown or warehouse buildings secreted out in less-populated areas.

After five years of working together, Ann and I decided to open our own public relations/advertising business specializing in real estate. We had some sizeable clients and did quite well for five years but the drag of a recession and life's changes convinced us to move on.

After years of real estate, learning the ins and outs, doing ground breakings, and topping out ceremonies, it was time to make a change. Of course, I didn't segue into anything real estate related - that would have been too easy.

My next gig was as a consultant, for Uni Health Corporate Marketing and Communications.

Ann was consulting for them and had called me and said, "Why don't you try this? I think you'll like it."

This was akin to the backdoor of healthcare, working for IPAs (Independent Practice Associations) and medical groups. Basically we helped groups of independent physicians assert the bargaining power of large groups.

After a year, Ann decided to change careers and go for a master's degree in marriage and family counseling and tried to convince me to join her. Abbie was too young for me to leave her for large amounts of time, especially for the five or so years needed to go back to school, study and put in practical hours. Instead, I took a position at WellPoint for the UniCare division which was Blue Cross of California working in other states. John and I skewed our schedules so I took care of Abbie and got her to school in the morning, and he took the afternoon shift.

What an education in insurance! I worked in the Marketing Communications Department in the senior department - Medicare supplement insurance for individuals and small (usually employer) groups- creating brochures. But to write the brochures, I had to understand the products inside and out. I also created slide presentations for traveling corporate VPs. I tracked and managed agent/consumer direct mail and budgets, compliance (each state was different so I worked with the compliance manager to ensure that we were complying with the local laws), agent fulfillment (sending the correct brochures to selling agents) and helped roll out their new "Final Expense" product.

A vice president there told us early on, "Insurance is a simple business: the money you take in, the money you spend and profit."

We sat right next to the actuaries. That never meant much to me until I met them. These were brilliant chaps, most with Ph.D.'s in statistics, whose job it was to make sure that the company didn't lose money. The team of five or so actuaries would spend hours plugging in statistics in the computer and hit "run." For the next few hours, they played a hidden game in Excel until the computer had finished. They taught me how to access the game but I have no idea if it is still active or not. Occasionally, we would talk about classical music experiences or other cultural events. It was a most impressive team!

Then one of the Blue Cross vice presidents Susan B. left to take a position as CEO of Maxicare another health insurance company downtown. She offered me the Director of Marketing position. I accepted with glee and increased my understanding of insurance and the nuances even more as I learned about different groups, government programs, and launching new products in different states including dental plans, all the while rolling out collateral material and brochures for these.

The Chief Financial Officer(CFO) had cooked the books, otherwise known as he illegally kept two sets of books, unbeknownst to us and to the CEO. Soon we were all laid off and the company as we knew it closed.

Secret Smiles of a Special Ed Teacher

I was happy Sand content I but still wanted to help others, and I always had a soft spot for children. I enjoyed working with kids, in addition to wanting to share my education in school and out. And I had another education altogether studying and watching Abbie learn. I looked into becoming a substitute teacher, credentials for which were not as stringent as those of full-time teachers.

It was the time of another recession.

While meeting with our financial advisor at the time, one of his assistants said, "Well Laurie isn't going to go back to work again."

I just looked at him, indignant while railing to myself.

"How does he know that?" I thought.

After thirty-six years in the corporate world - as an editor of national and local consumer magazines and then as a marketing director of a health care insurance company, I shifted gears. I was told that I qualified for the District Intern Program, LAUSD's accredited in-house credentialing program. This program allowed qualified bachelor's degree holding candidates to finish their teaching credential in three years while working under intense supervision. Classes were held weekly one night a week and monthly all day on Saturdays. This amounted to going back to school full-time, while teaching full-time. This was somewhat grueling with a small daughter and a husband, but I survived and so did they. John pitched in and picked up the slack, thankfully.

I did things backward. I should have taught first and then become a parent, but that is twenty-twenty hindsight and we don't always have the luxury to do things in order.

At age fifty-seven, I decided that I wanted to teach special education students. When asked why I wanted to teach special ed., I always said I wanted to give my students what I wanted for my daughter - a lofty expectation. I'm told I have patience, sometimes too much and, lord knows, I'm a softy.

Still what a ride!

As one of my professors told me, "Parents don't send these kids to school and save the best at home." My ten-year tenure as a special ed teacher of a middle-school special day class for students with specific learning disabilities, gave me a new outlook on life and shaped me.

My first year was a stunner. I'd spent six months as a substitute teacher for middle and high school, but I had just started teaching and was going to school full time.

I dreamed of magic lessons that would entice the students to learn. I wanted to market ideas and captivate this young audience. But this is not quite how teaching works.

I worked tirelessly each night crafting, creating, and simplifying concepts and working to present them in visual, audio if possible, or kinetic modes so the students would grasp the main ideas.

John had always teased me about being a kid at heart. He attributed it to skipping my teen years because I was so seriously dedicated to playing volleyball. Still I would like to think that I had a compassion for and an understanding of the tweens.

I had a mélange of students, five periods daily of sixth and seventh graders. I had students who had A.D.H.D., traumatic brain injuries, fetal alcohol syndrome, learning disabilities, autism, spina bifida, bipolar and obsessive compulsive disorder. And I had to know their personalities, histories and diagnoses thoroughly to teach them. They were great kids, some more mature than others and a splay of behaviors to match. They were first and foremost kids with all the normal growing pains of tweens.

My sixth graders were an incredible mix - mix matters, trust me. I had several students with A.D.H.D. who talked like auctioneers with no impulse control coupled with chattiness. Two arch rivals in elementary school and with the same name, the twin Andys, fought mightily and wound up in the dean's office. Voila, they became best friends and remained friends for years. A bussed-in student, Terry, was volatile and angry. His life had been chaotic. I found out that this young student had never had a bed, among a host of other basics, and I was crestfallen. How could I work around this and get him one? I worked behind the scenes with the therapist but there was no way without inducing embarrassment and pointing up poverty.

I leaned over one day to show Terry an answer on the page and his attention immediately departed. Instead, he reached up and started jiggling the skin on my upper arm. I paused, worked hard to keep a straight face, and agreed that I needed to exercise.

Even though this was my first year teaching, I viewed the world of hormone-hyped tweens through rose-colored glasses and classes.

I went home that night and John asked, "How was your day?"

I paused. "Fine, I think."

I was still reeling from the behaviors.

My eyes opened wide, and I said, "Oh, fine," as I replayed the events of the day.

Toto, I was no longer in the corporate world.

Classroom management is driven into teachers in school, and I took it lightly until my first year. In fact, student behaviors ruled, all manner of behaviors. I toughened a little each year clamping down on the behaviors.

One day before class started, my early morning comers, seventh graders, marched in and they were atwitter.

One student came up to me and said, "Mrs. H., we saw snail porn."

Science in seventh grade covers anatomy, human and otherwise.

With a straight face but chuckling to myself, I said, "So you saw a film of two snails getting it on?"

N immediately exploded, "Mrs. H., I don't believe you said that!"

They all seemed so shocked that I might know what they were talking about.

Dealing with immature middle schoolers has many fascinating facets and is prone to elicit secret smiles. During the first few years that I taught, I had a half-circle computer table in my room which typically seated one to two students during class. The table had a small circle hole through which computer wires were to be passed to avoid chord chaos. One afternoon just before the final dismissal bell, one of my lithe sixth graders with little impulse control, decided to start playing with the hole. He eventually stood up and stuck his arm through the hole acting as though his arm had been cut off and was severed. Hoots and laughs rang out. Then I told the student to remove his arm. He laughed and moved his arm up and down through the hole without fully removing it. He developed a sheepish look. I went over to make sure that he extricated his arm, and I could tell by the look on his face that he was "caught with his arm in the cookie jar," literally. He was stuck. I called maintenance who had no luck getting his arm out and so the school called the fire department and his parents. By this time, it was three o'clock. Nearby teachers were poking their heads in because they couldn't believe it, and were curious about the entourage of firemen.

By this time, the student was scared. All the up and down had irritated his arm, and it swelled slightly. The firemen took out a saw, and after a few short tries, abandoned the hack saw and pulled out the electric rotating saw. I worked to calm the student who by this time had eyes the size of saucers. He was getting panicky. The firemen finally took a chunk out of the table to the edge, and the student pulled his arm out. His mother was there to greet him. She rolled her eyes and talked to her son. I was late for class that night, but I figured I had a good excuse.

One time I fudged and took my seventh grade class to the library for a library orientation, usually reserved for the sixth grade. But this class was teacher deaf, and had little memory retention. Somehow they had managed the year before to miss all the hallmarks of English Language Arts that they were supposed to know. Research? Ha, they had just finished a "light" cross-curricular project on history, and only three had managed to open their history books for relevant information.

One presented a project on China, supposed to touch on the Silk Road. It talked about China a little and then digressed talking about the poetry of Italian poet Petrarch - just a continent away.

One time I took one of my sixth-grade classes to the library for an orientation. The librarian was a seasoned teacher/librarian, and we had conferred about levels of comprehension and more. She introduced the library and then set the kids off on a scavenger hunt. All went well until one girl unleashed her caustic remarks to another boy. He replied in kind and she counter attacked. I quickly quieted them both. The librarian asked if they were brother and sister.

"No," I replied, "They just like to fight."

The next day I passed the librarian and she said jokingly, "I don't know what you're on, but I want some!"

I took that as a compliment.

One afternoon, my reading-resistant sixth grade class was slogging through a story in the reader. I asked a question about the story, and several students raised their hands. One student seemed sleepy and inattentive. I walked from the front of the room to the desk in front of his and sat on the desk, repeating the question. He still looked dazed.

Later, my paraeducator clued me in that he had had his hand on his crotch for some time. Teachers are supposed to change the lesson or the pace under circumstances like that but my line of vision was not there. Next time!

About the beginning of my fifth year of teaching, I was in the midst of an open house, greeting parents and students. One of my most memorable students, now in high school, Jerry had come back to visit. I was elated to see him, hugged him, and continued talking to the parents of the new sixth graders. If nothing else, you learn to be flexible as a teacher and so I continued. The parents watched, smiled, and continued listening.

The entire three years that Jerry was in middle school, we had a tenacious, contentious relationship. He drove me crazy in class by talking constantly, answering every question with "Chuck Norris," all the while being at the ready to help me in any way possible. If I needed to get the cover off the thermostat, he worked tirelessly to figure out how to do it and would explain the process to me. He visited before class in the morning and would sit atop the cabinets. I allowed him to do this because he was agile, a climber and he needed this freedom to gear up for the day. Strict rule though, he was not to do this when anyone else was in the room.

When I met him, he was sitting crouched in the bottom of an audio/video stand beneath a T.V., wheeling in from the honors class from which he was transferring into my class. Incidentally, just before he graduated, he helped me return an AV stand and T.V. and he again rode in the bottom with another student pushing the cart.

Later when he was in eighth grade, he would finish his work and get permission towards the end of the year to hang out in my class. The class was full so he sat in the sink. (My classroom was formerly a home economics room.)

At the end of the night, I met with one typically concerned parent - middle school scares most parents, multiple classes and teachers, lockers, gym clothes and a host of other new experiences. This parent was the mother of a bright, attention-challenged, and very sensitive young boy. I was trying to assuage her angst when Jerry returned from his teacher visitations, entered the classroom quietly walking past all the empty desks and chairs and sat in the sink.

The parent looked and couldn't help but comment, "He's sitting in the sink." "I know," I said with a smile, "It's his spot."

The parent shook her head and continued. She seemed to calm at my answers and departed. He immediately hopped atop the cabinets.

About a year later, I had a call on my cellphone one evening. The voice said, "Who's this?"

I said, "You called me," chuckling. "My name is Laurie."

"Hi, this is Jerry," he said, two octaves lower than I had ever heard him.

Resourceful, he tracked my number back to a call I made to his mother – must have been two years or more before. He called to tell me that he had just returned from Washington, D.C. He and his team of five from high school had just taken second place nationally in a cybersecurity competition. He was doing well in school with three A's and 2 C's the latter in English and art.

He asked a favor, that I tell another teacher about his competition. "I want him to be proud of me too!" he said. "Oh, and tell him that I met X. He'll know what that means."

There is nothing like the ingenuousness of middle schoolers. What you see is what you get. I tried to respond in kind.

Teaching world history, Southeast Asia to middle schoolers was a challenge. What are the capitals of the countries? They falter on the capitals till they work their way to Thailand. There is a cacophony of laughter and periodically every few minutes until I stopped it. A student raises his hand and asks what the capital of Thailand is. Bangkok.

Teaching religious sects was another pleaser. Students were sure that I was saying sex until it's spelled out on the board.

A typical middle school day:

Two students are signing four-letter words back and forth to each other the word was not love.

Tessa breaks down crying because one girl won't be her friend. (Probably will change the next day.)

Uri talks the TA (teacher's assistant) into printing KFC bucket of chicken photo on teacher's computer. He stands and tapes it to the back of another student.

Jon sits through almost an entire class pounding his fist with his other hand. He was jealous that his "girlfriend" was talking to two eighth grade TAs.

Mika becomes upset because he thinks that the pencil lent to him by the teacher was taken by another student. He proceeds to the next class, picks up a desk ready to throw it at that student. Fortunately, he was stopped before it was airborne.

Teacher called Mika out of the classroom and explained that it is unacceptable to pass gas in the classroom, and that he should feel free to walk outside if he felt it coming on. He should also step out of line to do it as well. Mika said that he understood and continued into the classroom to loudly announce to the class and me that he has not taken his meds today and this is how he acts. There were a few others too who did not take meds and their behavior on those days was astounding.

Roger continued to act up talking and distracting all. He was sent next door to Mr. R's classroom. After a short time, my assistant was summoned to Mr. R's classroom. Chuckling to himself, he suggested that she retrieve Roger because the eighth graders were ready to beat him up for his laughing and comments.

As class ended, Eddie came up to me - a perfectly behaved and very bright student who spent four months in resource classes in which the teachers never heard his voice. He never spoke. Suddenly he blurted out, "If Mika comes back I don't know what I'll do. He was talking and teasing everyone"

"Wow!" I thought.

One day, I heard one girl wailing and crying outside my door. I summoned her in the classroom and asked what the matter was.

"I just broke up with my boyfriend, "she said tearfully.

"How long have you been boyfriend and girlfriend?" I asked.

"One day," she said.

Another day one sixth grader had irritated another student. As she left the classroom, the other student screamed out at her, "You're gay!"

She shrugged and started to continue on. I called both back into the classroom.

I asked both of them, "Do you know what the word "gay" means?"

Both looked at me and said, "No."

A talking to them about name-calling and not using words that you don't know the meaning of ensued.

At the beginning of one year, a wide-eyed sixth grader came into my classroom before the start of school. I said, "Good morning, Reed"

"I have a project to do," he blurted out.

"Really," I said. "Which teacher is it for?" I asked.

"Mrs. W.," he said. "I don't have a lot of decorating stuff at home."

I could tell that he was more than overanxious about his project. I sat down and read the instructions and said, "I can help you with this. I have plenty of decorating stuff."

"Really," he answered incredulously. "Can teachers help students?"

It was time to retire. John wanted to travel and embark on adventures. I was most complimented when my general education peers asked for copies of my lesson plans.

Heart and Health John's parents both had had heart problems so if he experienced severe indigestion or any symptom that may be heart-related, he did not hesitate, he went straight to the emergency room, for which I was grateful. Once when I was working in Camarillo, he called and said he had taken Abbie to lunch at McDonalds, and he would leave her at the neighbors. He was heading to the ER for just such a scare. I panicked. Traffic on the 101 Freeway was thick, and I was ready to get out of the car and start running - foolhardy but that's how I felt. Fortunately, all turned out ok.

Another time, his cardiologist, whom we both loved, Dr. F. took him in the cardiac catheter lab for a blockage. She discovered an aneurysm and with seven stents reconstructed the artery before any severe complications.

Once after he had had an arterial heart procedure at the catheter lab, I had been told, that if there was any blood at the incision site, to call 911 immediately. I was terrified. Every hour on the hour, I checked his groin incision.

After a few hours of this, he lifted my blouse and said, "If you get to look, so do I!" cutting through my terror with humor.

He read me like a book. There was little I could hide from him.

Whether it was a liver biopsy for a suspected fatty liver when he was in his forties or knee surgery at age seventy, I always brought him home, and we weathered all together.

When we first met, I told John I would not ask him to keep up with me since I have a great deal of energy. I was always strong and in good health. But when I turned fifty-seven, my heart started beating fast. The ER nurse asked who my cardiologist was.

I said, "I don't have one."

The nurse said, "You will now."

John worried about the atrial fibrillation, he fretted and took me to the emergency room numerous times to ensure that I avoided a stroke. I had two ablations to counter the A-fib. The first was a breeze but the second knocked me for weeks. It had been a four-hour ordeal and the technology and knowledge had advanced significantly since five years before when I had my first.

I went to see a cardiologist whom I referred to as my "plumber" cardiologist, whom John had seen years before and who was revered by hospital staff. When the subject of an ablation came up, I spoke with his partner but decided to see another specialist, an "electrician" cardiologist, who oversees the electrical impulses of the heart, for this procedure. My plumber cardiologist told me that the rule of thumb was an eighty percent success rate with first and a ninety percent with the second. Knock wood, the second has held so far thankfully. My heart is strong so I've stayed positive. Heart problems were a post-fifty gift that I was not too fond of and it cut into my coffee drinking.

John was a white-knuckle dentist goer. He told me that he saw a dentist named Dr. Ivy when he was younger. Dr. Ivy was a wizened older man. John, at the time, was robust and dentist phobic. Dr. Ivy put John in the chair and started examining his mouth and teeth. John had grabbed the arms of the chair and held tightly - so tightly that he pushed one whole chair arm off on the floor. Dr. Ivy ran out of the room.

The Northridge Earthquake of 1994 was a hallmark on many fronts. Saint John's shut down for nine months due to structural damage. John understandably was incredibly upset and with great support from family and me, he took a job at Grossman Burn Center in Sherman Oaks. He interviewed there and was told that they would hire him but that he had to account for his 300 glucose level. He was diagnosed with Type Two Diabetes. At least I knew the reason behind his newfound fondness for gulping down fruit juice. So John had diabetes, high blood pressure and high cholesterol, quite a combination. I set about studying dietary considerations. I had already switched to sweet butter (butter with no salt) and made other changes for blood pressure, but now a new wrinkle. I set out to learn about diabetes and diet.

His time at the Grossman Burn Center had a big impact on him.

"I thought I'd seen it all with stroke patients and others. Here the burn patients can be happy and alert one day and overnight turn toxic and die. And there is a whole floor of AIDS patients who are suffering," he lamented.

Geoff Returns and Retires

Geoff returned to live with us during the week and commute home on the weekends, when Abbie was a teen. The corporate headquarters, where he worked, was near our house and we no longer had a cat. He quickly found out how humbling dealing with a teen is.

Geoff's witticisms were never ending. He categorized everyone and liked referring to John and Abbie as my "competitive eaters." They both had a fondness for food.

Despite the fact that they met while working in a hospital, Geoff's distaste for most things medical didn't wane. He had no love of doctors other than for those he knew personally. While in his late twenties, Geoff was playing softball and broke his finger. He visited the emergency room, had it set, and hopped a plane for a distant continent and never went back to a doctor for his finger, which healed crookedly.

A world traveler, he had just returned from a trip to Machu Pichu with his brother Doug. His fondness for food had expanded to include wine since he and his brother were planning on opening a winery. As FedEx delivered these vineyard treasures, he generously shared.

When I finished a three-year program to get my teaching credential in special ed, I was bowled over when he came home early one night and announced that we were going shopping. Voila, a top-of-the-line new refrigerator! A graduation gift he claimed.

Geoff also had a lifelong fascination with Native Americans. In fact, as he groused about the machinations of the health insurance company where he worked, he avowed an interest and dedication to writing a history book.

All three of us celebrated Geoff's sixty-fifth birthday at Saddle Peak Lodge, a restaurant known for its fine cuisine, particularly game. He kept talking about retiring, but discovered that golden parachutes were soon to be given out. He decided to stay for a time. A half year trudged by and just after Christmas, he came home one day and announced that he had retired.

"Do you have the number?" I asked, referring to the book and the amount needed to retire comfortably.

"Yes," he smiled.

Geoff then moved permanently to Phoenix. He promised he would be returning to do history research at UCLA's Powell Library. He sold his deceased mother's car (he had three at that time) to us for two dollars for Abbie. He had sold us a Jeep a decade earlier for one dollar just before John was to drove him to LAX to catch a plane to Phoenix.

When they arrived at the airport, John leaned over and said, "Geoff, I have to borrow back the single dollar to get out of the parking lot!" This time Geoff insisted on two dollars cash for the car, no returns!

We talked frequently by phone while he was working to clean out his late mother's belongings and organize her condo in Phoenix.

One night in April, John and I were sitting in front of our house much cooler in front than back in the San Fernando Valley and I called Geoff. He was his usual dry-witted self. He told us he had cut back on some of his activities since he was almost done cleaning out his late mom's place, but he explained that he had developed swollen feet.

I immediately jumped on him, "Geoff, swollen feet are nothing to play with. It's not like a bump or bruise. It could indicate that something is going on with your heart."

"Yes, dear," he responded. "I'm fine. Just resting."

These regular conversations continued through May and early June. John and I were both on him to go to the doctor.

"I couldn't go to the urgent care center," he said. "I spent half the night ironing my pants. Didn't have any to wear."

The next time we talked, he said, "I've screwed up my Medicare card."

"You wait much longer, and your Medicare card won't matter," I said.

John got on the phone and talked to him in his soothing tone of voice and cajoled him to go get his swollen feet and now his raspy voice from bronchitis taken care of.

"Do we have to come over there and drive you?" John asked.

"No, I'm fine," he assured us.

Mid-June, John and I called and there was no answer. Nothing unusual for Geoff, who often returned calls in a day or so. No call. We called again and again over a three-week period. No response.

"John, I have a bad feeling about this," I said.

He agreed.

Finally, we dug out his brother Doug's number. We dialed the Denver, Colorado, prefix and got him. "Hi, Doug, this is John. How are you? Have you heard from Geoff lately? We've tried to call and haven't been able to reach him nor have we gotten a call back," John started.

"You know; I haven't heard from him either for a few weeks. I thought I 'd go down in a few weeks and visit," Doug said.

"It's been quite a while," John said. "We actually thought of calling the police and asking them to do a wellness check. We thought maybe it would be better if you, his brother, called."

"Ok," Doug said. "I'll call and call you back."

John and I started dinner. A while later, the phone rang.

"Hi, Doug," John said. His demeanor turned serious. "So, he is dead and he has been so for a while? He threw a blood clot to his lung."

My heart sank.

Snapshots

John and I were dedicated to Abbie who grew up with Dad's adventure rides and ice cream cones. John would scoop her up, and they would hop in the car and head off to the top of the nearest mountain or the beach or whatever struck their fancy. Of course, an ice cream cone was obligatory on the way home.

John arranged his work hours so that he could be home in the afternoons and help Abbie with her homework while I worked corporate long hours downtown. Consequently, for a time he got up at 3 A.M. and left shortly after showering. Later the scenario switched and I was home earlier to take over homework chores.

When Abbie was in high school, she spent more time with friends out and about and John and I were freed to spend time alone at home or going on our own adventure rides.

He was an avid T.V. watcher and loved the Food Channel. He would say, "Laur, take a look at this recipe. Sounds good."

Food initiated our meeting so it was only natural that we would continue the tradition.

We would try it and we would unofficially rate it. And yes, he did occasionally fry baloney and take-out pizza was a staple in our house. Both John and Abbie loved pizza.

He also loved grilling and developed a penchant for smoking food. As he grilled we would sit on the back patio, listen to music on the portable speaker, and talk. I would sometimes flashback to when Abbie was a tyke.

One night he checked the barbecue, turned around and said, "The grill is ready. Hop on, Abbie!"

I chided him for the remark since she had just barely learned that fires, stoves, and grills could be hot. Abbie just smiled. Even at a young age, she had sized up dad's sense of humor.

John's humor permeated our lives. When she started making noises as a young infant, he'd walk by and say, "Say Dada first and I'll buy you a Mercedes."

An older Abbie would watch T.V. with John and the two would joke through the show. Occasionally their taste in shows differed. She tired of food, travel or house renovation and wanted to watch murder shows. We adapted.

Over the years, John and I grew together and closer with time, anticipating each other's needs, wants and well-being. He loved to shop while my tolerance for shopping was about an hour. We ran errands with each other, explored, and took adventure rides. And when we were going to purchase something of import like an appliance, he wanted to shop every available option. He was very thorough.

Together was the happiest place to be. John and I spent almost all our time together. He did not lobby for a night out with the "boys," and I managed to duck out of non-mandatory evening meetings. When I had to go, I resented spending time away from him.

All of our alarm codes and pin numbers for accounts were John's birthday. He had no trouble remembering that, and he was not good at writing codes/pins down. I received his continuing education requirements for his radiology license via email as well as alerts from the big and tall clothes shop that he liked. I was forever on the hunt for information on type two diabetes and dyslexia. Our lives were intertwined.

Saturdays were the day we picked up sandwiches for lunch as a treat. All three of us enjoyed them. John would tease the local sandwich shop owners who laughed in return. Then we would watch "The Kitchen" for inspirational ideas for that night, later or whatever holiday season was pending. Abbie too developed a love of cooking and frequently cooked for her friends.

John helped his friend David Saxby build two houses, but still John had little confidence in his fix-it skills. When there was an imperative fix-it job around the house, John would go to Home Depot or Lowe's and buy a tool belt or tool bucket. He would then fill it with whatever tools were necessary for the job. Later he would ask me where the specific tool was.

"What does it look like and when did you last use it?" I would ask.

After a description, I would hunt down the tool.

Sundays, while Abbie slept in, John and I would watch the political shows on T.V. and discuss them. I probably drove him crazy since I would turn them on or news if ever there was a lull in T.V. watching. He managed to stay up on what was going on but was rarely discussed with others. John and I though would share ideas. He offered insightful analysis, a different perspective, thought provoking nonetheless.

One sizzling 113-degree afternoon, John called me en route home from work to let me know that his car had died only a few blocks away from home. I quickly hopped in the car and sped over there to give him a respite from the heat with my car air-conditioning as he awaited AAA to get his car going again. We sat in the car for a while but then thought it might be compromising the car in the heat so we sat on the wall nearby. No doubt AAA was busy with the heat. Finally, AAA arrived and John and I drove home. John was fine. I was red-faced and sweating. It took about four hours for me to cool off and regain my normal facial hue.

John's impish side was always at the ready. When we first acquired iPhones with Siri, John had a great time. After a few simple questions and answers from Siri, he peppered her with irreverent questions.

"Siri, you don't know much do you?"

"I don't have an answer for that," she replied.

Alexa was another case in point. If John wanted to stop the music and turn on the T.V., in his deep rumbling voice, he would say, "Alexa stop!" This was the suggested command to turn her off. She never did. He couldn't say it gruffly enough to get her to stop. Abbie or I would have to intervene. So typical of John.

John was a protector and a worrier. I would say I was going for a walk on the metro path.

He would instantly say, "Wait till I come home from a doctor's appointment."

This fits with his brother's recounting of traveling as children.

His siblings would ask, "When are we going to be there?"

John would ask, "Do we have enough gas to get there?"

Our neighborly relations evolved over thirty years. Axel used to come down to our house and fix anything wood. He was a natural carpenter. He had a repertoire of jokes that kept us laughing. His jokes were from a generation or more before us so they were frequently new to us.

Over a period of thirty years, our neighborhood changed. Tom and Martha lived next door, and had become Grandpa and Grandma to Abbie. Tom died when he was in his late seventies, and Martha moved away.

Lilly and Mike were almost part of the family with their blended family. The girls Leah and Timolyn would play with baby Abbie and half-brother Derek joined in sometimes. I drove the girls to school. Lilly staged Easter egg hunts for Abbie and showered us with child-friendly Tupperware. I frequently fed them all, but I had hard and fast child rules: "You don't have to like or eat the food but you do have to taste it. And, if you eat with your hands, you move to the floor with the cat."

It was rather like living in Mr. Roger's Neighborhood.

Eventually Lilly and Mike moved away as did Joyce and Barb and others but Axel remained. He had heart issues and was wheelchair bound from an amputation due to peripheral artery disease.

Deb, John, and I adopted Axel. Deb drove him around when needed, after Axel decided in his mid-eighties that he should stop driving. We made sure he was active and entertained.

He came over on the weekends, and I would fix brunch and frequently took dinner over to him. John checked on him daily. When Axel became less self-sufficient, our mutual friend Deb moved in with him. John spelled her when she had to go out. My job was to organize his meds – a most nerve-wracking job since his prescriptions were very powerful. One error could be catastrophic.

Deb would take Axel gambling at major casinos in the area which he loved or on her rounds cleaning pools, but then his health declined that much more and he became homebound. Deb was there, and John would go up daily or when needed.

Deb had to check on something one weekend, so John went up to cover. John became so anxious I thought I was going to have to take him to the ER. After I called, Deb returned. Two days later, the hospice nurse stopped by. Deb called me at three in the afternoon and alerted me that he had passed. I immediately alerted John and went up there. Deb sat with Axel for several hours. The three of us reminisced about Axel and bid him goodbye.

Unbeknownst to me, Axel had left his house to Deb and John.

It is ironic that we had all our neighbors for dinner nightly in the early days, when our kitchen was somewhat closed in. When we inherited money from the house, we decided to remodel. We gutted the kitchen, bathroom and installed new windows, a bay window, and French doors. By that time, though our entertaining pace had slowed, we had the kitchen of our dreams.

John and I collaborated on every detail, but I acted as the project manager while John was at work. I had an exciting chance to raid my imagination which had been fed during my time at Architectural Digest. I scheduled the workers and kept a good working relationship with all. I frequently scooped up sandwiches for lunch and plied them with sodas. Some even did piece work for us later. And we were lucky to have had help and support from our nephew Tom, an architect.

One day the head of the electrical team/company appeared at our door and introduced himself. I wondered if he was here to check in on his guys.

"We have been working on a huge project in Northern California, a retirement home and they didn't put us on a schedule, but you did! I had to come meet the lady who put us on a schedule," he said.

I chuckled.

Retirement

John and I were in our late-sixties and time had not been kind to his joints. He walked with a hike since he had arthritis in his knees. Along with years of being overweight, the stress of lifting patients had taken their toll. He was thinking about retiring. Both of us had slowed down.

He retired in 2018. I wanted to work one more year, which I did. We made plans to travel to see our good friends in California - John and Kathy in Nipomo, Lynn and Mike in Fresno, Laura and Tom in Carmel and north to Los Altos and Oakland to visit family. Should we do it in one trip or break it up? John wanted to plan a trip to New Orleans, a destination that had always fascinated me. He wanted to see the trees change on the East Coast. I wanted to visit antebellum houses in the South.

This was fun! Once I got over the feeling that I had to be somewhere every morning stemming from working since I was seventeen, I settled in adapting my schedule to him. We spent all day together.

John looked at me one day and said understatedly with a smile, "Well I guess our marriage has withstood us spending 24/7 hours together."

There were no hiccups. We loved spending time together.

John's knees became worse, particularly his right knee. He had already put off knee replacement for two years and his mobility was sorely reduced. Finally, in 2020, he decided to go ahead with the knee replacement. Great! I thought. Now he can walk with me daily, and we can move ahead with travel plans.

In September, he went through with the surgery. That evening, he was prodded to get out of bed and walk, as I watched. The anesthesia and implanted pain killer were still active. He walked up and down the hall and said, "This is great.! Let's do the other knee tomorrow." Pain set in shortly after, dampening his enthusiasm for doing the other knee right away.

John was reticent about walking up the three home steps when he was released from the hospital. Richard and Arlene drove out for moral support.

John kept saying, "Arlene, standing behind me is probably not a good place to be."

He maneuvered the stairs and into the house without a snag. We all talked for a short time before they left. John was sitting in his new recliner chair, and after a time, decided to go lie down. The only problem was that he could not get his knee bent enough to propel himself out of the chair.

Argh! I was beside myself. I could not pull him up but spied a postal worker in a truck outside. I ran outside and begged this young man to come in and help me to get John, just home from knee replacement surgery, out of the chair. The postal worker looked at me incredulously perhaps wondering what I wanted from him. He came in and together we lifted him out of the chair. I thanked the postman and tipped him handsomely. I was so grateful.

We were both impressed with his team of doctors, the preparation and follow up. He had a home health nurse and physical therapist, both of whom were caring and knowledgeable.

The physical therapist, Yonnis, arrived the first day and said, "Just think of me as Mr. Pain."

That was John's cue to tease him unmercifully. He and John developed an entertaining repartee joking back and forth. John wanted me to observe all of these sessions so I could duplicate them in between the twice a week sessions. He was making good progress with excellent knee range, and Yonnis wanted him to walk a block.

John grabbed his cane and off we went. For several days, he walked a little more each day.

Then one day we were about four or five houses away and John said, "I'm going back home. I don't feel well."

A cold chill overtook me. His words scared me. Trying not to jump all over him, I said, "What does that mean? Where don't you feel well?"

There was nothing in the knee surgery binder about not feeling well.

He began to lose weight, quite a bit and quite unusual for him. When we were first married, he left his wedding ring home when he went on the horseback trip, since he didn't want to lose it. I immediately swooped in and had it engraved: "9/10/88 Onederful 11/24/88." The only snag, the engraver put '89. Since it was summer, which pre-dated September and November, I wondered what the jeweler was thinking. John and I just chuckled and subtracted a year whenever we checked his ring.

He told me that he had lost his wedding ring around the house. He had lost so much weight that it fell off his finger. I immediately went on the hunt and found it tucked under the trash bag fold on our trash can. I quickly put it in a secure place and so hoped this was not a portent.

One night in late October his internist called and said, "John, your liver blood panel is way off."

Curious, I thought since his blood work before the knee replacement less than a month ago was fine. We saw the internist just days later.

Dr. G. took one look at me and said, "Hmmm, usually when the spouse comes there is greater urgency."

I whipped out my list of worrying symptoms. He suggested we see the gastroenterologist and so we set up an appointment just a few days later. Dr. K. wanted to do an endoscopy and a colonoscopy. The colonoscopy was postponed but he did undergo the endoscopy, and all was fine. Good news.

John suddenly insisted on listening to Christmas carols whenever we drove somewhere. I never said anything, but deep down I think he thought this may be his last Christmas.

Tests were scheduled at a good clip, but Thanksgiving delayed his MRI for a few days. Meanwhile, I was peppering his gastroenterologist with questions: Can bile ducts be stented? Can a portal vein be stented? Still, I was frustrated since nothing had been done to treat whatever it was that was making him feel ill. Was I asking the right questions?

Richard and Arlene checked in regularly to talk to John and check on him. He had dropped almost forty pounds.

"Is Laurie taking good care of you," Richard asked.

"I have to go to the bathroom to get away from her," John responded.

I smiled when I heard this for, I have never been the good nursemaid. I was trying. Unfortunately, my first instinct was panic, what can I do to help? My next instinct usually was to run, but not this time.

We sent the MRI to our nephew, my sister's third oldest of six, who was finishing up his residency in radiology at Johns Hopkins. He basically went over the MRI with us on the phone and confirmed the report and mentioned a possible blockage.

Dr. K., the gastroenterologist recommended a biopsy and scheduled it shortly. The biopsy confirmed our worst fears, it was cancer of the liver. Dr. K. suggested we see the Liver Transplant team at Cedars Sinai Hospital. That was Wednesday. We set up an appointment for the following Monday. I worked to keep John's spirits up and fanned my trust in medical knowledge and innovation.

Despite his discomfort, he was never cross, short-tempered, or cranky.

Family rallied. Mary Beth, his sister, called to talk to John. Nick, Tom, nephew Tom, and others called too. That family closeness came to the fore. My sister and brother checked in regularly.

Monday, we saw the transplant team who said there are options. I asked why his liver couldn't just be removed.

"His body wouldn't tolerate it," he explained.

John was having a tough time that Monday, retching and not feeling well.

That night the transplant team called and said his blood work was way off and the doctor wanted me to drive him to the ER to admit him to the hospital. It was five o'clock, terrible traffic hour in Los Angeles. Off we went.

"I have a bad feeling about this," he said.

After months of cheerleading his mood and nurturing hope, I was at a loss for words. I could think of nothing to counter his feelings.

He was scheduled to undergo tests, and later called me to ask that I bring the iPad on Tuesday so he could do some Christmas shopping. Tuesday night he was up to use the bathroom and to prevent himself from falling, he grabbed the countertop injuring his shoulder and leg. He was plagued by pain. Wednesday, he could only hold still for forty-five minutes during the MRI of his abdomen due to leg pain. I was waiting to hear if that was enough, and what the x-rays of his leg showed. He was on his third day of a heparin drip for a blood clot in his lung, typical they told me of this type of cancer.

Early in the week, John called me at night and said, "Laurie, you need to call the administration here and tell them that there is a man who comes in in the middle of the night and steals all the chords."

I was stunned, knowing that he was hallucinating. He had high levels of ammonia hence the delusions. They gave him medication for that, which quelled it.

Wednesday the oncologist talked with us and told us his liver needed to be able to slough off or flush out poisons before he can start immunotherapy. The cancer has spread throughout liver, and there was a blockage.

John asked, "How long do I have - three months, six months?"

The oncologist answered, "I don't like to talk in time."

My mind went blank. This wasn't what was supposed to have happened.

I kept asking questions, "Can the portal vein be stented? Can the bile ducts be stented? When can we start chemotherapy?"

There were no answers, and little was done to treat his liver. It had been two months from when he said he didn't feel good. Surely this couldn't take him so quickly.

The Liver Team called. They were going to give him meds to reduce confusion from elevated amounts of ammonia in his system. They were trying to get his bilirubin down to start chemo. His blood level was three but now has jumped to eleven. His liver portal vein was occluded from cancer.

I found out later he had hepatocellular cancer with portal vein thrombosis, usually an aggressive form of cancer and difficult to treat. John had been diagnosed about fifteen years before with a fatty liver. I had no idea what that meant nor did he, I think. I was figuring out.

John wanted me to stay longer at the hospital Wednesday evening after the doctor's bad news.

"John, Sweetie, I've been here since 9 A.M. I'll be back bright and early tomorrow, I said.

I couldn't stay. I had to go home and cry hysterically. I was numb. No chemotherapy and no hope extended. I called him about an hour after I had arrived home and finished crying.

"John, truth be known, I had to come home and cry hysterically. I wasn't going to do that in your hospital room."

He said nothing. I think he understood.

Thursday his brother Richard came to visit.

Only one visitor was allowed at a time so when I returned John said, "Wasn't that nice of Richard to come and visit?"

It was never about him.

It was high Covid time, so I was masked, and they kept putting a mask on John as well. I stroked his forehead and cheeks as he dealt with the pain. Kissing through a mask was most unrewarding, especially when I am such a "touchy feelie" person.

Friday morning Nick sent a beautiful poem and asked me to read it to John. Stephanie sent a text asking to talk with him. My brother was ready to drive down from Redding in Northern California to sit with John. My sister, the hospice nurse, had been in regular almost daily touch via phone asking about every detail and offering to come to the hospital to advocate for John. Brother Tom also had been on the phone with me regularly.

Early Friday morning, John had the nurse dial our house line. Uh oh, I thought, why didn't he use his cell phone? My heart sank.

"Laurie, they are not letting in any visitors tomorrow because of Covid," he said.

Terror struck. I felt John's angst over being alone.

"John, don't worry. I'll find a way to get in if I have to scale the outside of the tower," I said.

I was up early and on my way to the hospital, when the radio played "Celebrate Me Home" I quickly shut the radio off and prayed that John would come home with me. He always had before. I cried and couldn't imagine life without him.

When I arrived, he seemed lucid. I was so pleased.

"Have you seen the Saxbys? They just called." he asked.

"No," I said, "They're driving here."

He liked that. Their drive was over an hour.

He was fitful, uncomfortable, and kept asking me to move his legs, raise and then lower his bed. Finally, after about a half hour, he calmed and seemed to doze off. I rejoiced that he was comfortable enough to sleep. I went downstairs to check in with family by phone, and his best friend David Saxby went up to sit with him. I called Abbie to let her know that her dad wasn't doing well.

Nephew Tom had come by the hospital in the hopes of seeing him but since only two visitors were allowed, he had been turned away. We spoke in the parking lot, and I told him how sorry I was that he couldn't see John.

"Will he be starting chemo today?" I asked the doctor and nurses at the station.

"No chemo today. His blood work is worse and his kidneys are shutting down," she said. I teared up. I knew that meant organ failure from the cancer.

"I'm sorry," she said, "I know it's a lot to process at once."

I knew then. My mind was racing but I said little.

"Should I take him home?" I asked.

"Oh, no. He needs strong meds," the doctor responded.

John had a dread of being put in a nursing home. And I wanted him to be as comfortable as possible.

"I will be giving him morphine. Please know that his heart could slow, and his breathing may become shallow," said the doctor.

They also counseled me to see the lady in charge of hospice and to put him in hospice care to ensure that he was as comfortable as possible, which I did immediately after talking with John for a while.

Later that morning, I finished talking with David, and meeting with the hospice lady who said they would take care of all and make sure he was comfortable. I transferred him into hospice care.

David sat with him for a half hour and then came down to the rendezvous point just outside the South Tower of the hospital. He reported that John was sleeping. I breathed a sigh of relief and returned to be with him. He had also been given a shot of Dilaudid for pain, David explained.

As I entered the room, four nurses were tending to him. They applied warmers to his hands which were cold.

"He is in full code," said one.

I looked at the monitors, his heart rate had dropped, and his breathing was very low. He rallied. He opened his eyes and his breathing and heart rate rose. No paddles or other measures but an oxygen mask was placed over his mouth and nose.

I leaned over and said, "I love you."

Through the mask, he said, "I love you." His eyes closed, he dozed off to sleep. In a short time, he was gone.

Saudade *Saudade*, a Portuguese word with no direct English translation, means a deep and intense longing for someone or something no longer present.

I had the time of my life with John. Shortly after meeting, I asked John what his goal in life was.

"To be a good person," he said.

He was indeed. And he made me a better person.

Later our nephew, Derek, said that ours was a marriage of two remarkable laughs - John's deep resounding guffaw and my loud chortle - a high compliment. Humor was always a valued cornerstone of our relationship.

My memories of John are precious and shared memories more so. A year or so after his death, I found a handwritten note on an envelope: I think of you as not a part of my life, but my whole life. Fifteen years later, I just remember going to Alice's Restaurant and kissing on the pier. I love you. John

My heart warmed and I missed him all the more.

John was my heart and soulmate for more than thirty-two blessed years, finishing my sentences, enlightening my life, and bringing happiness and humor. He was a gift.

There's so much I still want to tell him, to share.

Saudade!

Printed in the USA
CPSIA information can be obtained
at www.ICGtesting.com
LVHW011959181023
761451LV00011B/727

9 781916 770560